Time and the Hour

TIME AND THE HOUR

Nigeria, East Africa and the Second World War

૭૩

R. T. KERSLAKE

The Radcliffe Press
LONDON • NEW YORK

Come what come may,
Time and the hour runs through the roughest day.

Macbeth, Act I, Scene iii

Published in 1997 by Radcliffe Press
An imprint of I.B.Tauris & Co Ltd
Victoria House, Bloomsbury Square,
London WC1B 4DZ

175 Fifth Avenue, New York, NY 10010

In the United States and Canada distributed by
St Martin's Press, 175 Fifth Avenue, New York, NY 10010

A full CIP record for this book is available from the British
Library

A full CIP record for this book is available from the Library of
Congress

ISBN 1 86064 154 7

Printed and bound in Great Britain by WBC Ltd, Bridgend,
Mid Glamorgan

Contents

Foreword by Anthony Kirk-Greene   vii

Abbreviations and Glossary   xi

Introduction   xiv

PART I Initiation, 1937–39   1

1   Voyage to 'The Coast'   3

2   Colonial Lagos   8

3   A Change of Course   15

4   Into the North at Last   20

5   Katsina: Province in the Bush   25

6   Administering the Lugard Legacy   32

7   Disillusion and Hope   39

8   Bush Life is Better   44

9   Locusts, Cattle and Humans   59

10   Rivers, Nomads and War   68

PART II A Taste of Army Life, 1939–42   77

11   Joining the Regiment   79

12   Sahara, Home and Bletchley   86

13   Round the Cape to Kenya   90

14   Towards Somaliland   97

15   Training with Monkeys and Crocodiles   102

16   To Mogadishu without Love   107

17   Preparing for Action   114

18   Marda Pass: an Impromptu Battle   118

19   Into Ethiopia   124

20   Liaising with Italians   129

21 The Omo Gorge 134
22 A Blue Nile Tributary 138
23 The Regiment Goes Home 141
24 Farewell to Arms 149

PART III Muslims, Tribes and the Secretariat 155

25 Quick March to Bornu 157
26 Worthwhile Work and Agreeable Associates 169
27 Prematurely a DO 178
28 Personalities and Problems 186
29 Relieving an Outpost: Nguru 196
30 Sand and Swamp 206
31 A Remote Work-station 216
32 A Wife to the Rescue 225
33 Yola is Worse than Katsina 229
34 Escape to Independence: Numan 235
35 Anthropologists' Paradise 243
36 Final Scenes and Farewell 252
37 Return and a Postscript 265

Index 274

Foreword

❧

THE post-imperial period has been marked, in so far as its one-time civil servants and their families are concerned, by a remarkable upsurge in the writing of memoirs. Not that those overseas administrators, engineers, agriculturalists and so on were ever reluctant to put into print accounts of their work or their opinions on the political future of the countries where they served. Autobiographies of viceroys and proconsuls have long enjoyed a distinctive niche in the imperial literature, from time to time complemented by the reminiscences of their senior subordinates. Among them all, too, were a few who preferred to record their experiences in fiction, sometimes even in verse. Indian Civil (ICS), Sudan Political (SPS) or Colonial (HMOCS), the Service has never been a silent one.

But what has made such a distinct impression on the auto-biographical literature in the forty years or so since the end of empire is the wealth of memoirs written not only by the high fliers on their rapid rise to Government House and beyond, but also by the middle-ranking and run-of-the-mill overseas civil servant, the typical District Officer or Forestry Officer, the doctor and the policeman, and often by his wife, too. Often the origin of the memoir lies in the determination to make available to the family – children and now grandchildren – a record of what their parents' life and work in the Colonial Service was all about. The historical value of such an eye-witness account is substantially enhanced when the reader realises that here was a lifetime career under the Crown, at once respected, sought after and satisfying, which is today little known by, and unavailable to, anybody in this country under the age of fifty. For those who never knew the Colonial Service experience, such memoirs help to open the door to understanding what overseas civil servants did – and were expected to do – in their day's work, what they hoped they achieved and believed they bequeathed as part of the colonial legacy to the new states.

Yet, I would argue, for all the undoubted worth of such memoirs in setting the record straight on what Britain's overseas civil servants accomplished and felt they were contributing towards a better tomorrow for the emerging Third World – a record chronicled not by armchair analysts or conditioned critics but by those who actually did the job – there is a deeper vein of value to be explored in many of the memoirs. This is the sub-text, the ideas and the doubts, the non-mentions as much as the thoughts expressed about the work and those they worked with. A memoir allows the writer to step back, certainly now in retrospect and often then in actuality where he kept a diary or has come across a sizeable deposit of letters home, and reflect on what he was doing, the whys and wherefores and – equally significant – the why-nots.

Trevor Kerslake's memoir, when I read it in its draft form, immediately struck me as a winner on both these counts, the narrative and the reflective. Here is a detailed yet unpretentious account of the experience – commonplace and in no way unique – of a young colonial administrator in Nigeria just before and immediately after World War II. As a bonus, it so happens that much of this took place in the very same remote districts, Yola, Numan and Maiduguri, where I was to follow in the 1950s. At the same time, here are many revealing glimpses of puzzlement and self-questioning about the purpose, the context and the operation of colonial administration. The alternating moments of 'Disillusion and Hope' reach far beyond the so-titled Chapter 7; Trevor Kerslake's diary from which his text is derived reflects, he honestly concedes, 'the varying degrees of isolation, physical, intellectual and spiritual' which he endured for much of the time.

For instance, as a probationer at Oxford, he was worried why Margery Perham, the great apostle of Lugardian Indirect Rule, never invited L. S. Ward, one-time Resident of Sokoto – the heartland of classic Native Administration – and now teaching Hausa on the Colonial Service Training Course, to address its members about his encounters with Indirect Rule in action. Again, Kerslake found himself debating how significant it might be that the two pre-eminent Colonial Service theorists of colonial governance in the twentieth century, Sir Frederick Lugard and Sir Donald Cameron, whose writings constituted prescribed texts for all newcomers to African administration, had had no experience whatsoever of the realities of that district administration which they so vaunted.

A year later, as a mere cadet, he was exercised by the possible reasons for the Colonial Office's sharp break with tradition in bringing in an outsider as the new Chief Commissioner of the Northern Privinces. Nor was he slow to identify the bureaucratic absurdity which, in the single division Katsina Province, regrettably left the energetic and interfering Resident with too little to do and 'in complete ignorance of the range of tasks devolving on the Assistant District Officer additional to that of general assistant to the Resident'.

Moving from up-country ADO in 1938 to a posting to the promotion platform of Lagos Secretariat in 1946, it did not take Kerslake long to assess his new post as a dead end. It was not only the dullness and disappointment of the work, it was also 'the new and rising power-holders', African as well as European, 'brash, hard faces and loud clothes to match'. Even the new Governor seemed to him a different kind of senior officer under whom to work, noticeably lacking the warmth of his predecessor. Soon Kerslake was spending his evenings 'making a thorough review of "the life colonial" as I had known it, and as it promised to be in the future ... I could not avoid the conclusion that the best years, almost certainly, lay behind me.'

His letter of resignation quickly followed. Trevor Kerslake's return visit to Nigeria in 1973 did nothing to dissuade him that he had made the right decision in 1946, and in no way can it be said to have helped him recapture the proverbial best years of his life thirty years earlier. At the end of his memoir he asks, now as then, 'was any of it worthwhile?' His answer, qualified but unambiguous, is thoughtfully set down as the finale of his memoir.

In the fifteen years since I was Director of the Oxford Colonial/ Development Records Project, when I interpreted part of my remit as being to encourage former members of the Colonial Service to give thought to writing down their experiences now that Her Majesty's Overseas Civil Service (HMOCS) was no longer a career on offer to university leavers, I have studied several hundred such memoirs in manuscript, typescript, on tape and in print. It is a pleasure which has yet to pall. Now and again a one-time District Officer's memoir stands out as something special, signalling that extra star which, at least among hotels and restaurants and some wine lists, denotes a deservedly higher category. Keeping to my home ground of Northern Nigeria, I still rewardingly revisit such sterling latter-day memoirs, gubernatorial reminiscences apart, as John Smith's *Colonial Cadet in Nigeria* (1968), Elnor Russell's *Bush Life in Nigeria* (1978), Nicky McClintock's *Kingdoms in the Sand and Sun* (1992) and Neil Skinner's *Burden at Sunset* (1996).

To these I shall now be adding *Time and the Hour*. Here is a book not only to be enjoyed and learned from but one to consult and invoke, too – an important record, in the author's own words, of 'a unique and now vanished way of life'. To me, Trevor Kerslake's memoir confirms the message behind the opinion I tentatively advanced a decade ago:

> It may well be that by 2066, the centenary of the closing down of the Colonial Office, our great-great-grandchildren will find the most telling image of Britain's empire in memoirs and in biographical studies, rather than in the weightier imperial archives at the Public record Office in Kew or in the Rhodes Library at Oxford.

Anthony Kirk-Greene
St Anthony's College
Oxford

Abbreviations and Glossary

ᘓᕓ

A and Q jobs   Staff appointments relating to army administration, stores and supplies
ADC   Aide de camp
ADO   Assistant District Officer
Ajiya   Kanuri name for a district head
Alkali   A Muhammadan judge in Northern Nigeria
Ardo   The head of a group of Fulani families
Bachama   A tribe living in the Benue valley near Numan
Batta   A Benue valley tribe, neighbours of the Bachama
BBWA   Bank of British West Africa
Chief Commissioner   Effectively the Governor of Northern Nigeria, stationed in Kaduna
CO   Commanding Officer (in a battalion, a Lieutenant Colonel)
CSM   Company Sergeant-Major
DH   District head
DO   District Officer; the administrative officer in charge of a division of a province, subordinate to the Resident thereof
Emir   The head chief of an Emirate
Fulani   A widespread, mainly Muslim cattle tribe of Northern Nigeria and adjacent territories; their leaders waged a jihad in the 1820s and displaced the former Hausa emirs
Haraji   The main (occupation-based) annual tax in Northern Nigeria
Hausa   The main tribe (and language) of the emirates of Northern Nigeria (except for Bornu)
HE   His Excellency (the Governor), stationed in Lagos
HH   His Honour (the Chief Commissioner), based in Kaduna
Ibo   The major tribe of south-east Nigeria
IO   Intelligence Officer

xi

Jangali	Cattle tax, levied at a rate of about two shillings per head. The value of a cow was roughly fifty shillings
Kanuri	The major tribe (and language) of Bornu; they are Muslims, and their present chief, the Shehu, has considerable religious influence to the east as far as the Sudan
KAR	The King's African Rifles: the East African Force comprising regiments raised in the East African territories, having an organisation and command structure similar to the RWAFF
Ma'aji	The Treasurer of a Native Administration
Magaji	A town head, also used of a village head
Mallam	A man of some Islamic education
Mukaddam	District head of Maiduguri town and environs; a member of the Shehu's council
NA	Native Authority: a chief or chief-in-council. Or Native Administration: the organisation operating under a Native Authority
NCO	Non-commissioned officer
NR	The Nigeria Regiment; 1NR standing for the 1st Battalion thereof
OETA	Occupied Enemy Territory Administration
OP	Observation point, normally an elevated position from which an officer is able to control the fire of an artillery unit
OTC	Officer Training Corps; most public schools had one, as did Oxford and Cambridge
PS	Private Secretary
PWD	Public Works Department
QM	Quartermaster
RE	Royal Engineers
Resident	The senior administrative officer of a province
RQMS	Regimental Quartermaster Sergeant
RSM	Regimental Sergeant-Major
Rumfa	A rough shelter made of plaited reeds or straw, fairly sun-proof but not rain-proof
RWAFF	Royal West African Frontier Force; it had regiments in each West African territory, Nigeria having the largest establishment; known throughout the West Coast as the 'Waff' (pronounced Woff)

SAAF	South African Air Force
Sarki	A chief; attached to a territory or a calling with 'n', e.g. Sarkin Katsina, Emir of Katsina; Sarkin kasuwa, the market overseer
SDO	Senior District Officer, frequently an acting Resident
Shehu	The Sheikh, ruling chief of Bornu
Shuwa	A tribe of nomadic Arabs living in the area of Lake Chad
UAC	United Africa Company, a subsidiary of Unilever
VH	Village head
Waff	see RWAFF
Wali	A member of the council of the Shehu of Bornu expert in Arabic and Muhammadan law
Waziri	A vizier; an Emir's chief executive officer, and senior member of his council
Yoruba	The major tribe of south-west Nigeria: some Muslims, but mainly Christian

Introduction

❦

WHEN I started work in Nigeria in 1937, the regulations, procedures and traditions of the imperial government were thoroughly established and were accepted by the majority of the inhabitants, certainly in the Northern Provinces and probably also in the South, as an improvement on what they had experienced before the British occupation. The rigidities and excessive formalities of the Lugardian concept of Indirect Rule had been softened by decades of human contact and understanding between the British and the Africans who shared their work-load and, increasingly, their responsibilities. Government's version of the future was of steady improvement in all areas of public service, with increasing African involvement as higher education services developed. However, Independence was still considered to be so remote that it was rarely discussed outside Lagos, where local politicians and their press maintained some virulent opposition to the government.

My service with the Nigeria Regiment lasted from September 1939 to October 1942, and, following a year in East Africa, was mostly spent in Southern Nigeria, where I heard very little from my old contacts in the North. Nevertheless, life in the regiment, where most of the rank and file were Northerners, remained for me an important continuity with experience as a District Officer in the bush; one was living very close to the Africans for whom one was responsible, came to know them intimately and fondly, valued their trust and tried to deserve it.

In 1942, the Governor, Sir Bernard Bourdillon, demanded the return of the Colonial Service officers who had been mobilised into the Nigeria Regiment, and about a dozen administrative officers, including myself, were returned to our former employment. In my case, this included posting to remote Bornu, and Adamawa, and finally to the Lagos Secretariat, where I became fully and finally aware of all that had been happening to the vision of the future since 1939.

So, my brief career in the Service began at the peak of the imperial tradition, with its virtues and its failings, and spanned the years to the beginning of its decline and the early dawn of new nationhood for the African. The sadness, indeed the tragedy, for Nigerians, has been the loss of much of the freedom they experienced under the British, the harsh experience of civil war, corruption and military dictatorship. This, and the disturbing evidence of damaging environmental change, was made plain to me during a brief visit to Nigeria in 1973, since when the decline in the quality of life for the 'ordinary people' appears to have continued, with little present hope of improvement.

There has been much denigration, in recent years, of the aims and achievements of the Colonial Services during the first half of this century. This book is dedicated to the men who were my respected and admired seniors, and their successors, who spent so much of themselves, in the prime of their lives, in the hope that Nigeria might have a better future than it appears to have today. Without the support of my wife it would probably not have been written, and certainly would not have been typed!

Fawler, Oxfordshire, 1996

PART I

Initiation, 1937–39

❧

Resident to Assistant District Officer: 'We don't want more spanners thrown into the machinery of Government, do we?' (Katsina, Northern Nigeria 1939)

I

Voyage to 'The Coast'

❧

A SHIP'S siren can be a dismal sound, and so it seemed on a grey January afternoon in 1937, when the MV *Accra* swung away from its berth and headed down the Mersey, bound for West Africa. I watched the coast of England disappear into the gloom and began to realise how decisive was the step I had taken, but I had no conception of where and into what strange encounters it would ultimately lead me.

I suppose it all started when an Oxford friend joined the Colonial Service and infected me with his enthusiasm for the opportunities and satisfactions which it seemed to offer, in doing a useful job with a wide range of responsibilities concerned with people and their needs. In the spring of 1936 I made a tentative application for an appointment in the Colonial Administrative Service, and was disappointed, but not surprised, when I did not receive an offer of one of the year's cadetships for which there was strong competition. After graduating in Physics I was invited to join the research team in the Clarendon Laboratory where I wrestled with my apparatus for some months without conspicuous success, and became convinced that I was not a born practical experimentalist. My mind turned again to the possibilities of overseas employment.

In December 1936, following an application suggested by the Oxford Appointments Board, I was offered, and accepted, an appointment by the Colonial Audit Department as an assistant auditor in Nigeria. There followed an induction course of about six weeks' duration at the Colonial Audit headquarters in Queen Anne's Gate. The purpose of the course was not so much to teach me the techniques of auditing as to demonstrate the principles of budgeting in a colonial territory and the role of the auditor in ensuring that expenditure was controlled within the allocations which had been approved by the appropriate authority in the colony (usually the Governor in Council) and sanctioned by the Secretary of State (to whom the auditor was ultimately responsible). I was set to apply these principles by examining the accounts of St Helena, little changed perhaps since Napoleon's time, and graduated from there, northwards, to the Gambia. My equipment consisted of a green pencil, to tick entries which were deemed to be correct and to put ? against anything considered to be questionable. In the Colonial Service, I was told, only an auditor might use green pencil or green ink. This exercise gave me quite a good idea of the departmental structure of colonial government, and the allocation of responsibilities between departments. It was also clear that power, in colonial administration, was exercised through the authority to spend money, but I was later to learn that power could have other leverages when it was operating at some distance from headquarters. By mid-January, I had completed the course and had my fill of London smog, civil service tea, and multiple vaccinations, and a passage was booked for me to sail for Lagos on 27 January.

Now, as the ship began to leave the Mersey and enter the open sea, I went below and began to take in my surroundings. The Accra was a passenger liner of about 8000 tons which carried a fair amount of cargo in addition to about 300 passengers. It was one of a group of three ships of the Elder Dempster Line (the *Apapa* and the *Abosso* were the others) which ran fortnightly (and sometimes with a weekly interval) to the various ports along the west coast as far as Lagos, where they spent a couple of days before the return journey. The P & O ran larger and more splendid vessels to East Africa and beyond, via the Mediterranean, but the routines of the various lines serving the old empire from Liverpool or Tilbury were very similar. Travelling to remote and mainly tropical destinations in these fine, well-appointed ships is something that has gone for ever, like the special world of the passengers whom they carried. The 'old coasters' who made the trip many times were fully *au fait* with the class structure of the accommodation and of the passengers who occupied it, but it was all new to me, and I soon realised that I had much to learn, not only about the way of life on board, but also about the hierarchical structure of colonial society and the formalities and behaviour associated with it. The 'for'ard' two-thirds of the ship and its superstructure were

4

occupied by first-class passengers and ship's officers, cabins on the four decks being allocated by seniority, with the smallest fry on the lowest, 'C' deck. The 'aft' one-third was occupied by second-class passengers, who were the 'second-class' officials of the Colonial Service: foremen of works, well-diggers, sanitary superintendents, engine-drivers, plate-layers and others, of whose great merits I shall have much to say later, together with some people doing similar jobs in trading firms or mining companies.

Geoffrey MacBride (an Oxford friend) had told me to look out for his brother Desmond, who was a Northern Nigeria District Officer travelling to Lagos on the same ship. I went to find him in his cabin and we arranged to sit at the same table in the dining-room. Desmond was delightful; a former scholar of King's, Cambridge, he had many of the attributes which, over the years, I came to associate with men who matured in that college in the 1920s and 1930s: intellectual, eccentric, humorous, friendly but with a certain detachment; dedicated to his job in an unambitious sort of way, and with many interests outside it; rather spartan in his personal life. At our table there was, in addition to Desmond, a somewhat more senior administrative officer, Rex Niven.

We played deck tennis, for exercise, throughout the voyage. Niven, dark, good-looking, impeccably dressed in white shirt and shorts, concentrated intensely on the game. He had won an MC as a gunner in 1917–18 and now, at thirty-eight, was coming up towards a Resident's post. Considered to be probably the most able man in the Nigerian service, his outspoken critical attitude and unwillingness to suffer fools gladly had combined to provide him with more enemies than friends in some high places.

Also on board was Hugh Pellew, an officer seconded from a fashionable cavalry regiment, who was beginning a tour of duty as ADC to the Governor. In an unguarded moment, Hugh heard me admit that I played bridge and persuaded me to help him by providing a much-needed recruit to the Governor's bridge group, consisting of two tables in which the partners changed regularly to avoid monotony. Sir Bernard Bourdillon, tall, monocled, a man of great presence and natural manner, I liked enormously. He and his wife occupied the gubernatorial suite in the most exclusive reaches of the top deck. They were always very kind to me, and I imagine that he and other well-disposed people were instrumental in getting me transferred to the Administrative Service later in 1937.

There was a sort of farewell dinner on the last night before Lagos. In later years, I came to understand the rather special significance of it, for those who had been travelling briefly together may have been long-term friends, served together in some station, and now were to part again, perhaps for years. Of my new 'friends', Desmond MacBride and Rex Niven would be boarding the boat train for the north the following evening, but Hugh Pellew would be around in Lagos. After a convivial evening, I descended to the cabin and tried, against the heat, to complete my packing.

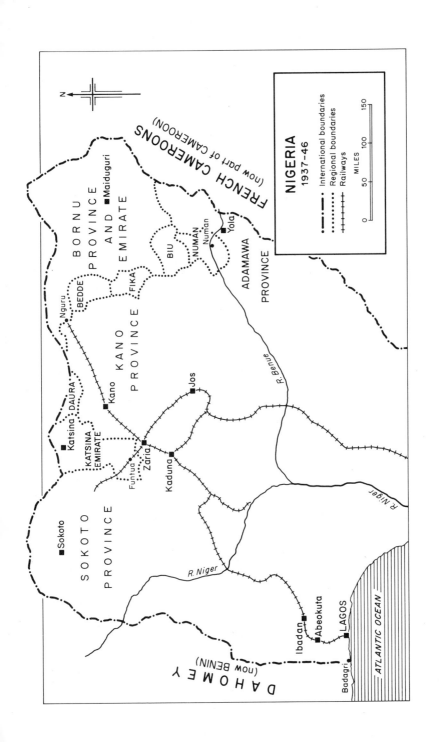

2

Colonial Lagos

❧

T HE following morning (I think it was 10 February 1937), we crossed the bar of Lagos harbour soon after dawn and sailed between the long lines of the two 'moles' towards the Customs wharf. We passed the many landmarks which I was to come to know well: the yacht club, the line of old wooden houses with their lawns fringing the water's edge along to the white façades of the Secretariat building and Government House, with more green verges and brilliant red-flowered trees set among them. This part of old colonial Lagos had a certain dignity and impressiveness.

While we were breakfasting, people began to come aboard to greet their friends and to seek out newcomers and guide them through the formalities of entry. I was met by a young auditor, Allison, who got me through Customs with remarkable speed, took me to the house on Ikoyi island, about three miles from the port, which we were to share, and left me to sort myself out. Before leaving the boat, Desmond MacBride had brought along to me a rather tall and rather ugly and very black Northerner whom he proposed as candidate for the post of steward of my household. This was Alhadji, whose former master had just retired, and who was now looking for another job. He was a Kilba (a tribe from the hills to the north of Yola) whose parents had been enslaved by the invading Fulani around the turn of the century and who had been brought up as a Muhammadan. He had served with several masters, including a District Officer who had been killed by pagan[1] tribesmen on the Plateau escarpment east of Jos in the 1920s. His departing master had helped him to make the pilgrimage to Mecca,

---

[1] 'Pagan': neither Muhammadan nor Christian, having 'primitive' religious beliefs.

from which he had just returned. He was a much-travelled man, who was to be an important figure in my life for most of my time in Nigeria. I took him on at once, and we spent the morning sorting out my belongings in the unlovely box which was No. 6 Glover Road. Allison's 'boys'[2] helped, until he came back for lunch, after which we drove into Lagos and I was introduced to 'the office', which was located across an angle of the upper floor of the Secretariat building. I spent a few minutes with the Auditor himself, H. W. Drake, a man of about fifty, very portly with a large round pale face and rather sharp eyes. He was very competent and was well supported by able subordinates, whom I went to meet. There were, in addition to Allison and myself, two senior men and a few assistant auditors, most of whom were on tour away from Lagos. There was also a considerable number of Nigerian audit clerks, some detached to work with the British audit staff, and some working in the main office under the supervision of the Chief Clerk and his hierarchy.

The work, in the Lagos area, soon settled into a regular pattern, much of it very dull. It took me into a number of government departments: Public Works (PWD), the Post Office, Customs and Excise, Land and Surveys, Income Tax, the Supreme Court, the prison, hospitals – these are the ones that I can remember. For every department and sub-department, the Audit Office had a type-written guide to the accounting system and the relevant procedures. My job was to check that the African audit clerks were following the correct procedure (they generally did it very well) and to carry out certain independent checks and cross-checks. Back in the office, I would draft queries on the points arising from the examinations, and would sign queries drafted by audit clerks. Most of the queries were relatively trivial. This was supposed to indicate (and probably did) that the accounting and audit procedures were effective and prevented any appreciable malpractice or fraud. Such as did take place never entered the books of account, and so were the responsibility of the administrator (as I was later to discover) rather than the accountant.

So, the daily work routine went on, and I got used to shuttling

---

[2] The word 'boy', used to mean a personal servant, was certainly not intended to be derogatory. The retainers of a Hausa chieftain were known as *yara* (boys).

back and forth to Ikoyi in the heat and humidity, the stuffiness of some of the offices I had to visit, and of the people who occupied them. The road from Ikoyi ran between the golf course and the 'European' cemetery, which appeared to be equally extensive – a depressing daily reminder of the West Coast's reputation as 'the White Man's Grave'.

Outside office hours, social life was considerable, even hectic. I was keen to play squash and tennis, and did so, almost every day, often with Hugh Pellew, the Governor's ADC, who would collect me in a large Sunbeam flying the Government House flag, to Alhadji's great satisfaction. For the first week or so, however, I was heavily committed to 'calling' on a large number of senior people, not only those in my own department, but also the heads of the many Lagos-based departments and banks with which the Audit Department had dealings. This convention had the result of producing a crop of invitations to dinner, which could be a pleasant change for a lone bachelor. This meant that I had to become familiar with the geography of Ikoyi where, apart from a few old houses near the race course and the Marina, together with the railway settlement at Ebute Metta, most of the European population was accommodated. 'Greater Lagos' consisted of the 'islands': Lagos itself, Ikoyi and Victoria. Lagos was the old settlement, containing the old African township and the various government offices as well as most of the trading firms and warehouses; it was bounded by the harbour, part of the 'lagoon' and a creek. Ikoyi island was separated from Lagos island by a creek; the European residential area was a grid of roads named after famous proconsuls such as Lugard, Temple and MacGregor; the remainder was still undeveloped 'bush' running down to mangrove swamps at the creek and on the shore of the lagoon. Victoria island was separated from Ikoyi and Lagos by creeks, and was otherwise bounded by the harbour and by the Atlantic beach, along which the ocean pounded with tremendous waves and surf, with a most dangerous undertow.

Every day, as I cycled or drove from the office to Ikoyi or to one of the departments under audit, I passed through some part of the African town. Much of it was congested, overcrowded, antique slums, something far worse than could be found in London or Liverpool. Although I passed through all this every day, I understood very little of the way of life of the residents and how they made a living. Many of them provided services of various kinds, especially in the operation of the many markets from which all who worked in the capital drew their supplies.

Most Sunday mornings I went to church at St Saviour's, the so-called Colonial Church beyond the race course and near Government House. There I met the colonial chaplain, Ruthven Wright, always known as Padre Wright or 'the Padre', who was a very good friend for many years. He was a remarkable man who did much to help lonely souls, particularly seamen who came to the port of Lagos, where there was an old and inadequate mission house, or to Apapa, where, before Ruthven's time, there was nothing for them. He stirred the conscience of the commercial community and made them find the money to build the Wharf Inn at Apapa which I used to visit with him about once a week. During the Second World War, when ships were held up in convoy, this place seemed literally heaven-sent for the sailors who used it, and it was the only establishment of its kind on the West Coast.

Some time in April, as a sort of convalescence from jaundice induced by yellow fever injections in London, I was told to accompany Allison on a tour to Badagry, a very old Yoruba town about sixty miles west of Lagos, near the Dahomey border. Early one morning we left the Customs wharf in the Marine Department launch and chugged across the harbour into Badagry creek through which we meandered, between mangroves, patches of taller forest, scattered villages with oil-palms and coconut, all the way to Badagry, long notorious as a slaving port and more recently known as a collecting centre for the local palm-oil trade. We disembarked at the oil wharf, where the smell of rancid palm oil was almost too much for my still tender stomach, and walked a short distance along the 'beach' to the rest-house, an old-fashioned wooden structure on stilts, where the smell seemed slightly diminished. We made the acquaintance of the DO who, *mirabile dictu*, was still there five years later when I arrived with a military detachment. He lived in another rather ancient but comfortable house on stilts further along the 'beach' at a tolerable distance from the smell-centre, and he and his wife were very hospitable during our stay. We audited, over several days, all the 'on the spot' finances of an administrative division, which I was to come to know all too well in a few years' time, but there were also some special features attaching to the semi-maritime nature of the place, such as registration fees for canoes and other craft, which were a means of raising some revenue from people who were, apparently, particularly averse to paying any form of income tax.

In the days of the slave trade, slaves were brought south along the established slave track into Badagry, where they were assembled before being ferried across the creek to the narrow strip of land which separates the creek from the ocean. Coconut palms had been planted on the strip, but the slave route was still easily discernible through the palms to the sea. Inland, from Badagry to the north for at least one hundred miles, the land was still very sparsely settled as a result of the slave-raiding which had denuded this relatively fertile area of its breeding populations and removed them to the plantations of Virginia and elsewhere.

Allison had brought with him a portable gramophone and records of the 'New World' Symphony which he played one quiet evening when the creek was bathed in moonlight and there was no sound but the singing of crickets and the occasional plash of paddles from passing canoes. The effect was magical and unforgettable and came to my mind most vividly years later, when my wife and I were visiting some of the old plantations on the James river in Virginia. The people of Badagry in 1937 were predominantly Yoruba and seemed friendly enough, but some of their forebears, presumably, had been involved in this trade, one of the most horrible ever carried on by man against man.

Sometime in May or June, Drake informed me that I was to go on a tour of inspection to Ibadan for about six weeks. Ibadan was considered to be the largest African town in the whole continent, with the possible exception of Cairo. I set off one morning with Alhadji in the back seat of the small car which I had bought, on government loan, a fortnight earlier. I was worried as to how the car would cope with the severely corrugated laterite surface of some sixty miles of the Ibadan road, but although the shaking was horrible, it survived. How different the scene then, compared with the chaos through which the road passes today, and the disastrous destruction of the environment. Carter bridge, linking Lagos to the mainland, was almost empty of traffic in the early morning, and within a few minutes we were beyond Yaba (then the site of the University College) and through Ikeja, a village with a thriving market, on to Agege, another village which boasted little more than a citrus research station of the Agricultural Department. Beyond Agege we were into the bush, with only Abeokuta and the odd village before we ran into Ibadan. Today, Ikeja has been developed into a vast industrial and trading area, with numerous factories and also breweries. Agege, that sleepy little place with its oranges and grapefruit, is now one of the several dormitory areas serving the ever-open maw of Ikeja.

I was glad to reach the rest house at Ibadan, a graceless concrete block, and to find it, as promised, fully furnished and moderately comfortable. Alhadji and I had just about finished unpacking, when the sub-treasurer arrived and invited me to lunch. He was a large man who perspired freely and breathed heavily, giving the impression of having recently imbibed several gins. We reached his house after a visit to the club (of which he was the hon. sec.) to ensure that 'everything was all right', including the gin supply. Lunch was very prolonged – my first experience of up-country entertainment of this nature – very kindly intentioned, but best avoided. I decided to steer clear of the sub-treasury, and concentrate on the other departments in the town area, leaving the sub-treasurer in suspense as to when I was going to check his cash and procedures. I enjoyed my visit to the Forestry headquarters beautifully situated in the low hills at Olokomeji. I checked the details of the timber extraction and the royalty arrangements, the rates of extraction and payments made. In some cases, there was provision for replanting, but I could only check the amount done from the paper evidence. The Forestry people seemed glad, rather than bothered, that I took so much interest.

I spent some time checking the accounts of the several courts, including one in the old Yoruba chief town of Oyo. The township of Ibadan sprawled over several hills, which at the time of my visit had been eroded to the bare red earth, possibly through over-grazing by goats, which seemed to be part of every household, even in this urban setting. Crowning one of the hills was the Town Hall, a monstrous, inappropriate building approached by a dirt road which was almost unmotorable in wet weather. I never fully understood the economics of the existence of Ibadan; it seemed to be the ultimate African example of one of those concentrations of people who take in each other's washing.

I made my first contact with the Nigeria Regiment when I checked the cash of the company which was stationed in Ibadan. The company commander was in a state of blue funk about it all, and, in fact, his cash was in surplus, an awkward situation which

I chose to overlook by simply handing over to him the few pounds involved. Accountancy was not one of the RWAFF's strengths, as I was to discover some years later to my cost.

And so, back to the sub-treasurer. I put him out of his anxiety by checking his cash (several thousands of pounds, all correct), and spent the last few days of my tour on the routine transactions of his office. I was not hard-pressed, and he most certainly was not, as I was able to see in observing his daily procedure. He arrived at 8.30 a.m., having driven via the club. He signed papers until about eleven, when he visited the club to inspect the grounds, returning to the office at about 11.30. At 1.30, he declared that there was absolutely nothing more he could do, and thereupon drove home to lunch and to relax for the rest of the day. As far as I could gather, this had been his routine for a decade or so, and would have continued until his retirement if the war had not intervened.

3

A Change of Course

~

I RETURNED from Ibadan to the departmental treadmill in
Lagos. There were compensations in friendships and the
delights of sailing, but my travels away from Lagos had convinced me that I had to change my way of life. I felt that I had
simply exchanged one kind of suburban existence for another, and
I didn't really like the job. I decided to make a formal application
for transfer to the Administrative Service. Drake told me that I
had virtually no chance of making the move; such a thing was
unheard of. However, he forwarded the application, and the reply
came back that it had been 'noted'. I was somewhat encouraged
that there was no immediate outright rejection.

August, with its tornadoes and rain, came and went, and then,
one day in mid-September, I was summoned to Drake's office. He
informed me that my application for transfer had been approved
and that I should be leaving the Audit Department and returning
to England later in the month, to take the Administrative Service
course. I left his office in a daze, almost unable to believe that it
had actually happened. Most of my colleagues and friends congratulated me, but a few, like Drake, said that I had made a
mistake, that I should find the life hard and lonely, and that I
should probably come to regret my decision. I knew from discussions with Desmond MacBride and others that there would be
hardship and loneliness, but that there would be many compensations, particularly the close contact with the people, and the
job itself was uniquely interesting and demanding. I felt greatly
privileged in having the opportunity to do this work, and in spite
of occasional periods of frustration and disillusionment, I continued to feel this sense of privilege, and still do.

I discovered that my application for transfer had been made at a fortunate moment. The old Treasury Department had been split into an Accountant-General's department and a Financial Secretary's department. The latter was a policy-making department, and would be staffed mainly from the Administrative Service. A few accountants had been transferred to the Financial Secretary's office and, additionally, three people, including myself, with accounting experience, were being transferred, with the requisite training, to the Administrative Service, for possible employment in the more distant future in financial posts. The two other men were Sam Bradshaw and Louis Bain, who had been working in sub-treasury offices in the provinces. Both were to become valued friends.

Very soon it was time to say my goodbyes. I found a good master for Alhadji and warned him that I would want him back again when I returned in 1938. I saw the *Abosso* sail in on the Thursday morning, and found the time pass very slowly until Saturday and the drive to Apapa, where I went aboard and began to feel that I was really making a fresh start. There was the usual festive atmosphere on board, with passengers entertaining their friends according to their means, the wealthier ones throwing champagne parties and the lesser fry content with well-cooled beer. It was true what was said about the view of Lagos being most delightful when seen from the stern of a vessel homeward bound, and I unreservedly enjoyed the voyage home.

There were, I think, about forty of us taking the course at Oxford, and a smaller number at Cambridge. At both universities, Nigeria had the largest group of cadets and, within the group, Northern Nigeria had more than half the total. There were eight of us who were learning Hausa (the lingua franca of Northern Nigeria) under L. S. Ward, a former Resident of Sokoto, a major province of Hausaland. Various other languages, including Swahili, Malay, Yoruba and Twi were also taught during the daily periods which were set aside for language study. The remaining five or six periods of each working day were allocated to a bewildering range of studies which were supposed to improve our understanding of, and competence in, our future jobs. The language teaching continued, more or less every day, throughout the three terms, but some of the other subjects were covered only briefly, though always by experienced, often very distinguished, lecturers. Next in importance after language were Law (Contract, Tort, Criminal Law, Law of Evidence), Colonial History, Native Administration, Tropical

Agriculture, Forestry, Social Anthropology, Ethnology, Tropical Hygiene and Medicine, Accountancy, Typing (I am still learning), First Aid, Surveying and Field Engineering. Criminal Law was presented by the brilliant but eccentric Stallybrass, later Principal of Brasenose College; Colonial History by the first Beit Professor, Reginald Coupland; Native Administration by the woman who practically invented the subject, Margery Perham, then about forty and a little shy of those of us who had already worked in Africa.

I enjoyed the course immensely. Its structure, content and 'staffing' were admirable and a great credit to the various 'directors' (some seconded from the Colonial Service) who had built it up over the years. Hausa was, and for a long time continued to be, for me, a fascinating study in itself, with its immense vocabulary reflecting the richness of Hausa tribal life and culture. Our teacher, L. S. Ward, became a friend and told me much about the job, pointing up the relevance of the course subjects.

Ward was not openly critical of Margery Perham but he was not willing to accept unreservedly some of the conclusions of her *Native Administration in Nigeria*, which had recently (1937) been published and was one of our 'set books'. The book, which came to be recognised as a classic and established her reputation, was based on her observations and research during a five-month tour of Nigeria in 1931–32; some of it was considerably out-of-date five years later. It seemed strange, at the time, that Ward was never invited by Perham to talk to us about his own practical experience, including his service in Sokoto, one of the holiest of the holy areas of 'Indirect Rule'; that is, the method of 'native administration' supposed to have been invented (and certainly firmly installed) by Colonel Frederick (later Lord) Lugard. Lugard's methods were very successfully publicised by his wife when she was Colonial Editor of *The Times*, and her mission was later continued by Perham, who hero-worshipped Lugard, and also had a great regard for Sir Donald Cameron, one of Lugard's chief lieutenants in the years before 1918 and a very supportive friend to her at the time of her tour of Nigeria, to which Cameron had then returned as Governor.

A cynical observer of the way British government works will not be surprised to learn that three of the people who most strongly influenced colonial policy in the 1930s, 1940s and 1950s – Lugard, Cameron and Perham – had little or no experience of administration at grass-roots level. Lugard had never personally administered anything larger than an infantry brigade. He had, however, been an expert in the use of the Maxim gun against recalcitrant Africans. Cameron had been a desk-based colonial servant all his professional life and never really understood the traditions of district administration in Northern Nigeria. Margery Perham managed to spare some time from files and provincial headquarters to descend upon District Officers in the bush, but her lack of understanding of the 'bush DO' and his problems is revealed all too clearly in *West African Passage*, the diary of her Nigerian tour, published posthumously in 1983.

I returned home at the end of the final summer term to take leave of family and friends, and to assemble my effects for transport to Liverpool docks, to await shipment in the MV *Abosso*. This time, I had to go very fully provided with all kinds of camp equipment, which filled a number of packing-cases, all of which, to my surprise, arrived intact at the far end of my journey. The voyage was pleasant, but inevitably less exciting than that of the previous year, until the time came to put our cadet friends over the side at Accra. As we saw them waving goodbye as they rode the surf towards the coast, it was plain that a new life was beginning for them in that moment, and that something similar awaited the large group of us who would disembark at Lagos on the morrow, and who had just received notices of our postings to the various provinces.

From this point in my story I have, for something over a year, the rather dubious benefit of a diary which I began to write within a day or two of my arrival in Nigeria. It provides a chronology, but is all too often highly subjective in tone, reflecting the varying degrees of isolation, physical, intellectual and spiritual (for want of a better word) which I experienced for much of the time.

We sailed up the lagoon in the early morning of 11 August and tied up at the Customs wharf, on the Lagos side of the harbour. With Bernard Hadow (bound, like me, for Katsina Province in the far North), I shopped around all the 'canteens' in Lagos, gathering stores and hardware of all kinds, and placing orders for much more to be forwarded to Katsina. All this, together with clearing Customs (a particularly tiresome ritual which got worse every year and is now an awful experience) occupied most of the day, but there was just time, after tea, for an hour's sailing, and then the drive to Apapa to join the boat train for the long, long journey to

Kano via Kaduna, where all the Northern cadets were due to make the acquaintance of the Chief Commissioner for the Northern Provinces.

4

Into the North at Last

❧

M Y previous experience of Nigeria had been limited to
Lagos and its hinterland. I was now at the beginning of
a spell of seven years of travelling and working in a
much larger area of Nigeria, and also in large tracts of East Africa.
I felt that I had been fortunate in transferring to the Administrative
Service in the Northern, rather than the Southern Provinces, and
subsequent experience confirmed me in this view. I shall not attempt to describe the state of Nigeria in 1938 in any detail. It was
well done in Margery Perham's *Native Administration in Nigeria*
(1937), which is still available in libraries. Suffice it to say that
Nigeria is a large country, about 350,000 square miles in area; that
it was considered to have a population, in 1931, of 20 million,
which was probably an underestimate, as the population fifty years
later was estimated to be 100 million. The Northern Provinces held
over half the population and occupied about three-quarters of the
area. The Hausa-speaking people in the north were mainly concentrated in the Muslim Emirates, of which the most important
were Kano, Sokoto and Katsina. Kano was the richest, with a
population of 2 million and the far-famed city of Kano as its
capital. Sokoto was larger in area, with a population of 1.3 million,
and had, as Sultan, the Muslim religious head of the Hausa North.
Katsina, though much smaller in area, had about one million population, a thriving agriculture, a considerable educational/religious
tradition and a 'progressive' Emir.

Hadow, Bain and I shared a compartment, in which an electric
fan stirred the air around, pushing some of it through the open
windows, day and night. The train was hot from standing in the
afternoon sun, and we felt little inclination to try to sleep before
midnight, preferring to look out on the little village communities

in the forest clearings near the track gathered for company or activity around their hurricane lamps, the youngsters shouting, ululating and holding out their hands for coins as the train made its weary way at about 20 mph. Finally, we had our bunks made up (with the windows wide open for maximum ventilation) and tried not to be completely roused by stops in the middle of the night. I suppose people were dropped off at Ibadan and at Ilorin (the southernmost of the Northern Provinces) around breakfast-time. By lunch-time we had reached the Niger, a brown swirling mass of water far below us as we crossed the Jebba bridge. We were in the height of the rainy season, and the river was in full flood, but the sun shone for us that day, and Jebba station, with its surrounding rocks, was like an oven. In the restaurant car, pats of ice-cold butter from the 'frig' rapidly turned to blobs of oil.

With the Niger behind us, it seemed as though the northern lands had arrived at last. The air in the evening was cooler, less humid, and Hausa traders were in evidence at every stop, with their bags full of leatherware, hand-woven cloth, carvings, silver-ware, brassware and mats. I met an amusing young DO who was on his way to Yola via Makurdi and the river Benue, a journey which could take up to a fortnight. Like the rest of us, he stopped off at Kaduna, the HQ of the Northern Provinces, for a day's refreshment before the next stage of his journey.

The Chief Commissioner, Northern Provinces, was T. S. Adams, who was appointed in 1937 after long service in Malaya. Various reasons were suggested for this strange break with the tradition of appointing from 'within the service': to emphasise once again (as the Governor, Sir Donald Cameron, had tried to do in the early 1930s) that the Northern Residents were not a law and a class unto themselves: to prepare the way to self-government by up-grading the status of the Northern Emirs to something resembling that of the Malayan Sultans; to remove Adams from Malaya where he was not too well liked. Anyway, it was kind of him to receive, house and entertain a dozen or so of us at Government Lodge, Kaduna, and to make an attempt to get to know us a little before we dispersed to our remote stations.

We arrived in Kaduna at about 6 a.m., and were met by the Private Secretary and driven to Government Lodge, set in its beauti-ful gardens, for baths and breakfast. Adams appeared at about ten o'clock, and made us generally welcome, after which we were given a rapid tour of the Secretariat, the museum, the prison, the club, all before lunch. The prison impressed me as being at least more modern, and probably better organised, than the one in Lagos which I remembered from the days of audit inspections. Kaduna was, in those days, still recognisable as the entity which Lugard had created: a government headquarters hacked out of an area of empty bush, with all the associated trimmings, including of course a prison and a club. It was also a military headquarters, and had begun to grow a small native town as an appendage, with the inevitable warehouses of the trading firms – United Africa Company, John Holt, Paterson Zochonis and so on – and a string of clerks and hangers-on from Yorubaland and Iboland. Still, the place had a sort of upper-crust suburban calm, like some tropical Wimbledon, and no one could have guessed the nature and extent of the development which was to transform it utterly within the space of a further thirty years or so. In 1938, the name Kaduna signified, for hundreds of staff, black and white, and for the functionaries of many Native Administrations, the centre of power and decision-making, more real, more immediate and, of course, much closer, than Lagos.

Before dinner, the PS informed me that I should be sitting on His Honour's left, and I divided my attention between HH and a Cambridge man on my left, who bombarded me with questions throughout the meal. Adams was, I suppose, like all colonial bachelors, essentially a lonely man, and he seemed reluctant to break up the party to allow those of us who had to join the night train to Kano to depart. He needn't have hurried, for we had a long wait on Kaduna station before the train arrived, two hours late, which was not unusual in the rainy season when bridges, culverts and embankments were frequently washed out or undermined. So Hadow and I, after an hour or so of a hot, mosquito-buzzing railway platform, piled into a compartment and tried to sleep away the night-long journey to Kano.

We arrived at about 8 a.m. and were most kindly met by Desmond MacBride, who drove us through the centre of Kano and out on the other side to his pleasant bungalow for beer, followed by breakfast. This was my first impression of Kano's scattered settlement of official housing, trading areas, military and police barracks, which I never managed to get fully sorted out in subsequent short visits. Desmond was one of a group of administrative officers engaged on 'special duties' in Kano (Zaria was a similarly favoured station), his assignment being the supervision of the Kano Native Authority printing press. This press did a wide range of work, including the printing of tax receipt books, licence forms and so on for all the Northern NAs, and this was regarded as a security operation, requiring a high degree of supervision. Desmond was about to take up a senior job in Benue Province, where horses could not live on account of the tsetse fly, and so he offered me the loan of his saddlery, which I gladly accepted. The Katsina NA lorry, one of the old indestructible Albions, arrived at about noon, and we set off in the full heat of the day on the 120-mile drive to Katsina, with Hadow by this time equipped with three boys, and myself as yet boy-less.

We jolted along over the corrugated laterite road, sitting on the hard 'passenger' bench in the front of the lorry, through the open, orchard bush country that is characteristic of the Western Sudan plain, and eventually arrived, hot, aching and tired, at Katsina, to find everything closed and sleepy at four on a Sunday afternoon. This method of travelling, with all its discomforts, was something I should come to accept as the norm over the next few years, thankful if the lorry was not too ancient, the road surface tolerable and the distance not longer than 150 miles. Travelling took many forms; it was always an important preoccupation as part of the job; it was often a kind of adventure, and could even be enjoyable.

We were made welcome by Russell, the ADO in charge of the Katsina Provincial Office, who was a year senior to us. We walked the fifty yards or so from the office through Russell's sandy patch of garden to his house, which was built, in the traditional fashion, of mud (sun-baked) and timber, and found it relatively cool within. As we conversed over a cup of tea, Russell gave us a rapid, amusing, but also slightly alarming survey of the state of the 'station' and its officials, the Emirate, and the jobs to which we had been assigned. Hadow was to go to the Southern touring area, working under Scott, a very senior ADO, who had his HQ at Funtua, on the railway line running north-west from Zaria. Hadow was delighted about 'going to bush' but rather concerned to learn that Scott was somewhat hypochondriac and could be difficult to deal with. I was to take over the Provincial Office from Russell, who was escaping to Daura Emirate, about fifty miles to the east of Katsina.

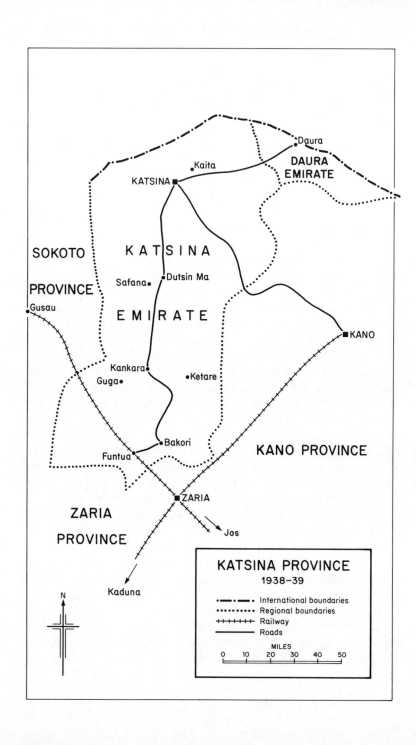

5

Katsina: Province in the Bush

☙

T HE substantive Resident of the Province was on compas-
sionate leave, visiting his wife who was seriously ill. In his
absence, the acting Resident was 'Toby' Drummond-Hay, a
senior DO, also somewhat hypochondriac, a major from the
trenches of Flanders, one of the large intake of officers from the
Services in the 1919–21 period. I soon found that it was *de rigueur*
to address people by the rank they had held in the Services and
that this rule applied to 'Captain' Macfarlane, the DO, and
'Captain' Campbell, the Senior Education Officer. We dined with
the Drummond-Hays that first evening, in the Residency, a very
large traditional mud building, with a truly enormous dining-room,
where we sat under a punkah which was pulled most vigorously in
a vain attempt to drive away the flying insects which were attracted
by the light, singed their wings, and nose-dived into the soup.
'Toby' and his wife were very agreeable; she had something of the
manner and appearance of Joyce Grenfell.

Drummond-Hay, like most of his colleagues, rejoiced in the
departure of Sir Donald Cameron (Governor 1931–35) whose memory as an anti-Northern desk-wallah and autocrat still rankled.
We were congratulated on having escaped the period of his alleged
misrule, which included a deeply resented cut in all salaries. I found
that Cameron was thoroughly disliked by all the British I met,
with the sole exception of Margery Perham. We talked about the
strange and (as Drummond-Hay saw it) somewhat unfortunate
association of Lugard, Cameron and Perham. Cameron had appeared determined to impose his own version of Lugardism upon
the North, and to do it autocratically, even offensively, to win at

25

last the many battles he had fought, and lost, with Northern Residents when he was Chief Secretary in Lagos from 1914 to 1924. Perham's reception in the North was somewhat chilly as a result of her sponsorship by, and obvious close association with Cameron. The views expressed at dinner that night have been little modified by my subsequent experience and reading. Perham's enthusiastic endorsement of Cameron's policies in her *Native Administration in Nigeria* is to be contrasted with Robert Heussler's presentation in *The British in N. Nigeria* written thirty years later. Anyone wishing to correct the fulsome praise of Lugard in Perham's biography of him should read *The Administration of Nigeria 1900–1960* by L. F. Nicolson.

Russell kindly put me up and I spent the following day in the office with him, reading files and picking up the office routine 'as it happened'. Russell was very patient and helpful, and this was, in fact, one of the few occasions on which someone made a real effort to tell me what a new job involved, what the difficulties were, or might be, and how to tackle them. In this case, the difficulties and problems were individually small, but they were unremitting and numerous, and their cumulative effect, by the end of any working day, was vexatious. The ultimate frustration was the rigidly-enforced requirement to wear long trousers and a tie. A jacket was also required in the court-room, or to receive a VIP such as the Emir or the Waziri, but this we all recognised as 'convenable'.

The offices, built of mud with a corrugated iron roof stretching over a narrow veranda, were strung out in a long line. At one end was the court-house, about twenty feet square, with the DO's office next to and communicating with it. The Provincial Office (my own) was next, and it also had a door, generally left open for the circulation of air, into the DO's office. An opening in the opposite wall led to another room which housed the three 'general' clerks, with a cubby-hole for the treasury clerk. One of the clerks was a native of the Gold Coast (now Ghana); the other three were from the South, all Yorubas. The Chief Clerk, Awafeso, tried hard to operate efficiently under great difficulties, and generally failed. All the clerks complained bitterly about their housing (in mud and thatch, which often leaked and tended to be infested with white ants, bats, rats, occasional snakes and other pests). They also complained about the food, the climate, money and the lack of social life, and they longed for transfer to the South. Sometimes, I felt some sympathy for them. Margery Perham said in *West African Passage*: 'I never saw a worse office, except in Kenya; a dirty, discoloured, crowded shack. The European housing in Katsina is the worst I have seen anywhere in Africa.'

The contented chaps, who helped to keep us all cheerful, even when things seemed quite intolerable, were the messengers. The two senior ones, Mallam Yahaya and Mallam Bello, were literate, knew some Arabic and had particular skill in the transliteration of Ajami (Hausa written in Arabic script) into Hausa in Roman characters. The other two messengers, Sali and Nakunda, were not literate and on them fell most of the burden of sweeping the offices (transferring dust from one place to another using a bundle of fine twigs) and carrying files between the various offices. All of them helped in the tedious task of counting money in the form of coin, to check the amount, and also to detect counterfeit, of which substantial amounts were being manufactured in the Ibadan area and spread around the country. Yahaya and Bello were kept almost continuously employed in the DO's office, writing out the details of complaints which were delivered verbally and with much histrionic effect by the complainants seated on the veranda. Good messengers were very valuable members of the 'political' team, acting as interpreters for little-known languages, and as intelligence agents, particularly in the bush when a DO or ADO was on tour. There was, of course, always the possibility that they might be unduly influenced, or even bribed, and it was part of the DO's expertise to be able to detect this, or any other situation in which someone was trying to hide the facts or misrepresent a case. Bello was considered to be pretty reliable in Katsina, but, as a distant cousin of the Waziri of Kano, might have been less useful if employed in that Emirate. He was a lively, amusing little man, whose heavily pock-marked face evidenced his survival from smallpox as a child; he was always impeccably turned out in a white or blue gown and turban. His Hausa was very clear and full of humour, and I found him a better teacher than the schoolmaster whom I employed at first. All the messengers spoke Fulani, an essential qualification when touring with a DO or ADO in the rainy season when Fulani and their cattle would be roaming in large numbers over all the Northern area.

The office staff, the nature of their employment and their relationships with the British officials were characteristic of the

27

strengths and weaknesses of the administration of government in Northern Nigeria. The Southern Provinces, as a result of early and continuous missionary effort and other influences, had very much more schooling and Western-type education (including the teaching of English) than the North, which retained an Islamic bias in all but a sprinkling of 'middle schools'. The Native Authorities managed to staff their own clerical establishments with Northerners by pitching their own standards below those set for equivalent government posts, but the number of the latter which were filled by Northerners was very small indeed. The administration and the clerical labour associated with it were therefore divided into quite distinct operations. In dealing with the NAs, the chiefs, their offices and all their departments, the normal language was Hausa. The records of the tax office, the Treasury, the Alkali's court, and even technical departments such as Works and Veterinary would be written in Hausa. Letters passed from the NAs and the Emir to the DO, but received only the briefest replies. Communication was usually by meeting, and a minute recording agreement and/or action to be taken would be issued by the NA official concerned immediately afterwards. On the other hand, all communication between the Resident or DO and other British officials would be in English, as would all government Treasury business, and would pass through the files and clerical procedures of the Provincial Office.

The government clerks were relatively well paid, compared with the messengers and many of the NA officials, whose work was often very responsible in political or financial terms. There was no love lost between the two groups, and one of my earliest and strongest impressions was the attitude of near-contempt of the Northerner staff towards the Southerners. The attitudes of the British probably did little or nothing to improve matters. Occasionally, one would find a clerk with a sense of humour and a cheerful response to the difficulties of life in the North, but for the most part they took themselves too seriously, often complaining, pernickety, awkward, even whining, and all this in a form of biblical English with the odd inflection of 'pidgin' which seemed rather graceless by comparison with Hausa, which is a language with a rich vocabulary, full of idioms and proverbial expressions. I have to admit, with regret, that the Northern DO (and other British officials based in the North) generally had little sympathy with the

Yoruba clerk and even less with the Ibo. The Northerners were aware of this attitude and could compare it with the easy, friendly relationship which most of them enjoyed with the British. I tried hard to like the Southerners, and came to be very fond of Francis, my cook, who was an Ibo, but the relationships were usually uneasy and there was undoubtedly a complex psychology in all this which would need many pages of explanation. Sadly enough, these antipathies, expressed as tribal antagonisms between groups of Africans, were to have tragic consequences, not only in Nigeria but elsewhere, and they continue to this day.

All this is something of a digression, but it is part of the attempt, which I must make, to describe the scene in which my work, for the next six months, was to be carried on. It remains to complete the picture of my most immediate working relationships by including the Resident and the DO. Katsina was an unusual province in that it contained only one division, and so the geographical areas of responsibility of the single DO and the Resident overlapped completely. Most provinces contained one large division (often sharing the same headquarters with the Resident) and two, three or four smaller ones, and there was always a tendency for the Resident to have a rather undue influence on events in the large division where his own headquarters would be based. In Katsina, this had become an absurdity; the Resident had too little to do, and would irritate his subordinates by too much attention to detail and non-essentials; his staff, on the other hand, were overworked, and their irritation was often increased by lack of understanding of their difficulties. Katsina was one of the provinces where the Resident was still able to retain an Olympian detachment from the all-too-frequent surges of hectic activity in the Provincial Office by isolating himself in his personal office in the Residency. Messengers walked or cycled all day long the half-mile or so between the Residency and the Provincial Office, and the telephone which (unfortunately!) connected the two places seemed sometimes to be in constant operation. The impatience often displayed by the man in the Residency was bad enough in itself, but seemed to imply a complete ignorance of the range of tasks devolving on the ADO, additional to that of general assistant to the Resident.

The DO, Brian Macfarlane, was a quiet man who always seemed to be fully occupied, either investigating complaints or functioning as a magistrate, together with some touring and prison inspection when the ADO simply couldn't find time to do it. In Katsina, as in any other Emirate, the DO was the man immediately responsible for the supervision of all the activities of the Native Administration relating to finance, including tax assessment and collection and law and order. He had also to maintain close liaison with all the provincial departmental officers, medical, education, engineering, agricultural, forestry, veterinary, geological survey and others, to ensure their satisfactory cooperation with the appropriate officials in the NA.

The Emir, as the paramount chief, was assisted by a council, including the Waziri (Vizier) who was the senior administrative officer, the Chief Alkali (judge) and two or three senior officials, who were sometimes aristocrats. There were about twenty districts in Katsina Emirate, each in the charge of a district head who was sometimes hereditary, as were the village heads who were answerable to the district head for the collection of tax. The district heads were directly responsible to the Waziri, and were supposed to keep a diary and report all matters of any significance. They brought tax collections as cash to the Beit-el-Mal (native treasury) in Katsina.

The Resident was responsible to the Chief Commissioner in Kaduna for all aspects of administration in his province. Residents and District Officers did not always agree on the handling of Emirs and their officials, and this could sometimes lead to quite serious friction.

The celebration of the installation of electric power was my first opportunity to see something of the old town. Dusk was falling, but there was moonlight against which the great mass of the wall loomed up as we drove towards and through one of the main gates. The 'palace', a large walled enclosure with its own great gate, lay on our left, and to the right, across a broad open space, lay the NA offices and the various 'wards' of the town, with its market. It was all very like Kano, on a somewhat smaller scale. A platform had been erected in front of the palace, and it was there that we met the various notables, all splendidly attired, some of them in robes and turbans stiff with shining blue-black indigo. The Emir, an impressive figure in white, was the only person with whom we shook hands; all the others, including the Emir's sons, made a deep obeisance, with the traditional greeting, 'Ranka shi dade' ('May your life be prolonged'). The Emir's courtiers stood around, echoing the greetings, which were again re-echoed by the long trumpets which are always played on ceremonial occasions. From the platform we looked out over a vast crowd of people who seemed to fill the whole square. All this followed the evening prayer, which was just finishing as we passed through the town gate. When the Emir, after a brief speech, threw the switch, coloured lights came on over all the main buildings, and a loud shout of wonder went up from the assembled populace, which sounded like 'Wallahi' in unison.

The Emir, Muhammadu Dikko, had held the chiefdom since 1906, when he was appointed by the British, following the dismissal of his predecessor who had failed to cooperate, after the occupation of Katsina. He had the presence and dignity which one expected of a man of such experience, combined with a personality of considerable warmth and charm. His eldest son, Usuman Nagogo, had a lively, exuberant manner, and somewhat staccato speech – the words seemed to tumble out of him. A very intelligent, gifted young man, he was probably the best polo player in Nigeria, and played the game with a style and dash which was quite characteristic. I saw a lot of the Emir and Nagogo during the next six months, and found them to be a very impressive pair.

Alhadji arrived by the mail-lorry from Kano, and Mrs Drummond-Hay found a cook for me, an Ibo who was a relation of her own cook. There was a proliferation of such relationships among domestic servants in the British community; the resulting intelligence network was sometimes useful in obtaining information via one's own servants about, for example, one's own further movement to another station! Alhadji and Francis had considerable respect for each other, and came back to me, after my army service, to travel with me and my wife into remote bush areas, cheerful and uncomplaining.

Now that I was provided with boys, the time had come for me to fend for myself, and I was allotted a large empty house until such time as Russell moved out of the house which 'belonged' to the Provincial Office. Within a week or so, I had taken over Russell's duties; he had gone off to Daura and I had moved into the ADO's house, which was smaller, more convenient, and had a few items of furniture for which I paid Russell £6.

6

Administering the Lugard Legacy

ɛ⌍

L IFE in the Provincial Office was a never-ending struggle to cope with many different demands and a variety of tasks and duties without completely losing one's temper or one's sense of humour. My diary records that I sometimes lost both, but fortunately not for very long. Of all my many Pooh-Bah responsibilities, that of being Local Treasurer was the most tedious, demanding and unrewarding. The treasury clerk, from the Gold Coast, was responsible for typing vouchers, but all the remaining responsibilities – checking the correctness of payments, writing up the cash-book, maintaining cash-balances, controlling the flow of currency between the NAs and government, paying officials' allowances, cashing cheques, settling government accounts, keeping the postmaster in order and checking his cash, issuing petrol for cash and replenishing stocks, paying station-labourers, pensioners, reservists, clerks, messengers – all these and more that I can't remember were mine. The poor clerk was very, very dense, extremely ugly, unloved and, unfortunately, to my senses, generally unwashed. I found collaboration with him very trying, and made worse by the fact that he tried hard.

Work done on behalf of the Resident consisted of the general running of the Provincial Office, and the supervision of the clerks and their work (including coping with the many complaints and squabbles among themselves); drafting memoranda, distributing incoming mail and ensuring that 'important' papers were 'put up' with the appropriate files without delay and that replies, duly typed and signed, caught the outgoing mail (this was a never-ending source of fuss with a Resident who was anxious to impress Kaduna with his efficiency); preparing and checking endless returns (weekly, monthly, quarterly, annual; some of these for the DO as well) – these chores coincided with much end-of-period treasury work, and could make month-ends and quarter-ends quite unbearable. In addition to all this, I found myself loaded with the preparation of the Native Treasury Estimates (the budgets, in effect, for Katsina Emirate and for Daura) in ridiculous negation of all the basic principles of the system of Indirect Rule. According to theory, the estimates should have been drafted by the NA and approved by its Council before being passed to the DO for his comments, discussion and possible amendment, before submission to the Resident for any changes he might have to suggest, before sending them to Kaduna. Katsina, which was supposed to be a well-organised emirate (it was, in fact, the first to have a Native Treasury, and might claim to have invented the idea), should have been able to follow this procedure, but the drafting was apparently considered to be beyond its capacity. In that case, the job should have fallen to the DO or, failing him, to the Resident, but these two gentlemen, with great modesty, considered that it might best be done by the ADO.

The DO was senior to me, and so, of course, there was always work to be done for him. These tasks included checking the Alkali's court records and visiting the prison, but with the Provincial Office work still to be done in addition, I never felt that I gave the time and attention to them which they required for a full and critical understanding. Sadly, too, I did not have time to get to know the NA officials as people, as I did later, when working in Bornu Province.

Prison inspection was instructive and saddening. It was one of the few opportunities which I had, at this time, of getting close to the ordinary people and understanding the problems in their lives. I was sometimes joined on these inspections by the Emir, and always by the Waziri and his chief scribe, who were responsible for the prison administration. The general routine was first to see, individually, all the prisoners on remand, to find out why the remand was continuing and when it was likely to end, and to see any other prisoner who had a complaint. Remands often ran on for long periods owing to the difficulty of locating and transporting witnesses from remote areas, and it was necessary sometimes to insist on the release of someone who appeared on remand month after month. Some prisoners showed a lot of courage in complaining of injustice, or of having been 'framed' by some authority. Quite often, this was a try-on, an attempt to take advantage of a new and inexperienced ADO, and this was generally revealed by a little questioning. Occasionally, I was impressed by the apparent sincerity of the complainant and asked to see the court record, or to discuss the case with the Alkali. Occasionally, too, one could be impressed by the skill with which the authorities mobilised their defences, and attempted (often, no doubt, successfully) to pull the wool over one's eyes.

For the physical inspection, the prisoners were assembled in the central courtyard which appears to be an essential architectural feature of all the prisons I have known. I looked at some of the faces and tried to guess the nature of the crime, ranging from perjury through theft to homicide, which had brought them there, and found that prison uniform, in the early morning light, gave them all the same cold and hungry look, so that I hurried on to bring nearer their breakfast, and mine. On later occasions, I was sorry to recognise men whom I had exposed in some crime or other (generally embezzlement of tax) and would exchange a few words, confirming that there were no hard feelings on either side. Women were housed in a separate small building, and here it was sad to see them (normally there were very few) nursing a child; in such cases there appeared to be no possible alternative arrangement. A few leper prisoners, mostly burnt-out cases, were also housed separately, and were, perhaps, glad to be fed and accommodated away from the hard outside world. (There was, however, a leper colony run by an American mission a few miles outside Katsina.) The last building to be entered on this doleful tour was the lunatic enclosure, where a few inmates (mostly women) were cared for with a surprising degree of understanding and compassion.

With September, the rains were coming to an end, and the harvest hot weather was beginning to build up. Most days I left the office at some time between 2 and 4 p.m., very hungry but too jaded to eat much. After a short rest, I had to pull myself together and work for an hour or so at Hausa, and also at the handbooks of General Orders, Financial Instructions and selected Ordinances (Acts) in all of which subjects I was due to be examined before taking Hadow's place 'on tour' in five months' time. In the evening, the folk who were quite undemanding and restful just to sit with were the 'second-class citizens': Shepherd, who let me listen to symphony concerts on his radio while he smoked his pipe and drank his whisky, ignoring the music; Len Wileman and his quiet, good-natured wife with their dry, North Country humour; and John Hall, the Scottish well-digger and music-lover, who became a good friend.

In spite of all this sociability, loneliness could be a problem, as indeed it was for all colonial bachelors, even the most exalted ones, as I came to realise later. The social hour of tennis or golf was usually relaxing, and I rode occasionally. On other days, I walked in the Forest Reserve which bordered the road between the station and Katsina town and was quiet, shady and cool. Unfortunately, I never met anyone knowledgeable about birds, which might have become an absorbing interest.

We were, of course, a long way removed, geographically, from the Munich crisis at this time, and in the absence of London papers which took at least three weeks to reach Katsina we depended on the BBC for news and comment on the situation. One undesirable and very unwelcome outcome of our apparent weakness in dealing with Hitler was a rumour reported in the Lagos press to the effect that the British government had agreed to hand over Nigeria to the Germans as a gesture of appeasement; there was a strong and immediate official disclaimer.

Drummond-Hay may have decided that my experience as an auditor should be used. He had no head for figures, and was obviously relieved that I managed to cope on his behalf with the drafting of the Native Treasury Estimates for the coming year. One used the current year's figures as a guide, but there were variations, inspired mostly by directives from Kaduna which indicated that particular attention should be given to certain items. Rightly, increased interest was being taken in rural development, which meant, in particular, wells, dispensaries, schools. I spent much of September on this work, and quite a lot of it was done in my quarters 'after hours'. It was not without educational value, and D-H and I (as my diary records) had some long discussions about the money allocated to various purposes in relation to their importance, and the urgency of need. At this time, I had very little knowledge or experience of the way of life of people living in the villages and small towns of the province, but I was shocked, even appalled, by the very small sums of money allocated to welfare and the development of amenities both in absolute terms and in proportion to what was spent on the salaries of NA chiefs and officials. When I gained first-hand experience of conditions in the villages by touring for several months on horseback, my discontent with the way money was spent, with the pitifully small return (apart from Pax Britannica) which the family in the bush had for the tax they paid, was a constant preoccupation, and remained so throughout my service.

The financial details for Katsina Emirate, as I recorded them in my diary, are worth comment at this stage, because they are, to my mind, a sufficient summary of the inadequacy of resources available to the handful of Britishers who were trying to cope with an enormous task: to improve the quality of life for the ordinary people. Of the total tax of about £120,000 paid by the people of the Emirate, about £50,000 or so was paid over directly to the central government. Of the remaining £70,000 which was retained by the NA, nearly £50,000 was spent on the salaries of the chief, councillors, district heads, alkalis, scribes, police and so on, leaving about £20,000 available for purposes of welfare, amenities and development generally. I asked: 'Is it any wonder that there is so little progress, that the land continues to desiccate for lack of preventive measures, that the death-toll from cerebro-spinal meningitis was 25,000 last year in this Emirate alone (population one million), to say nothing of the thousands of lepers, and people suffering from hook-worm, guinea-worm, sleeping sickness, fevers, and eye infections causing blindness. Isn't it to be expected when the expenditure on medical services is £2,000, and that on education even less?' One should mention that these figures do not include the salaries of British officials (such as medical and education officers) which were paid by the Nigerian government.

Drummond-Hay seemed interested to hear my views on the allocation of resources, being the views of a newcomer not yet inured to the enormous disparity between the funds available and the multiplicity and scale of the many urgent needs. It seemed to me then (and still does) that three things, at least, were wrong or needed review. First, the proportion of tax levied by the Native Authority which was syphoned off into the government Treasury was almost certainly too large in relation to the services provided by central government (being chiefly the government officials operating in the province) and bearing in mind that the government collected a large revenue in Customs dues (at the ports) on goods finally sold in the province. Secondly, the salaries paid to the Emir and the district heads were too large. Third, the natural resources of the country being modest (this was before the discovery of oil), Nigeria would take a long, long time to pull itself up by its own bootstraps. Some subvention from UK government funds was required, and was justified by the considerable trading advantages which the UK enjoyed in Nigeria.

Drummond-Hay said that he would raise these points, among others, when he discussed the Estimates with the Chief Commissioner during his local leave in Kaduna. A year or two later, Bourdillon, the Governor, wrote an important paper on the division of the tax revenue between NAs and central government, which led to a considerable improvement in NA resources. I like to think that I may have given a small push in the right direction.

As far as I know, the salaries of chiefs were never reviewed downwards, although inflation may have had some effect in later years. The theory was that chiefs were well paid so that they could support their proper status without resort to corruption to augment their incomes. In practice, many of them used their positions to help to line their pockets, and all too often their malpractices were not sufficiently investigated, nor were they sufficiently punished when detected. Indirect Rule could be made to work reasonably well if Administrative Officers were actively touring at full strength, knew their districts, and had their ears close to the ground. For various reasons, particularly shortage of staff, these conditions rarely obtained, and we could claim only that corruption was kept within bounds which were just acceptable.

Nigeria, and other territories at similar stages of development, had to wait for the post-war years to gain access to money, in amounts undreamed of by the old-style administrators, from the Colonial Development Fund. Much was then spent by the large NAs, too much, as ever, in the large towns and too little in the bush. (Polly Hill's book *Rural Hausa* shows how little a Katsina village was changed for the better between 1938 and 1966.) It remains for me very much an open question whether, within the time-scale available, the provision of substantial extra money would have helped Northern Nigeria better to prepare for the coming of Independence, which became the vital problem for the North in the 1950s. I and my younger colleagues would have chosen to see more money spent on the urgent needs of the common folk in the villages, on wells, dispensaries, markets, schools, dry-season roads or tracks (for transporting produce after harvest and bringing in consumer goods). This might not have done a great deal to help the Fulani aristocracy to deal with Ibo and Yoruba politicians, but it would have helped to create more awareness and spirit at the grass-roots. Without some such development, the villagers could have little hope of achieving even a local degree of democracy, still less of mitigating the power and influence of the Emirs and their retainers at district or higher levels. For my part, from the little that I knew already of the way things were moving in Southern Nigeria, I hoped that the North could avoid the kind of 'development' which might mean the loss of the great virtues of its people, their honesty, innate dignity and attachment to a traditional way of life that had many simple pleasures and satisfactions.

There was (and probably still is) an influential school of sociologists which held that the 'modernisation' of traditional cultures was inevitable, leading to a breakdown of loyalties and departures from accepted beliefs and values. I suppose that most of us, in supporting, with reservations, the Lugardian principles of Indirect Rule, and applying them in our daily work, were implicitly rejecting the concept of inevitable 'modernisation' and believed that we could help the people of the North to hold at bay the worst influences of Western culture while they built up their own material and cultural resources. If we could do this, not only would traditional values be protected, but ways could be found to modify the power structure of Indirect Rule which in the Emirates had become increasingly unsatisfactory and outdated, depending as it did on a great deal of institutionalised office-purchase and associated corruption. I, and many others like me, felt that we were not moving fast enough in these directions, not only because there was a lack of money, but also because there was a lack of purpose and will among those from whom we had to take our orders. For us, the frustration was greatest when we were nearest to headquarters of any kind, with limited freedom of action. In the bush, we were away from all that, and, as I shall relate, even with limited resources, we managed to get something done.

7

Disillusion and Hope

എ

I LONGED to get away to the bush, but could not expect release before February, and in the meantime had to cope with the increasing boredom and exasperation of the Provincial Office routine. Frustration caused me to think of resigning, but I had to admit that the world outside was full of unpleasantness and that sweating it out in Nigeria was probably the better option. The 'wireless news', as we called it in those days, mentioned on 9 September: 'France, calling up reserves; Russia, adopting a firm attitude; Great Britain, consultations among Defence Ministers; China, new Japanese offensive; Spain, new counter-attacks; Burma, martial law; Delhi, ditto; Palestine, more rioting.'

I managed to keep working throughout October and November, in spite of low fever, various aches and pains and, finally, boils! Drummond-Hay, who had been quite affable, began to get nervy and fussy about every detail as the return of the Resident became imminent, and this did not help. He arrived at last, in November, a rather short, physically energetic fifty-year-old whose speech came in brief, disconnected bursts, often unintelligible to the clerks, who would later badger me to interpret his requirements. He made himself very agreeable to everyone but Drummond-Hay, who was in a state of gloom following the hand-over. It didn't take the Resident long to show his true colours, oscillating between affability and bad temper, depending on the circumstances, including particularly any supposedly critical comment from his masters in Kaduna. Macfarlane left to take up station in the other small emirate in the province, Daura, and Drummond-Hay took over the Katsina Emirate in an uneasy relationship with the Resident. I bore the brunt of their mutually generated ill-humour, but the clerks and messengers also took a large share of it.

39

Throughout November, the messengers and my excellent Alhadji were enduring the rigours of the fast of Ramadan, and I did what I could to reduce demands on their energies during the worst of the heat of the day. For the messengers, this was difficult if not impossible, with files to be carried at all times between the office and the Residency. The hardship was borne with great good humour (and perhaps some mild contempt for the infidel British) and within a few days of the festival which marks the end of the fast, I was approached by my boys and messengers for advances of pay to enable them to purchase clothes, kola-nuts and other traditional items. This meant, of course, that money had to be given as well as being lent, but other debts were also incurred, and I began to understand how it came about that most of the African community seemed to be in debt to someone for most of the time. The day of the festival, 24 November, found the Resident fully in the saddle again, and I drove down to the town with him to join in the celebrations. The scene is described in my diary as 'a great sight, full of colour and life'. Several of the Emir's bodyguard were wearing chain-mail, which is supposed to have been handed down, across the Islamic world, from the time of the Crusades. The Emir, standing at the porch of his 'palace', was greeted in turn by each district head galloping up with a cohort of horsemen waving spears – all this to the accompaniment of drumming and the blowing of long trumpets. I recorded a fine blue sky above massive red walls and earth; clouds of dust from flying hooves, brilliant robes, assertive youths and shy maidens – definitely something not to be missed. This kind of spectacle, on a far greater scale, was laid on for the Queen on her visit to Kaduna in the late 1950s, and apparently made a lasting impression.

The following day we were again in the town for the unveiling, at the Yandaka gate, of the memorial to Lugard's entry into Katsina in 1903. There was more interesting ceremony, with many townspeople watching from the ragged top of the city wall on both sides of the gate. Drummond-Hay was very busy, taking photographs to be sent to Lugard. After the ceremony we walked through a long maze of passages and ante-rooms in the palace to the women's quarters to greet Madaki, the Emir's chief, and very young, wife, to whom he seemed to be particularly devoted. She was a shy, charming creature, gorgeously clad in a robe of scarlet silk. I gained the impression that 'visiting Madaki' had become a regular feature of ceremonial meetings in the town, which seemed to be surprisingly unorthodox behaviour in a high-ranking Muslim household. Later I was to find that Madaki accompanied the Emir to tea at the Residency (I was there) which seemed to be even more irregular.

After the Lugard ceremony, I accompanied the Resident and Drummond-Hay to the Council Chamber for a meeting with the Emir, Waziri and all the assembled district heads. There was much discussion on a range of topics, from the harvest and tax to epidemics and the reliability of census figures. Some of the district heads seemed to be very intelligent, including the new Kogo district head whose predecessor, a Katsina College graduate, had been executed in June for murder, after a trial which disclosed an alarming level of corruption.

December brought some variation to the station scene. By the end of the month, I was glad to have the blaze of a fire in the evening, and tried to close the great 'window' gap in the sitting-room with a curtain made from several widths of homespun cloth sewn together. Early in the month, I had completed, successfully, all the exams in Hausa, law and Colonial Regulations and now had these tedious matters behind me – a considerable relief.

There was a round of parties that stretched through Christmas into the New Year, the sizeable number of Scots in any station always ensuring that the latter festival received its fullest recognition. It is, perhaps, not surprising that these parties were so important to some people; after all, there was little in the way of other forms of entertainment. But I was not alone in finding them tedious. John Hall piled his kit and staff into the back of his old lorry and went off bush and to work, digging his wells. In Bornu in later years two of my colleagues took their horses or camels and withdrew into the remote sandy wastes on the northern border near Lake Chad, incommunicado, until it was all over.

However, such absenteeism was not allowed for *any* Katsina staff for the New Year of 1938–39. By Royal Command, all had to be present and correct, in the station, to meet the Governor, Sir Bernard Bourdillon, who was to spend two days in Katsina in the course of a tour of some of the Northern Provinces. The Resident vacated the Residency and lodged with the Drummond-Hays, who received him without much enthusiasm. On 30 December the Resident set off with Drummond-Hay to meet HE at the Kano boundary, where he was 'handed over' by the Kano Resident. A cavalcade of cars arrived at about 12.30, and HE, Lady Bourdillon, Joy Bourdillon (wife of young Bernard, then an ADO in Zaria, and later to be killed in the King David Hotel explosion in Jerusalem) and their staff settled into the Residency, where we all 'signed the book' during the day. Later we attended a polo match, in which HE played very well, after which we were presented to him and Lady B., who were as charming as ever and remembered me from our voyage in the *Accra* in 1937.

The next day I was dashing around, combining my office job with that of escort to Lady Bourdillon during the Governor's official visit to the town to meet the Emir, district heads and NA staff, to open a new ward of the hospital, and to drink a ginger-beer at the African Club. (We did *not* visit Madaki!) Then, after a quick lunch, we drove to the lake at Kaita, and were disposed around its perimeter in such a way as to ensure that our shooting drove the birds in the direction of HE, who secured quite a good bag. Back to Katsina for a brief rest, bath and change into black tie for HE's New Year's Eve party, which was held in Drummond-Hay's house and was made very enjoyable by the amiability of the Bourdillons.

The following morning, the first of the fateful year of 1939, was a Sunday, and the Bourdillons were on their way back to Kano and Lagos bright and early. At the time, I did not know that this visit was part of HE's appraisal of the Muslim North as a cultural, political and religious entity, and the problems that it raised for his plans, which he was trying to formulate, for constitutional progress for the territory as a whole. Bourdillon produced two memoranda setting out his ideas, which were supposed to be made known to all administrative staff. They were never brought to my attention during my service, but made interesting reading many years later.

In 1937, Bourdillon decided to try to involve the senior Northern Emirs in the legislative process in Lagos. (The Northern Provinces were not then represented on the Legislative Council, and the Governor simply decreed those parts of any legislation which were to be operational in the North.) He asked Chief Commissioner Adams to discuss with the Sultan of Sokoto the possibility of his sitting in the Legislative Council with some of his brother Emirs. However, Adams briefed the Sokoto Resident to broach the matter with the Sultan in a way which seems to have produced a negative response. It is sad to think that a positive response could have had important consequences for the future of Nigeria.

Unfortunately, Bourdillon did not then have the vision, or possibly he was not a hard enough man, to go for what might have been the best solution, to divide the North into perhaps three regions, to provide a better balance with the two in the South. This might well have reduced the sense of political polarisation, and the fear of 'Big Brother', which was felt so strongly in the South, and would have been more manageable administratively. Whether it would have provided a more effective unity in the ultimate federated territory as it exists today is more questionable. The world is full of examples to show how difficult or even impossible it is for peoples of very different beliefs, traditions and racial origins to sink their differences and cooperate in government. The most that any of us could do in the 1930s and 1940s was to make the benefits of Pax Britannica as widely available as possible, and to prevent undue exploitation of it to the detriment of the under-dog.

Before this long digression, I had been saying farewell to the Bourdillons and had returned wearily to the office in recognition that, although it was Sunday, it was also 1 January, and the inevitable due day for the Board of Survey on my Treasury cash. As far as I can remember, it was Drummond-Hay and Scott who constituted the Board, and we were none of us in very good humour before, during or after the session. It was all rather typical of the tiresomeness and artificiality of the office routine, with its mixture of physical discomforts, work pressure and personality problems.

My transfer to bush touring was scheduled for 7 February, when I was to hand over the office and Treasury to Scott, which was achieved, as expected, with a minimum of consideration and a maximum of bickering over every petty detail. At this time, I could readily shrug off my difficulties with him in anticipation of my escape to bush within a few days, and concentrate on enjoying, for the little time left, the company of John Hall, the Wilemans and good honest Shepherd.

8

Bush Life is Better

❧

O N the morning of 7 February, Alhadji completed the packing of all our kit and few belongings, while I had breakfast with the Wilemans, this being a sort of traditional valedictory hospitality among friends in the service, and one of the things I like to remember about it. Then, clad at last in khaki bush-shirt and shorts, I sat down alongside the driver of the old Albion lorry, and we set off, at a speed of at least 25 mph, heading south for Kankara, mostly along a rough dry-season road. As we approached Kankara, the HQ of Fauwa District, through orchard bush, the country was much more hilly than the open farmland around Katsina, with rocky outcrops and many dry river-beds through which the lorry toiled in bottom gear. We drew up at Kankara rest-house in mid-afternoon, very travel-weary and covered with dust (the 'staff' on the back of the lorry even more than myself), to find four other people already in occupation. Bevan, a short square Welshman with a very loud voice and inexhaustible energy, had replaced John Hall as foreman, Geological Survey Department, in charge of well-sinking operations in the province. Harnett and Williams, an oddly assorted pair, were officers of the sleeping-sickness survey, in charge of anti-SS operations in the south of Katsina Province. Harnett, brawny, red-faced, hearty and amiable, had formerly been a sergeant in the Royal Army Service Corps. Williams, a slight, dreamy intellectual, had recently come down from Cambridge and was still suffering from withdrawal symptoms. Hadow I had now known long enough to like and respect. He was rather smaller than average, and determined to be tough and resolute to compensate. He had a very able elder brother who was making a good career in the Gold Coast, and was striving constantly to model himself upon him. As a result, his attitudes and opinions were somewhat establishment-oriented. When four such different people (and I must count myself as a fifth) live in very confined quarters, they tend not to show their better qualities, and for a time I wondered whether I had jumped out of the Katsina office frying-pan into the Kankara rest-house fire. I soon realised, however, that the rest-house was very popular because it was one of the few relatively comfortable ones in southern Katsina, and was bound to be overcrowded occasionally.

Macfarlane had given me a very limited briefing on my duties. As far as I could gather, I was expected to carry on with the work which Hadow had been doing, that is, liaison with the well-sinking and sleeping-sickness teams and speeding up the collection of tax (*haraji*, a sort of income tax assessed communally on everything except cattle).

The measures which were being taken against sleeping-sickness in Northern Nigeria were part of a concerted drive to reduce the incidence of the disease throughout British Africa, and elsewhere, following international conferences in 1925 and subsequent years. The most important tasks were: to discover cases of human infection in the villages and isolate them for treatment; to map the incidence of the disease and of the tsetse fly and to clear dense vegetation overhanging stretches of water where the flies would breed and constitute a danger to a neighbouring community. Tsetse flies are carriers of trypanosomes, transmitted by bites, which are pathogenic to humans (and to some animals). By the time I arrived on the scene, the preliminary survey stages were largely completed, and Harnett and Williams were mapping in detail the areas of dense cover, mostly along the banks of streams adjacent to villages or near points from which water was drawn. Clearing vegetation for health reasons was a task for which forced labour could be required of the local community and my job was to persuade the village heads to produce men, as needed, to work under the guidance of headmen who were employed by the survey, which also provided axes and machetes. It was important to get on with the work while the stream-beds were dry and before seasonal farm-work began.

The clearing work was hard and even dangerous (poisonous plants and snakes were fairly plentiful) and was unpopular with the villagers, who regarded *rani*, the dry season before the rains, as a period for resting, relaxing and visiting friends and relations. The village heads and district heads were preoccupied with the problems of completing the collection of tax and were disinclined to apply further pressure to the villagers. Hadow, in the few days we spent together, complained bitterly of the laziness and incompetence of some village heads who were also suspected of embezzling tax. The head of the district, Sarkin (chief of) Fauwa, was a very old man, a scarred veteran of war and slave-raiding, in fact, and most of the responsibility and work devolved upon his son Sule who had the rather fragile and even effeminate appearance which in the Fulani sometimes belies their capacity and endurance. Sule gave me much of his time, and was the appropriate intermediary in negotiations with village heads, but in his absence I had often to rely on the services of Mallam Mani, the Emir's representative who stayed on after Hadow's departure. The procedures of Indirect Rule as laid down in Lugard's Political Memoranda and elsewhere required, *inter alia*, that I should use the Emir's representative as the channel of communication with district and village heads. Mallam Mani was an amiable old buffer and I soon found that he did not carry much weight with the district heads, or even the more important village heads. However, I used him for all formal communications and especially where criticism or a rebuke was required, but in all practical matters left the local authority in no doubt about what was needed, and how quickly, by expressing this in Hausa which was equally understood by all parties, including Mani, who would sagely nod his head, saying, 'Thus it is'.

The management style at district head and village head level varied enormously, as I found in all provinces throughout my service. The Sarkin Fauwa, unable to travel, was now for most village heads a remote but still formidable personality, and Sule's ultimate sanction was to threaten to bring a village head before his father. The district head of neighbouring Bakori district, whose villages were also in my touring area, was a man of considerable intellect and commanding presence (he was about six and a half feet tall). He bore the hereditary title of Iya, which in Hausa means ability or capacity, and certainly lived up to his name. His head-quarters town of Bakori (on the main road to Funtua from Katsina) was a model of its kind. The school and dispensary were clean, cheerful, lively places, and the town and market were well laid out, free from the dust and rubbish which was all too obvious in Kankara during my first inspection with Hadow.

Some village heads were poor creatures, cringing dependents of the district head, with soiled gown and turban bearing the evidence of many prostrations before those deemed to be superior, and much hard travelling and hard lying, in both senses, collecting tax. Others, who lorded it over the larger village areas, were well-groomed and relatively self-confident, especially those who could claim descent from one of the Fulani who conquered the area in the Usuman dan Fodio *jihad* (the 'holy war' of the previous century). The messenger, Sali, who had been working with Hadow, had elected to stay on with me and proved to be a most valuable source of intelligence. He was familiar with many of the office-holders, great and small, in much of the province, having toured with officers of all ranks since leaving the army to become a messenger in 1919. His knowledge of the antecedents and past performance of district and village heads, Alkalis, and their scribe/ assistants was encyclopaedic and his assessments of their current performance remarkably shrewd. Half Hausa, half Fulani, he spoke both languages well, but was illiterate apart from a smattering of Ajami (Hausa written in Arabic script) which enabled him to stumble through a census list. He was a wiry, tough little man, with a pock-marked face, and a great sense of humour which was often revealed, to the general delight, in the course of a long trek from one village to the next. Sali was one of several messengers who served me well and devotedly in various stations, and I became fond of them all. It made me angry that they were so poorly paid in relation to the value of their services, but long experience since those days has convinced me that this kind of inequality is wide-spread, and probably has been from time immemorial. Of Sali, one can only say, with gladness, that he was happy in spite of his poverty and enriched the lives of people who, like me, were fortunate enough to know him.

Hadow stayed on for several days, and we visited various centres of activity together, staying with Harnett and Williams in two villages, Ketare and Guga, each about twenty miles from Kankara. In Ketare we were accommodated in a mud hut with a thatched roof in the main street. The hut had been extended by the addition of a *rumfa*, which was a sort of porch, larger than the hut itself, made of tough grass matting, with a roof of the same material, which was neither sun-proof or rain-proof. As a place for rest and refreshment after a day's work, it was most unsatisfactory, being noisy, dusty, draughty and, after sunset, very cold. The harmattan was still intense, with wind and dust-haze persisting through most of the day but with a brief spell of fierce heat around midday and early afternoon. In spite of the substandard accommodation, provided by a substandard village head, I was happy in Ketare during our short stay there, because it was such a complete change from the Katsina station routine. The poor living conditions were made bearable by the interesting activity all around us, from before dawn until well after sunset. There was a thriving market on the river-bank a short distance away, and there one could buy all the considerable range of local produce, from a horse to a bundle of sugar-cane. I bought a lively-looking young horse for trekking (a light chestnut, which I called Gingerbread), and some sugar-cane to still the pangs of hunger between meals. I soon became adept at peeling the bark of the cane and chewing the succulent pith.

Guga was a small town rather than a village, and was largely contained within the remains of a defensive wall of sun-dried earth, rather like the Katsina wall on a smaller scale. The village head was a man of substance, quiet and efficient. He had completed the collection of tax, whereas the Magajin (head of) Ketare was still far behind and under suspicion of misappropriation. Magajin Guga had built a splendid *rumfa* camp, incorporating two roofs of thatch, just outside the town, away from the road but with good access to it, and here we stayed. We enjoyed our visits to Guga, where we could buy paw-paw which grew on trees dotted about the town; this was a great treat in an area where fruit of any kind was hard to find. I had firm and immediate support from Magajin Guga in all that needed to be done, and it was a pleasure to work with him. One had simply to explain the reasons for doing something and provide some stimulus from time to time. The problem villages like Ketare were, unfortunately, in the majority, and it was very difficult to do much to improve them, within the context of the machinery and procedures of Indirect Rule. I tried, from time to time, to introduce a little democracy into the nomination of a new village head, while touring in Katsina and later in Bornu, but I suspect that I did more harm than good; the time was not ripe for it.

Bush-clearing along streams and well-sinking were being carried out over a wide area in places which varied greatly in accessibility; some were on or close to a motor road, some were approachable by a motorable track during the dry season and the remainder could be reached only by the age-old bush path, about two feet wide, worn and kept open by the passage of man, donkey and horse. Occasionally, an intrepid cyclist, perhaps with a white (or red) face, would toil along a twisting, sandy, stony bush path to save time, uttering, with his little remaining breath, a prayer to be spared punctures. I had a horse and a bike, and reckoned that, using one or the other, I could visit a place up to twelve miles away, do some work and return the same day. Harnett and Williams had motor-bikes and Bevan had a Ford V8 kitcar, so I planned my movements to combine with theirs, to share their transport when possible, although riding pillion along a rough road or bush path is not something I would recommend. Travelling with Bevan was quite different – one's main concern was for the vehicle, and whether it would survive the trip. Bevan didn't really need my help, but he liked company as he jolted, bounced, skidded and slithered through the bush at about 12 mph in bottom gear. His way with village heads was simple: 'If you want me to dig your well, you must clear me a track so that I can drive to it.' In the face of such a threat, or inducement, village heads achieved miracles of co-operative voluntary effort, and bush paths were widened to accept the sorely-tried axles of Bevan's Ford and the much-enduring Albion lorry which carried his cement, reinforcing steel and work-men. My diary records one occasion of driving to a well-site with Bevan, who was singing at the top of his voice most of the way. Just short of the village we encountered a string of girls of all ages, each of them carrying a calabash full of sand or gravel on her head, led by a male drummer, who of course was carrying nothing but his drum. They had collected the material from the river-bed a mile or so away, and were delighted to receive an *anini* (one-tenth of a penny) for each load. They were a pretty and a happy sight.

The benefits which followed from the provision of a supply of good, clean water were immense, and were always greatly appreci-ated by villagers and townsfolk alike. The wells sunk by Bevan and John Hall and others were built to a standard design, about four feet in diameter with concrete walls and a concrete 'head' with rollers to take the ropes on which the leather buckets were lowered into the well. The buckets were emptied into a channel at the top of the well, which fed the spouts from which the waterpots were filled. In this way, the water was preserved from the contamination so often found in 'native' wells where the top of the well was at ground level and was surrounded by a wet, muddy mess. I became very enthusiastic about well-sinking programmes, especially some years later in Bornu, where water was scarce and wells very deep.

The stream-clearing programme was also very important for the health of the villagers, but it was hard to make them understand the benefits. The stronger and more intelligent village heads did understand, and somehow they persuaded their folk to turn out in large numbers and get the work done. With the weaker village heads it was a different matter, and I found it possible to make progress only by completely ignoring most of the canons of In-direct Rule, spending hours at the actual scene of the work and participating with axe or machete where necessary. My diary records one occasion when I arrived at a programmed work-site to find nothing happening at all, and was told by the village head that all the men were in the market. We were able to muster seven or eight determined horsemen who cleared the market very rapidly and drove its customers down to the stream. We got a good day's work done and, thereafter, I found that the threat of closure of a market, in the event of work being shirked, was sufficient to ensure that the programme was maintained. However, I did have sympathy for those who were attacked by wild cats, bees and snakes which resented the disturbance of their habitat.

My own habitat, in climatic terms, became very trying from mid-February throughout March. Days of harmattan alternated with days of heat and humidity, when rain seemed to threaten but did not bring its blessing. Some days combined the worst of weathers, and one had a hot dusty wind, which was most trying to nerves and temper. I began to sleep in the open, and twice, in February, was drenched by a freak storm of rain, too early to be the beginning of the true rains, but not, apparently, unusual in the hilly country of southern Katsina.

The harmattan season ended at last, and the worst of all the heat, the build-up before the rains came in earnest, was upon us. I travelled around, getting the stream-clearing finished, investigating complaints and shortfalls in tax collection, reporting on the con-dition of the villages. Some villages which were remote from motor roads, schools and dispensaries also lacked even the most modest amenities such as properly engineered wells, space between houses, and trees for shade. I became convinced that bad and inadequate water supplies were associated with the high incidence of two horrible diseases, leprosy and guinea-worm. The peasantry were woefully ignorant of the causes and modes of transmission of disease; leprosy was regarded as something inherited from an ancestor, and without segregation (as practised by the Jews in biblical times), the disease reached high levels in some communities. In one quite small town, I found eight lepers, including two who were circulating freely in the market and even selling food. I remember even now the intense despair I felt when seeing a woman suffering from guinea-worm drawing water from a 'native' well, with some water, almost certainly infected, seeping back into the body of the well.

The heat, particularly in the afternoons, became almost unbearable. I could not rest or sleep unless physically tired, and the simplest way I found of achieving this happy state was to travel hard and work hard. I visited villages which had not seen a touring officer for years (if ever), as well as the places which were toured more regularly, and everywhere rode the hobby-horses which I considered to be important. The best of the district heads and their subordinates began to understand what it was all about, co-operated splendidly, and even began to operate their own schemes of improvement. My formula for developing or redeveloping a village or town was a simple one, and I applied it with what seemed to be happy results in many areas throughout my service. The cooperation of the headmen was, of course, essential for success, and for continuity of action after one had left the district. The elements of the formula were: first, water supply; second, town or village layout; third, market improvement; fourth, provision of shade trees; fifth, emphasis on cleanliness.

Water supply was always the biggest problem, the rate of sinking new wells being limited by the availability of money and of the expertise of the well-sinking teams. I discussed this with Bevan, and we agreed that it should be possible, in the rocky terrain of the hill country, to reduce the specification for lining the wells, and so to sink more wells for the same money. Of course, we had no authority to change the specification, and ran the risk that we might be found out if a senior official from the Geological Survey made an inspection, but in our remote location, this seemed unlikely. So, we half-lined some of the wells, relying on the hard ground, and rock, down to the water level to resist the erosion by constant use sufficiently to prevent a subsidence of the upper concrete structure. In practice, this modification seemed to be quite successful in the short-term, and I am sorry I cannot find out how well it worked long-term, or whether the other improvements survived, for the general benefit.

Some towns, like Guga, had existed within their walls for centuries, and had become seriously overcrowded, with only the narrowest of alleyways providing access to houses and movement within the town. The health hazards were obvious, and received practical demonstration in periodic outbreaks of cerebro-spinal meningitis and smallpox. The wealthier citizens could afford to maintain a mud wall around their compounds but the others made do with fences made of *zana* (woven reed) mats or guinea-corn stalks, which greatly increased the risk of fire. People had a great fear of fire, having seen all too often how disastrous it could be, destroying houses, humans, livestock, and stocks of corn (stored in corn-bins in every compound), but they took no measures to prevent the spread of it, which could be terrifyingly rapid. Even the newer villages, set up in the bush under Pax Britannica, were too crowded, compounds being subdivided for the accommodation of relations and the alleyways between them sometimes so narrow and choked with rubbish as to be impassable.

About this time, Mallam Mani, the Emir's representative, returned to Katsina and was replaced by Mallam Turare, a lively, intelligent fellow who jollied the village and district heads into getting things done. On the day before a move, he would send a messenger to the next village, warning the village head to ensure that all rubbish was collected and burnt, and all alleyways swept clean before our arrival. It was a common experience, and a cause of some amusement, as we approached the village the following day to see the horizon full of clouds of dust and billowing columns of smoke. After the dust had settled, we would walk round the place in solemn procession, measuring distances here and there, and finally sit down to consider the matter, drawing a rough plan of the village, perhaps on paper, but more often with a stick in the dust on the ground. We would agree that the town was overcrowded, that the market was congested, too close to houses, too difficult to keep clean; there was no open space where old men could sit and chat in the evening, or if there was one, there were no trees, no shade. The *manyan gari*, the 'great ones' of the town, that shadowy authority of the people whose advice or counsel was sought by most sensible village heads, would shake their heads wisely and mutter that something should be done to correct this state of affairs which they had allowed to persist.

If all went well, the following day brought forth ideas and often a degree of enthusiasm. Much of the day would be spent in measuring out the areas for change and development, in agreeing how the work was to be done, and by whom, how long it was likely to take, and when I should return to monitor progress. Once the decisions had been taken, it was surprising how quickly the work could be done, given the cooperation of the people and some energetic direction on the part of the village head. Rebuilding mud walls was the most time-consuming operation, but all the other materials, including fences and thatched roofs, could generally be moved quite easily, given several pairs of willing hands and a drummer to provide some rhythm.

In spite of the heat and the poor living conditions, I enjoyed touring in southern Katsina; the people were delightful and un-spoiled, and in helping them to improve their lot, I felt that at long last I was doing the kind of thing that I really wanted to do. There was, too, a certain excitement, difficult to describe, about moving from village to village (normally anything from five to twenty miles apart) in this interestingly varied hill country. The early mornings were always delightfully fresh; even in the hot, dry weather; the horses were glad to be moving, and here and there would be some level ground with the opportunity for a canter or even a gallop, in which I was often joined by the district head or some other notable, gown and turban flying in the wind.

My domestic staff coped very bravely with this hard way of life. The day of a move would begin at about 4.30 a.m., when I was vaguely aware, from my camp-bed, that Francis, the cook, and Sali, Alhadji's assistant, were leaving with the carriers. (All except one, who stayed behind to carry my bed-bag.) The carriers were recruited on an ad hoc basis, as the situation required; a few would travel with us for a whole round trip, and the remainder would be found among local folk, from one village to the next. An amiable, competent chap called Moman attached himself to us from the beginning of our travels and became the unofficial headman of the carrier party. His was not an easy task; he had to allocate the loads (including the heavy ones) in relation to the strength and likely endurance of the individual carriers, always under the watchful eye of Alhadji or Francis who would not permit any breakables to be entrusted to a clumsy-looking fellow. Two heavy loads, my box of books and a 'case' of kerosene, when full, were particularly unpopular, and were switched around the strongest carriers in the course of the journey. Considering the hazards of the terrain, the amount of breakage was remarkably small (in the cupboard above me as I write, there are three pieces of glassware which survived). I was entitled to fifteen carriers, and generally needed at least twelve. It was amazing that Moman managed to keep them all together (sometimes helping out by carrying a heavy load himself) and I often thought that he would have made an excellent NCO. He wore an old army greatcoat in cold weather, saluted smartly, but would never admit to army service, so perhaps he was a deserter!

At daybreak (6 to 6.30 a.m.), Alhadji would rouse me with a cup of tea. I would dress quickly and go outside to find Andia, the groom, waiting with Gingerbread, restive and dancing a little. Sali the messenger, Mallam Turare, the district head, or his representative, and the village head would already be mounted and waiting, and we would set off at once, with the sun just appearing above the horizon. In single file, we would move to the edge of the village, looking across the fences of the compounds where people were just beginning to stir, until we found the path leading first through farmland and then into the open bush. Occasionally, we would pass through the remains of a former village, and I would ask about its history. Sometimes such places were deserted because of disease, or fire and loss of life, but more often because of slave-raiding in the nineteenth century or even earlier. As we approached our destination, my thoughts would be on breakfast which, if Moman had driven the carriers hard enough, Francis would have ready shortly after my arrival.

Rest-houses in Katsina were fairly plentiful at district HQs on the motor roads, but were almost non-existent elsewhere. At this time, there seemed to be no tents available in Katsina Province, but later I made a great fuss about it, and got one for touring in the rainy season. In the meantime, some improvised form of camp was needed at each overnight stop. Mallam Turare made himself responsible for ensuring that the camps were reasonably comfortable by sending on a well-briefed district head's representative to make the arrangements. The ideal site was under a shade tree on the edge of the village. The ground would be levelled, stakes would be driven into the ground, and matting attached to them. Round roofs of thatch would be borrowed from somebody for the duration of my stay, and would be carried, intact, and positioned on top of the stakes. *Rumfas* would be added to the thatched huts to give more space for the kitchen and living quarters for myself and for the boys. Quite an operation but, with materials to hand and plenty of helpers, all done in a matter of an hour or two. Apart from heat, flies and flying insects around the lamp at night, a major annoyance and hindrance to sleep was the howling of many dogs which the villagers kept as some sort of protection against thieves. We tried to persuade them to keep them quiet in their huts overnight, with limited success, for it was enough for one dog to start howling to set off all the rest.

Food was always something of a problem, and I should have been more grateful to Francis for what he managed to produce in the way of meals with such limited raw materials and such primitive cooking arrangements. Tough beef or mutton was sometimes available on market day in the larger towns, and Francis was quick to secure offal which was more edible than steak or cutlets. Chicken, always of the tough and stringy variety, was the unfailing standby, and a pair of wretched struggling fowls would be brought to the camp by the village head or a minion shortly after our arrival, along with eggs, and even milk if Fulani were in the vicinity. I would often go out shooting in the late afternoon, guided by a local hunter, and accompanied by Moman, who would carry the gun until it was needed. The hunter, often a very wild character wearing very little apart from a girdle of charms and armed with bow and arrows, would try to locate bush-fowl (a sort of partridge) or guinea-fowl or, rather rarely, bustard in the dry season. Sometimes one would cover several miles with little success, but patience was generally rewarded, and often there was enough for the boys as well. In the rainy season, whistling teal were fairly plentiful near rivers and ponds, and geese could also be found, the best of these being the knob-nosed and pygmy geese. The rains also brought fish to the rivers, the best being Nile perch, but a kind of catfish was more common and was acceptable.

Supplies of protein could therefore be described as plentiful but of rather low quality, with a tendency to monotony. In the arid North, vegetables were scarce and limited in variety. One ordered potatoes by the sack from the trading houses in Kano or further south; otherwise one had to be content with sweet potatoes or yams. Fresh vegetables such as tomatoes, onions and marrows might be found in the larger towns where some irrigated gardening would produce crops for consumption by Europeans, Lebanese and Indian traders and the more sophisticated Africans.

In the far bush, and particularly in the hills, there was none of this, and one was very dependent on tinned vegetables, fruit and also tinned meat for variety and reliability. It was a matter of bitter complaint that all imported food was subject to a Customs duty, and was, in fact, very expensive by UK standards. This, like so many discomforts and disadvantages of life in the bush, was supposed to be compensated within the five-shilling per day travelling allowance which was payable when travelling on duty away from one's headquarters. (The allowance ceased if one stayed in a place for more than seven days, no matter how great the discomfort.) Bread was made by the cook from imported flour, using dried yeast. It had the texture of cotton-wool, and was therefore generally consumed as toast. In some areas it was possible to buy locally grown wheat, and to get it ground by a market woman. The bread made from this flour was much more acceptable than the fluffy white, but it could be rather gritty, depending on the quality of the threshing-floor and the grinding-stones.

I had applied for permission to take three weeks' local leave in Lagos from about 11 April, but for some reason, perhaps because of the Resident's absence, perhaps because of the international situation, could not get it. My diary shows that I became obsessed with the need to get a real and complete change from the unremitting heat, the poor food and the hard travelling. I helped Harnett to complete his report on the season's operations, and then, to escape from evenings spent in increasingly unbearable boredom, pushed off on some long tours over the hills into the remote bush towards the Sokoto border. Here there were various jobs to be done; checking census lists; laying out village areas where new communities were developing; appointing village heads; examining crop-remainders from the last harvest and the seed situation. There was much dissatisfaction over the price paid for cotton which, in terms of the old money, did seem extremely low. There was the usual difficulty in finding good men for some of the village headships, and in later discussions with the Iya, and with John Stebbing at Funtua, we concluded that the pay was often inadequate and unlikely to attract a man of quality. Some men enjoyed the prestige of headship, but few regarded it as sufficient compensation for the hard work of tax-collection and the low remuneration.

I returned to Bakori and conferred with the Iya about a number of matters which had arisen during my touring in and around his district. My diary records my growing respect and liking for him: 'April 4th. Spent the morning with the Iya, going over the record book of the village administration, and had an absorbingly interesting two hours of discussion of policy and personalities, in which the old boy revealed more of himself than in fifty casual meetings. His heart is genuinely in this work, and he's got enough courage to resist interference from Katsina, whether on the part of Emir, DO or Resident, and is respected accordingly.' Stebbing joined me, and we did some useful, and overdue, work on the records of the southern touring area generally and tried, in particular, to produce proposals for a revision of village heads' salaries in relation to their responsibilities. A few days later, we talked to Macfarlane about our conclusions and he promised to try to get something done.

The Resident's wife died while he was on his way home, and he returned to duty. This appeared to clear the way for my local leave, and I cheered up mightily, readily tackling any jobs assigned to me during my remaining week. Rain had fallen further south, and its influence was felt in Funtua and Bakori where I rode for exercise every morning, enjoying the blue skies, scudding clouds and a fresh wet breeze. In Bakori, Stebbing and I met the Emir (of Katsina) on his way home from Zaria races, and in subsequent discussion could not reach any firm conclusion as to his worth or the nature of the inner man. He appeared to be, like so many of his kind, a master in the art of dissimulation, practised with success upon some of our senior colleagues.

Lagos had its agreeable aspects and, being a sizeable place, always contained some interesting people. I did not find many of them in 1937, but April 1939 was a time to remember Lagos for the enjoyments of its social life. It was a happy moment for me that brought so many agreeable people together, and I am sad to think that this could happen so seldom, and that, for so-called egg-heads, social life in Lagos and other large stations, as they knew it, was often extremely boring.

I sailed, and bathed at Tarkwah Bay (at the end of the inner mole, near the exit from the harbour) and was invited to join the Governor's party to Lighthouse beach one afternoon. I was amused to see that three bamboo changing-shelters were provided, one for men and one for women and one for HE, from which he emerged looking taller than ever clad only in bathing trunks and still wearing his monocle. The great attraction of Lighthouse beach was its surfing, but it was acknowledged to be dangerous, and we were supposed to keep together for safety and mutual support if necessary. When surfing, we did get somewhat dispersed, and I suddenly found that not only was I a long way from the others, but could not make headway towards the shore while carrying a surf-board. Eventually, I had to discard it and, after a hard struggle, got back into my depth again. It had been a close thing – one of the three or four occasions when I've felt that my last moment might have come.

I spent the last few days of this pleasant leave with Desmond MacBride, who was much preoccupied with the Annual Report on the Cameroons for the League of Nations but was otherwise delightful company as ever. I finally reached Funtua on 5 May, feeling much refreshed, and accompanied by Ruthven Wright's half-breed spaniel bitch, Jos, who was to be a faithful friend to me for the next four months. There was concern about the international situation and, locally, about the way that tax–embezzling village heads had been dealt with. I was informed that those who could find enough money to 'square' the district heads had simply been evicted, or had even retained their jobs. The small remainder were now living at the expense of the Native Authority in Katsina gaol. I was to tour Kankara and Yandaka districts and, among the tasks assigned to me, required to oversee the appointment of new village heads.

9

Locusts, Cattle and Humans

&

I T is fortunate that I have a detailed diary of events for the months of touring, interspersed with brief spells of duty in Katsina, which followed. It was a period of hard travelling and hard learning which stood me in good stead when I returned in 1942 after three years in the army. The rains were just beginning as I returned to work in Kankara district, starting with a realignment of the road through Guga, resiting part of its market, and planting branches of chediya[1] (they were in fact very large cuttings) to provide shade and boundary demarcation on the edge of the market in years to come. All of these improvements, except the road-work, could have been done by the villagers on their own initiative at any time, and I emphasised the point strongly, on this and other occasions, in the hope that they might feel encouraged to do more to help themselves in the future.

The road from Guga to Kankara was in a terrible state after the rain, but Bevan, generous as ever, sent his old Albion lorry to collect me, the boys and our loads. I went with him to a nearby village to help blow holes in the rock at the bottom of a well, using small charges of gelignite (Bevan always liked to have someone around on these occasions, just in case something went wrong!). Later, I discussed the village-head problems with the old district head and his son Sule, and agreed the itinerary of the tour which would cover the more remote villages across the hills towards the border with Sokoto Province. That night, I remember, Bevan and I sat

---

[1] A kind of fig-tree easy to grow from cuttings.

outside the rest house before dinner, counting, with mingled amazement, fascination and disgust, the troops of scorpions which emerged from the shadows into the lamplight.

On 12 May I trekked from Kankara to Sherere, about sixteen miles through the hills, with groups of black baboons barking at us here and there. Sherere, like Burmi, which we reached on the following day, was a new settlement, and at Burmi I was in time to be able to help them to lay out a model village, with much shared enthusiasm. A messenger arrived from Guga with a present of paw-paws (he had followed me for forty miles) in recognition of what I had done for them a few days earlier, and I left some seeds from the fruit for the Burmi villagers to plant and nurture. Perhaps the village has now matured, on the plan we laid out, with wide streets, a market square with shade trees dotted around and a paw-paw tree in every compound.

My diary records 15 May as a strenuous day. 'The loads went off at 3 a.m. I was up at 3.45, and we were in the saddle, following the small light of a storm-lantern, by 4.20. Dawn came at 5.30, and we pushed on to reach Dunya (a tiny hamlet on the edge of the forest reserve) at 7, passing through very pleasant bush on the way, following the line of the hills, well stocked with baboons as usual. Breakfasted on Ovaltine and sandwiches at Dunya, and then on to Kaiga, where we arrived pretty well dead beat, Alhadji declaring that the trek had been thirty miles. I lay down and slept until the loads came at 11.30, the carriers having been on the road for eight and a half hours. After lunch, we laid out sixty compounds on an excellent site, and finished about 6.30. After a drink, a meal, and bed with two aspirins, slept like a log until: 16 May 4 a.m. Trouble with the carriers, who had been wakened out of a sleep of the dead. They did not leave until 4.30, and we at 5. Breakfasted about thirteen miles out, and then pushed on another eight miles to Yangeme, where I rested stretched out under a tree. The "rest-house", which had been used by Hadow, was now dirty and quite unsuited to the rainy season. Furious wind came on in the afternoon, blowing dust everywhere, until I felt utterly filthy and miserable. After that, rain in sheets. Contrived to console myself with the *Sunday Times* while all this was going on, and then got down to the usual village-head business. A hopeless set of creatures proposed for the headship – we shall have to consider an outsider. Early to bed; the loads left just before a terrific storm set in. The roof leaked, but not much. Thank God for Kankara tomorrow.'

During this tour, I was greatly helped by the forest guard, Mallam Dodo, a cheerful, competent fellow with a great sense of humour and remarkable physical endurance. He and Mallam Sule became adept at laying out right-angles using lengths of rope and a few pointed stakes, and promised to apply their skills elsewhere when I had gone away. Dodo knew this sparsely populated area well and found his way unerringly, as I was to confirm when I returned there later to check the *jangali* (cattle-tax).

On 20 May I set off towards Yandaka district following instructions to tour it in some detail. At a village called Wawar Kaza (Foolish Chicken), the river was full and we had to ford it at the shallowest section, which even then was four feet deep. On the back of a horse I didn't get very wet, but felt very unsafe. I was to learn the techniques of negotiating flood water very thoroughly during the next few years, but my apprenticeship in Katsina is still memorable. Mallam Sule, deputising for his father, escorted me to the Kankara border with traditional courtesy, handing me over to the village head of Yan Tumaki, a son of the district head who was known simply as Yandaka among his equals. The rest-house had been 'repaired' for the Emir's tax inspection visit, but was now in a filthy condition, and not rain-proof. In the absence of the district head, who had been called away by the Emir, it took me hours to get some huts with thatches erected. All this frustration made me very annoyed, and I sent a rather pointed letter to the Emir, requesting Yandaka's presence. I woke the next day to the news that Yandaka had arrived overnight, and walked into the old walled town to find him and to point out the excessive amount of filth cluttering up the place.

Yandaka district in those days was very large and extended almost to the walls of Katsina. Like most districts near to administrative headquarters, it had been very little toured in recent years (perhaps that was why I was sent there) and Yandaka had become slack and rather arrogant withal, a situation which could not be allowed to continue. I spent half an hour with him that morning, explaining what was expected of him and of his village heads, pointing out that I had received the fullest cooperation in Kankara and Bakori districts and required the same degree of assistance in Yandaka. There was much nodding of the head, and praying that my life might be prolonged, but my touring experience of the following week revealed much that was wrong in the district. The HQ town, Dutsin Ma, had a pleasant situation, and had been town-planned by the Provincial Engineer a year or so earlier, but already the building lines had been encroached upon, and the shade-trees neglected; the school and its compound were filthy; the dispensary was untidy. The contrast with Bakori was striking, and so I told Yandaka, to his evident discomfiture. I found that comparison, to his detriment, with a rival figure was a most valuable means of leverage to achieve some positive action by a lazy individual and even a change of attitude, and I used this technique elsewhere in later years, with a fair degree of success.

From Dutsin Ma, I made my way back to Katsina by a zig-zag route, appointing new village heads on the way, circumventing, where possible, Yandaka's well-laid plans to install some unsatisfactory protégé or hanger-on. At Tsanni, about twenty miles south of Katsina: 'A rest-house here, the room itself in good repair, but the remainder all dropped to pieces. Must be ten years since anyone spent a night here ... This area was eaten up by locusts last year, and they have no corn at all. The people are living by practising various trades for money, and buying corn from outside. Despite all this, their tax was not reduced in the smallest measure. Not even a zana mat or a bundle of grass to be obtained – everything had been sold. But the people cheerful withal. Saw a terrific cloud of locusts on the horizon, a bad omen so early in the season.' The following day I stayed at Bakiyawa, where Polly Hill, a social anthropologist, spent six months some years later, and wrote her fascinating book *Rural Hausa*, full of information which would have been of enormous value to me and my colleagues. She discusses, among other recurrent problems, the poverty-trap which is created by the various hazards of farming, from the death of a father or brother in a partnership, to plagues of locusts or drought. My feeling is that the tax system pressed very hard on many of the victims of misfortune, and that the better-off townsfolk and villagers bore a quite inadequate share of the tax burden.

Back in Katsina, I was given a variety of trouble-shooting jobs, including the clearing up of some messy accounting at the Native Treasury, in anticipation of the arrival of my former Audit Service colleague John Cartmell to carry out an audit. I felt a measure of acquired ability to cope with the tasks assigned to me, including the investigation of some complaints against a district head which had the Resident wringing his hands again. (I was given the impression that I should somehow avoid the discovery of any dirty linen: 'We don't want more spanners thrown into the machinery of government, do we?') I shared a house with Hadow, which was inconvenient for both of us, and our servants, but I was glad at least to sleep with a rain-proof roof over my head.

On 8 June, we had a meeting of the Provincial Conference, a gathering of the provincial departmental officers, the Resident and his staff, and the Emir and his chief advisers. At the meeting, as my diary records, there arose the subject of locusts, corn supplies, cassava-growing and the supply of cotton-seed. Taylor (the Agricultural Officer) doubted the absolute efficacy of anti-locust measures, however well organised, and advocated the growing, for the current year at least, of cassava and sweet potatoes which were less vulnerable to locust attack. Taylor was anxious that corn from Katsina should be made available to Zaria where there was a serious shortage. He asked for money for more efficient distribution of cotton-seed. The Waziri said that there was also a shortage of groundnuts for seed, and unless something was done urgently many peasants would be without a cash crop in the current season. The Resident opposed Taylor's cotton-seed proposal on grounds of expense, and appeared not to understand the Waziri's comments. I intervened to support Taylor and the Waziri, and probably earned myself a bad mark. However, the discussion highlighted for me the essential difference of view of a Resident determined to be submissive to authority in Kaduna and an efficient departmental officer who was completely professionally motivated. In this case, Taylor had the best of the argument on logical grounds, and the Emir and the Waziri appeared to agree with him. The Resident perhaps didn't realise that he would have earned greater respect in Kaduna and among his own staff by fighting for what was urgently needed, and the money to provide it, even if he didn't get it.

During the rest of this spell in Katsina, I helped Macfarlane to catch up on various routines (the clerks seemed to be even slower than I remembered) and returns, and overhauled sundry accounting and stock-keeping procedures. (How I hated Boards of Survey of departmental stores, and still wonder whether similar procedures apply in this country. I'm sure they should!) Macfarlane and I had some long discussions, and I felt that I was well briefed for my return to bush, for which I was soon longing in spite of the relative luxury of station life and accommodation. My main tasks, for the next spell of touring were (a) to keep an eye on Musawa district which was being run by a wakili (deputy), the district head having been suspended from duty while various complaints against him were being investigated; (b) to contact the leading Fulani herdsmen and persuade them to take their cattle to Tareshi veterinary camp for immunisation against disease; (c) to organise swift action against locust infestations throughout the central districts.

I set off for Musawa in mid-June, in the inevitable slow-but-sure Albion lorry, much too small for stores, staff and hangers-on, with self sitting by the driver nursing little Jos, who was now my devoted companion. The Wakili, a quiet, competent man, mustered about thirty of the senior Fulani in the district, and I spent some time (with Sali translating into Fulani, though most of them seemed to understand my Hausa) trying to convince them of the benefits of having their cattle immunised at Tareshi camp. We sat under a tree, shaded from the afternoon sun, a dignified gathering in spite of the flies and the animal and human aromas which my guests had brought with them. They were polite, impassive and, through their spokesman, a tall impressive greybeard, formally acquiescent, but I wondered whether they regarded me as a Pooh-bah inviting them to put their heads on the block. My present role was that of friendly adviser, urging them to bring out their cattle for treatment, but they knew, and I knew, that very soon they would be hiding them to avoid paying *jangali*. At first, I attributed their lack of enthusiasm for immunisation to this obvious conflict of interest, but I was soon to learn that there were other factors involved.

My diary records further exhortation of the Fulani at various locations and, on 19 June, 'a violent dust-storm which made life not worth living from 11 to 4. Quite impossible to write letters; nothing to do but grin and bear it.' At Metazu a large crowd of about a hundred Fulani received my words of wisdom politely as usual, but at last I got below the surface and heard their complaints about the camp at Tareshi: 'Inadequate grass and little water, just higgledy-piggledy overcrowding of cattle somewhat feverish after injections and requiring careful feeding and watering which they can't get.'

I arrived at Dutsin Ma to receive further confirmation from

Yandaka and his Fulani of the unsatisfactory conditions at Tareshi, and rode out the next day to look at things. Hill, the veterinary stockman (another of the 'second-class' citizens, and a very pleasant, cooperative person) agreed with me that the Fulanis' complaints were fully justified, and that we should move the camp to the west, a long way from the motor road, but more central for the Fulani and providing water and better grazing. It seemed clear that the NA Veterinary staff had been against the whole idea of the camp from the start, since it removed them from the flesh-pots of Katsina for two or three months. (Hill and I were glad that the new arrangements would take them even further from Katsina!) I wrote a report on the situation and the action taken, expecting to receive some reprimand in reply, but it never came.

Census details – adults, children, livestock – were entered on printed forms by village scribes who were always underpaid, and frequently lazy, incompetent or even plain dishonest. The fact that the census forms were also used as a basis for tax assessment for each village certainly confused the situation and led to the entry of false or misleading information. I found that many lists were wildly inaccurate, and finally reported to Katsina that I regarded the system as very unreliable and in need of thorough overhaul and checking by competent supervisors. Needless to say, my views on this subject, as on others, were distasteful to the Resident (and probably to the NA hierarchy) as being likely to disturb the status quo, but I continued to do what I could to improve the quality of recording and the resultant equity of assessment.

Swarms of flying locusts are a terrifying sight to a farming community, particularly when they appear on the horizon in the late afternoon, possibly to settle on growing crops for the night, leaving them devastated on the following day. Creating smoke by lighting fires may divert them, but otherwise there is nothing effective that can be done. Hence the importance of destroying locusts at the 'hopper' stage when they are beginning to sprout wings but are not yet able to fly. My diary records on 15 June: 'Away on a rather fine young horse provided by Yandaka to Shema, about four miles away, to indulge in hopper-destruction, a worthy occupation for a Sunday morning. Came upon millions and millions of the brutes in two swarms, with 500 men assembled and already dealing with one of them. Finished them both off pretty successfully, about 25 per cent escaping to be dealt with tomorrow. Burning hot, and

I well scorched by the sun and covered with dust and sweat after active participation. A wonderful sight, all those men stripped to the waist, beating with palm leaves to the rhythm of drums, slowly closing in on the brown seething mass of hoppers.' Both swarms were eventually driven into trenches and buried or burned. The escapees gradually re-swarmed and were similarly disposed of, on the morrow. This was a well-organised affair, and showed Yandaka and his people at their best.

The next day was not so good. 'Went again to Shema, rather further, about seven miles, and did another locust-killing. But the people extremely stupid and rather unwilling. The great "technical" difficulty is to coordinate the efforts of some 500 men, say, over a large area, often screened from view by bush, and to keep track of the movements of the locusts all the time. Without many intelligent helpers, the job is impossible, especially if the hoppers refuse to gather together. Lost my temper eventually, and hurled abuse at one of the idiots; he just grinned on! Returned about 12.30, very hot, tired and dusty, with an enormous thirst, leaving the others to finish off the remaining swarm. They, poor devils, got back at 2 p.m., dead beat. In the meantime, I had two cold baths. In the afternoon, there was terrific wind, and, in the evening, rain at last. And so to bed, very tired indeed.'

Scott had taken over, temporarily, from Macfarlane in Katsina, and there was a marked increase in bureaucratic communication, together with the usual quota from the Resident, which added to the irritations of travelling in the rain. I would be urged to investigate something, such as apparent anomalies in the census lists, and then, having uncovered some maladministration, would be told to soft-pedal the affair, find some 'practical' compromise. I became increasingly cynical in my reactions to order and counter-order from HQ and increasingly committed to doing the things which seemed important to me and doing them my own way. It was, of course, necessary to maintain some sort of façade of compliance with Katsina's requirements, and this I managed to do.

The government was expecting prices to rise with the increasing international tension and threat of war. I had to inform Katsina (to the Resident's apparent disbelief and even disappointment) that most prices, with the possible exception of hides and skins, were falling. One had only to ride through the developing crops of millet to see the reason why; they were quite exceptionally good. It was too early, of course, to assess the prospects for cotton and ground-nuts, where the prices, even if the crops were good, would depend very much on world-wide buying demand. So I continued to supply HQ with the sort of information they didn't like, either because it didn't agree with what Kaduna expected, or because it revealed some failure in the administration. There were many complaints, some trivial, some hoary with age like the complainant, some silly or mischievous, and some apparently true and serious. I continued to report the latter to Katsina, but despaired of getting really appropriate action.

About this time, I came under much pressure from the Resident to join the Supplementary Reserve of the Nigeria Regiment. I had been hoping to enrol in the RNVR through my Lagos contacts, but there seemed to be endless delay in setting up the organisation. At the end of July, I had a letter from him, emphasising the army's desperate need of Hausa-speakers, commenting on the 'spirit' of the cadets in Kano, who were not only keen polo players, but had volunteered to join the Reserve. I gave in, joined the Reserve, and lived to regret it. The Resident obviously felt, from the tone of our correspondence on this and other matters, that a change would do me good, and that nothing could be better than a trip to Kano. I accepted because it offered me the opportunity of seeing the Bains and some other people whom I liked.

The Bains, who put me up, were living in the old Kano Residency, a rather splendid mud building with much more character than the new Residency in PWD concrete. They were well and happy, in spite of being desperately hard up, Louis having failed his Hausa exam and being therefore unable to move up the salary scale. This seemed unfair, considering that he was doing a very important job as Emirate Finance Officer. The next day, Louis showed me around Kano town in some detail; a fascinating and absorbingly interesting place, at that time still almost untouched by modern development and retaining much of its 'medieval' atmosphere.

10

Rivers, Nomads and War

❧

I MANAGED to get a lift nearly to Dutsin Ma with a Syrian trader, so avoiding a return journey with the Resident. It felt good to be back in the open air again, and I was soon off on a trek towards Safana, the headquarters of Yerima district. The date was now 10 August, the rains were in full swing, and the Fulani were scattered throughout the bush, grazing the vast areas of fresh young grass. By this time, all were supposed to have paid the tax (*jangali*) which was levied at a rate of two shillings per head of cattle. It seemed to me that this was rather high, compared with the six shillings or so paid by the average male villager, a cow being worth about thirty shillings, but herds were too large and there was undoubtedly much overgrazing, so if cattle had to be sold for slaughter, to pay the tax, so much the better.

I had paid a short visit to Safana on 24 June, and was very glad to go again, finding the town such a pleasant contrast to the dirty and congested towns in Yandaka and Musawa districts which I had recently toured and had found most depressing. My diary for 21 July records: 'Camped in the old rest-house at Kurfa [on the way to Safana] which was at least leak-proof, but full of noise of market-day ... Work after tea, and then went off to one of the nearby hills with Jos only, and looked at the countryside in the setting sun and the quiet, enhanced by the cawing of the crows as they wheeled overhead. The lovely sense of peace after the racket of town and market, the clean sweep of the hills after the filth and overcrowding of the narrow lanes helped to dispel that bloody-mindedness that comes too often now. At home, nothing but the threat of war and destruction, here, little more than squalor, poverty and misery.' (This must have been an off-day!)

At Safana I was received by Yerima, a charming man with a

most delightful smile, a son of the former Emir (who was deposed by Lugard when he refused to cooperate). He brought along his district diary, of which he was obviously and justifiably proud. The district diary was supposed to be the essential record of all important work done in the district: tax collected, crops inspected, schools and dispensaries visited, reporting of locusts, flood or drought, disease, crime, investigations, arrests and so on. All too often, the diary was kept in perfunctory fashion by the district scribe, with little or no interest on the part of the district head until the visit of a touring officer became imminent. Yerima, however, enjoyed both doing his job and writing about it, and it was a pleasure to sit down with him and discuss recent happenings and associated problems. The country to the west and north-west of Safana contained many square miles of orchard bush, forest and rocky hills, sparsely inhabited except for vagrant Fulani and big game. The diary made frequent mention of people being killed and carried off by lions and hyenas. Leopards were another hazard, as I was to learn in Bornu and Adamawa. The 'bush' farms which lay a mile or two outside the towns and larger villages were generally cultivated by the poorer farmers who were often old or infirm, unable to defend themselves against roving man-eaters.

My diary describes the rest house at Safana as 'very good indeed, and beautifully situated away from the town, which is almost entirely laid out with fine wide avenues'. It seemed as though Yerima was trying to show us what the whole of Katsina Emirate might have been if his father had not been deposed. The picture was somewhat spoilt, as usual, by the market, which I regarded as 'very filthy'. I never became reconciled to the inevitable association of the African market with dirt, rubbish, decay, flies, smell and general squalor, and fought a losing battle to the end. (Now, more than fifty years on, I am trying to prevent the British public from using country lanes as a rubbish-dump!)

During a late-afternoon ride from Safana rest-house, I came upon a remarkable sight, quite by accident. In a small clearing in the forest, a group of perhaps thirty to forty Fulani youths were assembled and were dancing in two parallel lines through which one youth ran while the others thrashed him with sticks. This, I was told by Yerima, was a traditional rite of initiation into manhood, something seldom witnessed, even by 'official' Fulani like himself. I was interested to see that the youths were wearing quite gay colours and anklets with bells, rather like those worn by English Morris dancers.

I had now to concentrate hard on one of the main tasks of the touring ADO, the check on the payment of *jangali*. Every district head was supposed to tour his district in detail during August, counting the herds in every Fulani encampment (*ruga* in Hausa), searching for cattle hidden in the bush, and establishing their ownership when found. The district head's retainers and hangers-on were pressed fully into active service for this operation, and formed a sort of sheriff's posse which scoured the countryside, following up scraps of information received from hunters and travellers and from tracks of cattle observed in remote places. My job was partly to help the district heads to cover the enormous areas over which the Fulani were grazing, and also to check the tax already collected against the size of the herds on which it had been assessed.

The touring officer knew that he was intervening in a rather delicately balanced situation. The Fulani regarded the whole operation as a battle of wits (in the early 1930s there had actually been some physical battles) against the taxing authorities, whoever they might be. The owner of a large herd had a number of options, depending on his own skill in deceiving the authorities about the size of his herd, and the reasonableness, honesty or rapacity of the district and village heads in the areas where he might choose to settle. Some district heads undoubtedly struck a bargain with the Fulani, and on a herd of, say, 100 cattle, would issue a receipt for fifty cattle, taking the tax for sixty head from the herdsman, and pocketing the tax on ten head for themselves. Obviously, the intervention of a third party in the shape of an ADO who would be counting cattle and checking receipts was a serious inconvenience, and involved hiding the 'surplus' cattle in the bush, in the care of the young men and the stronger boys of the group. Where such bargains were struck, it could be assumed that some benefit would flow, above and below, to the Emir and to village heads, so there was much vested interest in keeping the Fulani sweet by not pressing them too hard. If *jangali* income fell, the Emir would tell his Resident that touring officers had been too hard on the Fulani, and someone like my Resident would reprove his officers for 'interfering too much' or 'throwing spanners into the works'. It certainly wasn't easy to know where to draw the line, and each district presented its particular problems to someone doing the job for the first time.

It seemed sensible to begin by looking at the district records of *jangali*-collection for previous years. The Fulani appeared to recognise a pecking-order among themselves, and would attach themselves to a leader (*ardo*) who would generally have a large herd, owned personally or on a family basis. The ardo would make himself responsible for finding grazing, and for relations and negotiations with his district head and village heads, including arguments about tax. *Jangali* records were, for this reason, often grouped under the names of the *ardos*, each with his following of lesser herdsmen, which could vary somewhat from year to year. With the district head's help, I compared the current year's list with those of previous years, seeking explanations for changes, and agreeing the people, numbers and areas which required further investigation in the form of verbal interrogation of the Fulani, or physical counts of cattle at dawn before they were released to graze, or searches through areas of the empty bush where cattle could be hidden in large numbers. Some Fulani were partly settled, doing some farming and keeping cattle near their farms, the rest of the herd being despatched into the bush, with the young men in charge, to forage during the dry season. The others, the true nomads, known as *bororo*, would move over large distances, following the rain and the new grass, trading milk, butter and meat if necessary with the local inhabitants in exchange for grain and other necessities. The western marches of Katsina Emirate contained large tracts of wild hill-country, much favoured by the *bororo* Fulani. Kankara district had a high proportion of this kind of terrain, and I decided to help Sule, who was deputising for his invalid father, as much as possible in locating and counting the herds of the nomads.

The Fulani are a remarkable people, resembling, in physique and in their qualities of independence and capacity for endurance, some other cattle tribes such as the Shuwa Arabs and the Somali. They were, one imagines, particularly at home in Northern Nigeria, where most of the Emirs and many lesser chiefs were their blood-brothers and could speak their language. Their qualities (including their unwillingness to pay tax) were admired by British administrators, and one Education Officer married a particularly beautiful Fulani girl. Fulani were normally classified as Muhammadans, which seemed sensible in view of their tribal involvement with the jihad of Usuman dan Fodio (a Fulani) in 1810, but some of the *bororo* seldom if ever saw the inside even of a village mosque, and would be described as 'natural animists'. The true *bororo* are very shy people, and I have often wondered how they have fared in the increasingly urbanised and industrialised development of Northern Nigeria.

August was a month of heavy rain, and my diary makes frequent mention of storms, leaking huts, paths under water and swollen streams and rivers. In the search for cattle one had to start early, often before dawn, finding one's way out of the village and through the surrounding farms in which the guinea-corn was standing high and wet with dew or rain. Often, one emerged into the open country quite soaked and longing for the appearance of the sun to dry one's clothes. I started what was intended to be a month's *jangali* touring, moving south through Yandaka district towards Kankara, where I expected to spend much of the time. On 12 August: 'Set off in light rain for Dan Musa. Speed quite impossible as most of the paths are under water, and so we settled to a monotonous long walk – nothing more tiring than sitting on a horse for slow mile after mile. Millet is really wonderful in this virgin soil. We eventually reached the river Karadua [a tributary of the river Sokoto], a fearsome sight, full of rocks, rapids, and deep swirling currents.' I had crossed this river at this point twice before, once when it was completely dry, and once on horseback with the water washing around my knees. This crossing was to be something very different, requiring the mobilising of all the local expert resources. The chief actor in the drama was the Sarkin Ruwa (literally 'the chief of the water', the head fisherman, irrigation gardener, ferryman and general factotum in all matters relating to the river), a man in his forties, clad only in a loin-cloth disclosing a superbly muscled body. He was surrounded by a group of sons and relations similarly clad and similarly endowed, and stood waiting for us where the track met the river. After much traditional greeting, I was invited to seat myself on a raft which was being held close to the bank by three or four chaps who were half swimming, half standing in the water. The raft consisted of seven very large gourds in the form of a hexagon with one gourd in the middle and having a bamboo structure lashed to them to form a sort of platform. Yandaka joined me, and we were then propelled by the whole team, swimming hard, through the turmoil to the opposite bank about a hundred yards further down. The operation was repeated for the rest of the party, and finally the horses' saddles were brought across. The last and most dangerous part of the exercise was to persuade the horses, kicking and plunging, to enter the water and to swim with them until they found ground on the far side. As we saddled the excited animals, I thought of the effort required to ferry all the carriers and their loads, earlier that morning, and expressed thanks in my best Hausa. There were occasions, in the next few years, when I would dearly have loved to be able to draw on the services of men like the Sarkin Ruwa.

The following day, Sunday, 'at Dan Musa. Went off at 6 a.m., feeling very seedy about the tummy, on a cattle-hunt, and after a long search came upon a herd of some 500 head in a small tributary valley of the Karadua. Herdsmen stampeded them immediately and ran to bush. Followed the cattle on the run for miles, and eventually came up with the owners.' The 'owners' were, in fact, two young men of an *Ardo*'s family who had been running ahead of the herd, leading it by their calls for nearly an hour before we caught up with them. They were hardly out of breath and we were all amazed by their stamina. I remember vividly the difficulty of moving around this large number of restive, noisy animals, trying to count them, and hear what Sali and Mallam Turare were saying above the hubbub. Later that day we had the first of many long palavers with the Fulani, to decide how many cattle belonged to whom, how many had been taxed, and how many had to be assessed as untaxed (for which there was a penalty, up to twice the normal rate). I often felt sorry for the Fulani, who argued their innocence so persuasively, but not so my companions, who insisted on the fullest retribution. For me, there was always the problem of accepting that a man who had the features of an Old Testament prophet was actually a consummate liar.

The days settled into a steady routine, regardless of the state of the weather. We set off around dawn, and searched for cattle until two or three in the afternoon, visiting *rugas* as early as possible, counting the cattle on the spot and also looking for tracks leading out of the camp into the bush. The Fulani women, emerging from simple shelters made of branches pulled from trees, would be preparing the first meal of the day, and whenever I pass a herd of cattle, I am reminded of the mingled smells of a Fulani encampment: cattle-dung, wood-smoke and unwashed humans. We would press on until time for a picnic breakfast for me, probably cocoa from a Thermos and sandwiches. Some days we had luck, finding herds hidden with care and imagination, once in a cave approached by a narrow defile. Other days were less satisfactory: 'Followed a cattle-track for miles, but they must have gone on into Kankara. This bush is extensive, dense and baffling, but contains some delightful country. After riding from 6 till 2, came back expecting to find a new camp established and food and drink prepared, but met with boys and labourers still trekking, not having been provided with a guide. Have seldom felt so furious. Poor Tanko [horse-boy] was completely lost, having followed our tracks in the bush for some 25 miles, and did not get in until 4 p.m., by which time I began to fear the worst, with so many reports of attacks by lion etc.' Another day we came 'home' through a storm, utterly drenched, having found nothing.

By mid-August, I had crossed into Kankara, and was joined by Sule and his team, whom Scott had threatened with the loss of August salary unless the *jangali* target was met. I shot guinea-fowl and teal, on foot, at the end of a day's riding, to vary the diet. My clothes seemed very slack, and I must have been rather thin. We moved to Yangeme in the Forest Reserve, and I again pressed Mallam Dodo, the forest guard, into service. This I justified by 'his enormous competence, his obvious enjoyment of the change, and particularly my enjoyment of his drolleries (mainly quite unintentional!)'. Altogether, we were a fairly impressive group of about twelve horsemen, and Dodo, whose father had been a notable Fulani warrior, organised us into teams of three or four, moving across wide tracts of country, using hills and tall trees to scan the terrain and to keep in touch with each other. This commando-type manoeuvre he called 'banga-banga'. Dodo seemed to know every inch of this wild country and would collect information from local hunters about the movements of cattle, which would help us to plan each day's activity. After clearing up the day's work, and making arrangements for the morrow, a group of four or five, Dodo, Sule, Sali, Turare and perhaps one or two others would stay on for a time and we would have a chat and a laugh together. I remember with great pleasure our easy, happy relationship which had a special quality, hard to match in later years.

In the midst of the longest day's work, Hadow wrote to inform me that two of my reports had been lost, and would I please send copies. Of course, I had kept no copies, and had to produce the information again, from scratch, by lamplight, with the usual evening storm blowing up, and Jos snuggling against my knees for comfort.

On 23 August: 'Crossed the R. Turame on horseback, taking off shoes and stockings as usual – a very swift stream, but not so bad as the Karadua. Thankful for an easy crossing of self, boys and carriers, and God sparing us a thunderstorm in addition. Much cattle-sickness in this area. One ruga also had two lepers and two blind people – a depressing sight.' Later: 'Met with one herd in which over 100 cattle had died in the past year, of blackquarter. Cattle were just so many skeletons, and the prospect for the poor herdsman frightful. While I was there, a cow was seized with its death-agony, and its throat was cut before my eyes.'

The Forest Reserve ran along the border with Sokoto sultanate, and we cooperated with Dan Doto, the Sokoto district head, in trying to locate some of the cattle which were hiding there. Dan Doto was a fat man full of his own importance who tried to tax some cattle which had run from our searches, and I again transgressed the Indirect Rule procedures by informing the DO Gusau (in Sokoto Province) of the situation.

On 29 August I had reached the village of Mobei, in the hills on the boundary of Kankara and Kogo districts, where I expected to finish off the *jangali* touring. Mid-morning a letter came from the new DO, McCabe, recalling me to Katsina immediately because of the 'international situation' and the possibility of my being called up. I gathered that things were as bad as possible short of actual war, and felt quite ill with shock for a few minutes. I trekked off to the Kankara-to-Mallamfashi road, some twenty-five miles or so, and at the same time sent off a messenger to Constantinides, the Greek trader, at Mallamfashi, asking him to take me to Katsina in his lorry. I met him on the road at 4.30, and we reached Dutsin Ma at ten, after a hellish journey through mud and rain. The following morning, I loaded all my belongings, said goodbye to Yandaka, and reached Katsina in time for breakfast with McCabe, and to see Hadow about to depart to join the Regiment. My diary comment on the situation: 'Much surprised to hear about Russia's part in the present matter, in view of the state of our own negotiations.' How naïve we all were!

Now began a three-year spell of moving about and being messed about, an experience I shared with some of my colleagues and with millions of others. I was fortunate in that this period lasted, for me, only three years, and contained some months of great happiness, and that I emerged from it unscathed.

In Katsina I was at once given the job of interviewing Arabs, Syrians and Lebanese about their passports and resident status. Then Scott became ill, and McCabe went to Daura, and I was back to the familiar situation of running all the station offices and keeping the Resident happy. I got through the work against the background news of the invasion of Poland, the expiry of the ultimatum on 3 September, and my own call-up on 5 September. I was kept so busy that there was little time, during waking hours, to worry about the possibilities of air-raids at home and other horrors, and my diary entries became very patchy.

September 4–8: 'Spent sweating away at various jobs in the office, trying to soothe the Resident and retain a certain calm myself. Much fuss about organising a recruiting drive to raise new battalions for the Nigeria Regiment. Eventually got myself away and out of the place on Sept. 8th. Stayed the night with Louis and Catriona in Kano. A delightful, pleasant day with the Bains, to be the last such for a long time.' I had left behind, in the care of an agreeable newly-arrived cadet, my dear Jos, my horses and my staff, except Alhadji who had agreed to accompany me to Zaria. I had a shrewd idea, from my experiences of weekends dominated by the behaviour of the RWAFF in Kano, as to what life in the army in Zaria would be like, and I was wrong only in that it proved to be even more boring, lonely and uncomfortable than I had anticipated.

PART II

A Taste of Army
Life, 1939–42

ᥱᳱ

Regimental Sergeant Major to Acting Adjutant: 'This
Army will never lose its amateur status' (Kenya,
Tana River, October 1940)

11

Joining the Regiment

❧

I ARRIVED in Zaria in the late afternoon of 9 September and was dumped into a small round thatched hut, resembling the most primitive form of rest-house, with no furniture and not even the most elementary form of lavatory arrangements. It took several days to obtain even a modest degree of comfort, against the apathy and indifference of the depot staff, and the adjutant in particular. All my colleagues in the Supplementary Reserve were treated similarly, and learned their first hard lesson in the army code of 'looking after No. 1'. It seemed to us that the regular RWAFF officers (and the Warrant Officers and NCOs), known generically as 'the Waff', were determined to seize this opportunity to put the 'the civilians' in their proper place at the bottom of the pile. Perhaps they had considered themselves slighted or under-valued by the civil population, and by administrative officers in particular, in peace-time. Certainly, ADOs like myself with a knowledge of Hausa were given a very large share of the current chores of the depot, including the manning of the orderly office on a permanent twenty-four-hour basis. There was also the formal recruitment of large numbers of Africans who were now applying to join the Regiment, and were sent to Zaria from government stations all over the country. Quite a high proportion came, to swell the numbers already serving, from the French territories to the north and east of Lake Chad, and from the French Cameroons, with the object of avoiding *servitude militaire* and obtaining better pay. Others, like the Dakkakeri of southern Sokoto, came from the traditional recruiting areas of the North, but there were also Tiv, from the lower Benue, and other tribes who were alleged to be stupid or less amenable to discipline and proved a sore trial to those who had to train them.

Most of the recruits had some knowledge of Hausa, however rudimentary, but for difficult cases one had the help of an interpreter, usually a NCO from the same tribe. The 'recruiting officer' had to fill in a large printed form, full of details of tribal and geographical origin of the candidate, his physical appearance, height, weight and tribal markings (with, if necessary, diagrams to illustrate) and next of kin (a difficult interpretation). The MO would already have passed him fit, and there remained only the final and irrevocable step: the swearing of the oath of loyalty. For the relatively few Christians and Muslims who were recruited, the Bible or the Koran was used in swearing loyalty to the King and his officers. For the pagan recruit, the Waff had decided, many years ago, that the best substitute for the tribal fetish, if any, was a bayonet blade. The recruit seized the bayonet by the handle, put out his tongue, and drew the whole of the flat of the blade, from hilt to point, vertically downwards along his tongue. He would say, preferably in Hausa if understood, 'If I should break this oath, may this bayonet devour me.' The demeanour of the recruits led me to believe that the oath was firmly held and greatly feared, and it was indeed often proved on the battlefield.

When these chores proved insufficient to keep us occupied, the adjutant contrived to maintain our enthusiasm for military life by spells of square-bashing, either by being drilled ourselves, or being used to instil the elements of drill and movement discipline into the raw African recruits. When all else failed, there was always the open road, which stretched for dull red laterite mile after mile towards Kaduna, an excellent means of introducing the tender-footed ex-civilian to the realities of a route-march under a tropical sun. We were usually accompanied on these marches by a British 'regular' NCO who was perhaps being disciplined for some offence, and would be greeted on our return, limping and sweat-drenched, by the adjutant, looking spruce and cool in his well-laundered khaki drill. Two of our company were older, and fatter, than most of us, and deeply resented this treatment. They swore to be even with the adjutant, and managed, in the course of a mess guest-night, to deposit him, in full regimentals, into a roll of carpet and across the bar. Fortunately, we were all dispersed to other units on the following day and avoided retribution.

We were made members of the Zaria Club, providing squash, tennis, and the means of escape into a social environment somewhat preferable to that of the depot mess. The half dozen or so of us who were ADOs were completely ignored by our senior colleagues in Zaria, who never even asked us to take a drink with them. The Waff, also, made no attempt to be sociable outside the mess, for which, perhaps, we should have been thankful. The day's 'work' was sometimes physically exhausting, but never mentally demanding. I had plenty of time, including three days in bed with my first serious attack of malaria, to take stock of my own situation, within the general state of the world.

First, considering the job of ADO, which I had just laid aside, I had to admit to disappointment and considerable disillusion. Too much of my time had been spent in supporting, bolstering (if that means making comfortable) a system of 'native' administration which one knew to be corrupt and which was already under serious threat in the 1890s and probably saved from overthrow by the arrival of the British and the French. The job had seemed worthwhile because one could do a great deal outside the system, or in spite of it, *sub rosa* or by bending the rules. The alternative, judging by the examples of Liberia, Ethiopia, Haiti and other 'do-it-yourself' regimes, was generally an even worse fate for the underdog, and so I felt that the role I had played in the colonial government was justifiable. It was clear, though, that this whole structure in Northern Nigeria would be increasingly undermined by external influences, and the war would be likely to accelerate the process. I didn't feel at all certain that there would be a job worth staying on for by the end.

At that moment, the end of the war seemed very remote, and could, indeed, be deferred for ever if it moved at the Nigerian pace. In the meantime, I was committed to the tedium of army service, and also to enduring the company of people with most of whom I had less in common than with my former colleagues in Katsina and elsewhere. I felt angry and frustrated that I had allowed myself to be pushed into this situation by the Resident, instead of sitting tight until I could get transferred into a service where I could use my science training.

On 1 October, our depot days, to our great relief, came suddenly to an end and we reservists were all posted away to one of the three battalions, 1st, 2nd and 3rd (always known as 1NR, 2NR, 3NR) which were to make up the first Nigerian Brigade, available for active service. I was sent fifty miles down the road to Kaduna to join 1NR, along with several cadets of my vintage and 'Swig' Swainson, one of the adjutant's chastisers. We were quartered in a rather grand house, formerly occupied by the assistant command-ant of the Waff, which faced on to the racecourse and looked across to the club on the far side of the course, which also enclosed the polo-ground. Swig, as his name implies, was a man much given to drinking, which had, over the years, left its mark on his large, rather floppy figure. Before his balding and fattening, he must have been very good-looking and was still, with his lively personality and great sense of humour, rather attractive to women. He was a very senior Agricultural Officer and, like the rest of us, had his army pay made up to his civil entitlement, which was about three times the salary of a second lieutenant. It was alleged that he was the highest-paid subaltern in all the British forces – a distinction of which he was rather proud.

The barracks and parade-ground were about three-quarters of a mile from our quarters. There, on most mornings, we were met by Lieutenant Colonel Owen, the CO of the battalion, a tough, well-built, loose-limbed man of about forty-five with a pleasant, smiling, weather-beaten face and a delightfully easy friendly man-ner. He was the most agreeable regular officer I had met. He had carefully studied the campaigns and battles of General von Lettow Vorbeck in World War I in East Africa, and had convinced the Commandant, Brigadier Smallwood (who was also resident in Kaduna) that von Lettow's tactics and discipline of formation movement in bush country should be adopted as the basis of battle-training for all the battalions in the regiment. Naturally, the officer-cadets of 1NR benefited from the full, undiluted enthusiasm of Owen, who took us nearly every morning some miles away into the empty bush astride the Kaduna river, where we would study the ground in detail in relation to some military problem.

It was usually about 9.30 by the time we reached the mess for breakfast, in a state of ravening hunger. Owen appeared to avoid hunger by smoking cigarettes, and most of us were driven in sheer desperation to adopt the same pernicious habit. For the rest of my army days, cigarettes were a solace in the many times of waiting for someone or something, as a substitute for a meal, a drink, even a wash.

Between breakfast and lunch, at 1.30, our training was in the hands of Major 'Freddie' Fox, the battalion second-in-command.

He was small but had a compensating martinet manner, and was a great believer in the disciplinary virtues of square-bashing and bayonet-drill. The parade-ground squad-drill concentrated on formal movements which were never used in battle, and on developing in each of us the vocal powers of a sergeant-major. The production of loud war-like noises was also an essential accompaniment to a simulated bayonet fight, and especially during the charging and transfixing of a line of dummies stuffed with straw. We were never as good at any of these martial arts as were the African NCO instructors and Freddie was not pleased. His attitude to his profession was as far removed from that of Owen as one could imagine, and it was always a relief to escape from the Fox routines to do the daily stint with our companies.

I would, perhaps, be given some clerical chore in the company (B Coy) office but more usually would join one of the platoons in a weapon-training session. The old Lee-Enfield rifle was still the infantryman's best friend and was the basis of all weapon-training up to and including target practice on the range. We spent much time on the Lewis gun as well as the Bren gun, this latter being in short supply, and insufficient to equip the battalion fully in case of need. The British CSM supervised most of these sessions, especially the Bren-gun training, but the Nigerian NCOs were also very capable instructors, and obviously understood the weapons very thoroughly. We, the officer cadets, felt we had a special relationship with the Nigerian NCOs and rank-and-file in that we all spoke Hausa fairly fluently, knew something of their backgrounds, and had the Nigeria Regiment as our only army loyalty. All the regular officers, NCO's and Warrant officers were seconded from British regiments and were now longing to get back to them and to associated prospects of promotion.

To an impartial observer, 1NR must have seemed already to be a very mixed group of human beings, but by mid-October a further element had been added in the shape of a large contingent of white Rhodesians, sufficient to bring the battalion (and other battalions elsewhere) fully up to strength in officers and 'white' NCOs. The structure of rank and authority in the battalion also included a fixed establishment of Nigerian NCOs, ranging from lance-corporals to a very grand and well-polished individual known as the battalion sergeant-major (BSM). Most of these NCOs had some English, helped in the transmission of orders on parade or in the field, and were available to assume command, at the appropriate level, in the event of a white casualty. (In practice, they often did this very effectively.)

The Rhodesians, too, were a very strange mixture. Most of the officers had been commissioned as a reward for territorial service, often of very short duration, and they ranged from very immature ex-bank clerks to tough, hard-drinking veterans of World War I. A high proportion of these 'territorials' arrived with the ready-made rank of captain, which they retained. This arrangement ensured that 'Nigerians', like myself, had practically no chance of promotion so long as they stayed with the battalion. There was a roughly equal number of sergeants, some of whom seemed to be far better material than some of the officers. One of the sergeants, Basil Ledeboer, had been at Rhodesia's best school with one of my Oxford friends.

The weeks rolled by and, as Christmas approached, it became clear that the war was not going to be allowed to interfere with one annual event which was deeply embedded in the local Waff tradition, the Kaduna Fortnight. This was a famous (or infamous, depending on taste) jollification, organised by the soldiery around the mess and the club, stretching over Christmas and the New Year. Apart from a great deal of drinking and eating, there was to be, as usual, a polo tournament, with teams drawn from all over Nigeria, horse-racing, a gymkhana, football and, of course, golf, bridge, dances and all the usual pastimes.

In January 1940 the battalion marched some sixty miles to Kachia, near Zaria, for the annual Brigade camp and manoeuvres. At the end of the exercise, a number of people were very lame and the battalion was not really effective for several days; I was left with a lasting respect for the British soldiers who marched through, and pacified, this territory in about 1900. Life in camp gave us an opportunity to get to know each other better, black and white, British and Rhodesian, 2NR, 3NR, and the Light Battery (which carried its guns on its heads). It also gave the Brigadier the opportunity to play games with the 3000 or so men under his command, and our feet, even the black ones, became truly bedded into our boots. Perhaps all these troop movements proved that knowledge of Hausa was an asset, for it was decided to commission us at last. There was a shortage of 'pips' to put on our shoulders and makeshifts were made out of cloth; this was somehow typical of the way this colonial army was to be armed, supplied and equipped, as I was to discover later.

I continued to press for a date to be agreed for the commencement of my leave, and was told at last that I could go after our return to Kaduna in February. Passages by sea appeared to be irregular and rather unpredictable, probably in convoy and slow. Air passages by British Overseas Airways via East Africa were available, but very expensive, and so I negotiated for a passage by the only other alternative, Air Afrique from Zinder to Algiers, and Air France from Algiers to London. Miraculously, I got a ticket and then the only problem was to get myself from Kano over about 150 very rough miles to Zinder. Louis Bain helped me to find an Arab trader who was going to Zinder to fetch a load of hides and skins (and possibly other merchandise which would not be declared to the authorities) and then it remained only to say goodbye to Alhadji and my friends, whom I would not see again for many months.

12

Sahara, Home and Bletchley

❦

AT this stage in the 'phoney war' Mussolini was sitting on the
fence, but it was known that Italy had very considerable
forces in East Africa and the Waff would be needed in
Kenya very quickly if Italy entered the war. I was concerned that
my camp-bed should travel with the battalion if it moved, and was
assured that this would be arranged. Every officer's personal servant would also move with the battalion, and so, on return from
leave, one could be expected to slip into the routine, whatever and
wherever it might be. In the meantime, it seemed, I was a free
agent, answerable to no one but myself.

I travelled from Kaduna to Kano by train, and then had a seat
beside the driver in the usual bone-shaking lorry over a very rough
road to the border, after which the road was quite appalling for
the remaining seventy miles to Zinder, the headquarters town in
the *cercle* (province) of that name. The place seemed to consist of
a few buildings dotted among mounds of sand with sparse vegetation struggling to survive here and there (this was the middle of
the dry season). I presented my passport to the chef de division
who was very amiable and offered me a cigarette d'Indochine, a
slender cylinder of very strong, aromatic tobacco wrapped in a
wisp of paper. Zinder was drier, more barren, than the area around
Kaita to the north of Katsina, and the growing of even short-
season crops such as millet was hazardous. Desiccation was already
a serious problem, and by 1980 it had been recognised as a disaster,
over the whole Sahel area, on an international scale.

The next day, with two other British passengers, I boarded the
small plane which took us to Gao, on the upper Niger, for the first

leg of our journey. We made a stop at Niamey, also on the Niger, for long enough to stroll along the river-bank and admire the residence of the Governor of the Colonie du Niger which over-looked the river and was very much in the style of a Beau Geste fort. Touaregs and camels were very much in evidence, although Niamey is only a few miles north of the latitude of Sokoto. Gao was, comparatively, a lively place with a modern air in spite of its ancient origins as capital of the Songhai Empire. It was already established as the southern terminal for motor transport moving goods across the Sahara and also had a large airfield. Unfortun-ately, there was no opportunity to see the ruins of the medieval town, but we had time enough to walk along the bank of the Niger, where drivers of heavy vehicles were hosing them down after the long journey through Saharan sand and dust. The river here ran through a plain of sand, presenting an appearance like the Nile at Cairo on a smaller scale, in extraordinary contrast with the same river we knew at Jebba, with its deep valley, rocks, rain-forest and humidity.

In Zinder one was aware of the similarity to a British colonial station of the same size, but in Gao the flavour of metropolitan France was strong; 'Frenchness' had been imposed here and ap-peared to be accepted by the Africans, most of whom spoke French quite well. We were very comfortably accommodated in a small hotel with rooms arranged around a garden courtyard, run very efficiently by a middle-aged woman, and were given an excellent dinner, accompanied by wines served at the right temperature. The night was cool, and I awoke refreshed and ready for the onward flight to Algiers.

In Algiers the only indications of war were the numbers of French servicemen at the airfield and in the hotel where we were accommodated luxuriously. There were bright lights everywhere and the lounges and bars were thronged with officers entertaining pretty women so that one began to wonder whether there could be any officers to spare for the Libyan border. We were advised not to venture into the famous casbah by night, and indeed felt no need of further diversion, for there was so much of it at hand within the hotel, just observing the human spectacle. How the Waff would have enjoyed it all, and felt at home!

We left Algiers after breakfast by flying-boat and took most of the morning to cover the 500 miles or so to Marseilles. Paris was cold and dark in February 1940, and we felt that we had reached the war zone at last. We were driven to a small hotel, and then left to our own devices until the flight to London in the morning. My fellow-travellers had no French and relied on me to suggest a restaurant for dinner; they were delighted with the Relais de la Belle Aurore, where the food, décor and general ambience were still as agreeable as in 1938 when I had dined there with Oxford friends. The *patron* was *mobilisé* and stationed on the Maginot Line, where, with thousands of others, he would be immobilised when the German push through Belgium began.

The flight from Le Bourget to London (Croydon) was uneventful, but it was snowing when we landed. That evening, I reached my home at last, very cold in khaki drill and a light raincoat. As I sat by the fire, there was a strong feeling of unreality; I found it very difficult, nearly impossible, to tell my family much about my experiences. Even now, when I am, perhaps, more articulate, I find it difficult to describe the true flavour of West Africa when it was still relatively untouched, and the nature of the love–hate relationship one developed with it.

I learned that Jocelyn Bostock and another Oxford friend were both working at Bletchley and decided that a few days' stay there, perhaps at a local pub, would be an agreeable way of seeing something of two old friends, exploring the Buckinghamshire countryside and visiting nearby Oxford. Soon I found that life at Bletchley was much pleasanter than anywhere else, and began to look for some agreeable pad. Cycling around, I found a nice little pub in the village of Shenley Brook End about two miles from Bletchley. Mrs Ramshaw, who ran it, said that she had a spare bedroom and would be glad to let me have it, if Mr Turing didn't mind, and would I come again that evening when Mr Turing would be in. This I did, and met, and was approved by, Alan Turing, the mathematical genius whose contribution to the development of operations at Bletchley Park (BP) was later acknowledged to be outstanding. Over the next three months, we met almost daily at breakfast and supper, sharing the sitting-room that Mrs Ramshaw made over to us, and I used to marvel at the innocence, in worldly matters, of this man whose brain could cope with so much of mathematical or logical complexity. He had much charm and sweetness of disposition and a quirky sense of humour, all qualities which I appreciated after my experience of recent months. The later careers of many who served at BP, including some of Jocelyn's close friends, were very distinguished, reflecting the quality of intellect and dedication which they brought to bear on their war-time task.

A bitterly cold winter, so unkind to our troops in France, gave way at last to a wonderful spring. It was all carefree and idyllic. Not quite carefree, of course; we all felt that this phoney war could not last and, in April, the break came with the German invasion of Norway.

Events moved with staggering rapidity in May, and it soon became terribly obvious that the German gamble on the advance through the Ardennes was paying off, that the best of the French armies and armament were in the wrong places (too many in the Maginot Line) and could never be got to the right places in time. We all speculated privately about the implications of these events, but hardly dared to speak to each other about them – they seemed too awful. We felt almost guilty about our enjoyment of the glorious weather of May and early June, which was so helpful to the Germans in the rapid movement of their armoured columns. The heavy rain urgently needed by our troops in France did not come, and in the end we could only be thankful that the weather made possible the evacuation from Dunkirk. Two of my Oxford friends were flying Spitfires across the Channel and were lost at about this time.

I received orders to report at Southampton docks on 11 June, and was able to spend the last night of my leave with Jocelyn and her parents, who were most kind and welcoming when we announced our engagement during the evening. That was also the evening when Italy declared war.

Early next morning, Jocelyn came with me to Waterloo station, and on the platform we met Colonel Owen, who had come to say goodbye to some of us, since he was about to take up a brigade command elsewhere. He was as charming as ever, and helped to lower the tension of parting for both of us. The situation was already critical for France and could soon be very serious for Britain, and I was one of many who hated leaving England at that moment. As I sat down in a crowded compartment, I felt that I shared my loneliness with a trainful of people not unlike myself.

13

Round the Cape to Kenya

⁌

A T Southampton dock the P & O liner *Narkunda* was waiting
for us. I walked up the ramp and into the ship, a strange,
unreal, enclosed environment, all the more unreal because
of the frightful, earth-shaking events which were going on in the
world outside. I have described elsewhere the ritual of passage to
the West Coast by Elder Dempster line which was one of the poor
relations among the shipping lines that served the empire. The
Narkunda was not one of the jewels in the P & O crown, but it
did maintain the authentic style of the greatest, the most traditional, of all the imperial voyages, that to India and the Far East.
During the twenty-four hours or so which we spent at anchor
somewhere in Southampton Water, with terrible things happening
just to the south of us in France, the daily ship's routine was firmly
established, including afternoon tea in the lounge to the accompaniment of a string quartet playing 'Palm Court' music.

The ship was bound round the Cape; it would take five weeks
to reach Mombasa and much longer to reach Singapore, Hong
Kong, Kobe, the furthest ports on its proposed schedule. The usual
high proportion of sahibs and memsahibs, tuans and bwanas was
considerably diluted by numbers of unattached males travelling to
join their service units, a somewhat smaller number of unaccom-
panied females, including several on their way to join husbands
and fiancés detained overseas by the war, and a dozen or so of
young nursing sisters in transit to military and naval hospitals.
Several hundred rather oddly assorted people found themselves
enclosed, over quite a long period, in a small, artificial environment, cut off from home and family at a time when the latter

were suddenly exposed to unprecedented dangers, and the whole world order, as we knew it, seemed likely to collapse.

It was hardly surprising that emotional tensions in the ship's community were running high after several days in which each bulletin of war news posted on the noticeboards seemed bleaker and more alarming than the one before. For all of us in that ship, the French presence in Africa and a French willingness to hold out there and fight the Italians were of immense importance, not only for the winning of the conflict in Africa, but for the future of operations in the Mediterranean as a whole, and the influence of that upon the security of communications with the Middle East, Africa and the Far East. The realisation, following the surrender in metropolitan France, that a Vichy régime would also be established in most of French Africa, Syria and Lebanon was therefore a staggering blow, and the tragedy of it was soon intensified by the news of the action which had to be taken to neutralise the French fleet. By 8 July, the French situation had become all too clear and I wrote: 'It seems unbelievable that, in the space of a few days, a fascist government can seize power from one so surely established as that of Reynaud, make peace with the dictators, about-face with such speed as to become actively our enemies, start up a rabid anti-Semitism.'

Most of us had our daily ploys, including letter-writing and chess, for which we tried to secure, and defend, the odd quiet corner of the lounge or bar. A senior officer of the KAR (King's African Rifles) lectured us on the East African terrain and the possible courses of the campaign. Several of us got together to try to learn Italian, and discovered a teacher, a naval chaplain (RC) who had spent seven years in Rome. We had a formal lesson every day, following my copy of Hugo's Italian, and made quite good progress. I played chess with some delightful people bound for Malaya, Sarawak and Java, and enjoyed brief, happy and quite intimate relationships with them, as with so many one met in the course of the war. I remember the courage and cheerfulness of Mynheer Hymans, who had lost everything in the invasion of Holland, and, at sixty, was going to Java to start again.

One day I was watching some of the many children at play on the part of the deck reserved for them, and heard one child address another, 'You're second class, aren't you?' The second-class child blushed, made no answer, but looked on wistfully while the others played a game. The first child said, 'You know you're not allowed in here. They'll fine your father £5 if they catch you.' The other child's lip drooped, and he went away. More than anything else in this long voyage, so full of unreality, this incident convinced me that I was seeing the last of a world in which this degree of class-consciousness would be paraded, and accepted by the underdog. It could not survive the crumbling of the whole edifice within which it had its being and which had sheltered the virtues of the ruling class as well as its vices. For the moment, however, this ship, alone in an enormous expanse of sea, carried its freight of British and their values, good and bad, towards their distant duties. We still regarded the sea and the navy as our ultimate security whether in the Atlantic or the Channel and, having yet to learn the awful realities of air-power, faced our isolation in a hostile Europe and in a largely hostile Africa with resignation and a feeling that we should somehow manage to cope – as indeed we did.

According to the ship's radio news as we approached Cape Town, the Japanese were already beginning to take advantage of our weakened position, pressing us to close the Burma access route for the Chinese armies, and many people on the boat were suspicious of their objectives in South East Asia. Some wives and children were taken ashore, having decided to settle in South Africa for the duration. Husbands looked for accommodation for their families coming out by the following boat, to avoid the threatened bombardment and possible invasion of England which was a major cause of worry to all of us but something we hardly spoke of. This, for several families on board, was the hard choice of sudden separation, but a wise choice for those who made it. South Africa at this time was the great imperial bulwark in the South Atlantic, with naval bases, arms factories, military manpower and the great Smuts as its leader. The British were welcome. Apartheid was already a fact, but not yet an ideology. Groups of 'non-whites' in tattered trousers and jerseys, their faces every shade from off-white through saffron and brown to ebony, sprawled about on the quayside, unemployed, leaving one with a sense of sadness and deep unease. This, in our brief stay in Cape Town, was all that we saw of the other side of the South African experience.

Within a few days we were well into the tropics again and then there were the farewell parties for those who were disembarking at Mombasa, some lasting all night until we actually left the ship early in the morning of 13 July. We were quickly loaded into the boat-train on the quayside and, amid tears and waves and good wishes from our friends who were sailing on to Asia, we pulled away towards Nairobi. In the early months of 1942 I often wondered about the fate of those people whom I had liked so much, particularly those from the Malayan Service and the Sarawak Service; whether, like my brother-in-law, they toiled as prisoners on the Siam railway track, whether they survived. And the young nursing sisters?

I shared a compartment on the well-equipped, well-serviced boat-train with three of my contemporaries on the Colonial Service course at Oxford, Dick Greswell, who was joining the Nigerian Light Battery, and two others who were swept up into office jobs in Nairobi. After a night in the train, Swig Swainson and I were driven off to the Mbagathi camp some miles outside Nairobi, on the edge of the game reserve, which was being run as a base depot for West African troops by a reserve captain who was always regarded as something of an old woman. There was no sign of our kit or of our servants who were supposed to have been brought from Nigeria, and the captain could do nothing for us apart from allocating to each of us a bare corrugated-iron shack, with a concrete floor, about eight feet square. We walked over to the mess to get a drink and cool off, and there, the first and incredible sight, was the sub-treasurer from Ibadan, now 2 i/c of the depot, leaning against the bar with a large gin in his hand; I began to understand why there was no sign of our kit or our servants. It took several days to find camp-beds, and in the meantime we slept on the floor, and I was thankful for the sleeping-bag that Jocelyn had thrust into my baggage in London. Lions roared close by at night, and we took care to close the doors of our tin shacks.

I suppose we must have spent about ten days at Mbagathi, doing all the usual tedious things: orderly officer duty, exercising and training African troops (reinforcements awaiting, like us, movement to their units). We managed to get lifts into Nairobi, to chivvy the Army Post Office about our mail, to have the occasional meal at Chez Gaby, where the cooking was genuinely French, and to observe the frenetic life-style of the moneyed white Kenyans and of the army officers (many wearing the red tabs of the Staff) who swarmed around the Stanley and Norfolk hotels. There was no conscription in Kenya, and a surprising number of fairly young men of the remittance-man type, with appropriate female attachments, were living it up in Nairobi, in choice locations in the Kenya highlands and in a few places on the coast. Sometimes we wondered whether we had been brought to Kenya to keep the country safe for such people.

One day we were suddenly warned to be ready to move to join the battalion, and actually travelled forty miles or so before being returned to base camp. It was rumoured that 1NR had been involved in an unsuccessful action, and its present location was uncertain, necessitating our return. This provided a useful opportunity to switch one of us into a local vacancy, and our base depot captain, for reasons unknown, selected me. I collected my meagre belongings and was driven away to Langata camp, on the opposite side of the game reserve, several miles up the Ngong road. I reported to a major of the Gold Coast Regiment and his plump adjutant and was introduced to my duties: to take charge of about 120 raw Nigerian recruits and turn them into capable, disciplined drivers of heavy vehicles. This was not the first or the last time that I was to be thrown into the deep end of a messy, ill-managed situation, with no indication from my supposed superiors as to how to tackle it.

Having taken in the situation, cursing the army again and again under my breath, I got on with the job of trying to organise and discipline the outfit, even teaching some of them to drive on the few available Chevrolet trucks. After a fortnight or so of hard slog, the company training began to run more smoothly, though not the company's vehicles. The noise of crashing, grinding gears as our recruits tried to master the knack of double de-clutching rings in my ears even now, as do the Gold Coast instructors' admonitions such as, 'Make you no press de fire too much' for 'Go easy on the accelerator'.

The mess steward, a Kikuyu, brought along a young nephew, Atanas, in response to my expressed need for a servant. (My Gold Coast Hausa batman was very willing and competent, but not always available.) Atanas was mission-educated with amazingly good clear English, but he was only eighteen and I had doubts (later confirmed) about his ability to stand up to the rigours of army life. However, I engaged him, and found him immediately useful in interpreting our needs to the Kikuyu mess cook, which led to some improvement in the quality of our food.

Towards the end of August, I moved back to Mbagathi preparatory to joining the battalion. I visited the wounded officers from 1NR who were in hospital in Nairobi. One of them retained an arm and hand after some brilliant surgery, and the other, Willie Arkwright, a regular Waff captain, seemed likely to lose the sight of one eye. These wounds resulted from an unsuccessful action in which two companies had tried to dislodge an Italian force from a hill at a place called Dobel, a few miles to the south of Moyale (a village just south of the Abyssinian border taken by the Italians in July). The battalion was commanded by Major Fox and, at the time of the affair, was part of a brigade commanded by a KAR brigadier, who ordered Fox to mount an attack on the hill without artillery support. There was no effective reconnaissance of the position, but it was thought to be held by a company of Italian infantry, and A and D companies were committed to a frontal attack. A Coy, under the command of a very traditional officer, was soon pinned down by heavy machine-gun fire, while D Coy, under Arkwright, tried to work round to a flank. Suddenly, to his amazement, he heard a bugle sounding the 'Charge' and saw A Coy, with its commander leading, charging raggedly up the rough slope of the hill. The company commander and his 2 i/c were killed and there were many other casualties, including some in D Coy, which had tried to give support. Both sides withdrew in the course of the evening, and the bodies of the killed and the seriously wounded were recovered. This disaster had had a very bad effect on battalion morale. I was sorry to learn of this state of affairs; it seemed that I might be about to move from one unsatisfactory situation to another.

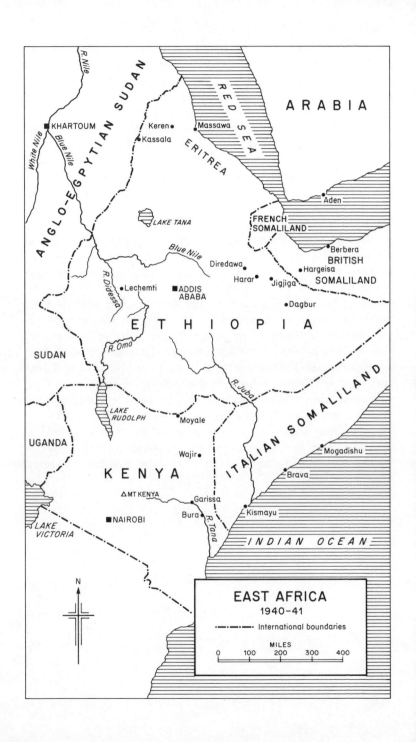

EAST AFRICA
1940–41

—··—··— International boundaries

MILES
0   100   200   300   400

14

Towards Somaliland

❦

I LEFT Mbagathi, appropriately enough, in total darkness, at
4 a.m. one day in mid-September, to join a convoy of trucks
which was about to leave for the Northern Frontier District.
We reached Nanyuki, near the foot of Mount Kenya, that evening,
after a pleasant drive through the highlands, and spent the night
in a tented camp. I woke early in the cold air, and went outside
into a brilliant crisp morning. Someone invited me to look at
Mount Kenya, and I stared around and could see nothing remarkable until I looked upwards, and there was this incredible snowy
peak, gleaming in the morning sun. There was little enough time
to admire it; after a hurried breakfast we were on the road which
runs round the broad base of the mountain to Isiolo, on the north
side, one of the main administrative centres for the Northern
Frontier District (NFD). The change in climate was dramatic; Nanyuki was cool, green, alpine in impression, whereas Isiolo was
parched, hot and sandy with sparse vegetation. From there we
ploughed on, along a rough track, with the landscape becoming
increasingly inhospitable, resembling the now-known lunar landscape of barren rocks and boulders with the addition of a few
thorn bushes. Places on the map were hardly more than names –
Archer's Post, Garbatula, Habaswein – a collection of shacks for
trading with the vagrant Somalis who somehow, somewhere, found
something for their livestock in this wilderness. Three days out
from Isiolo, I reached the battalion in its camp a few miles outside
Wajir, and was cheered out of my grimy weariness by the warm
welcome of B Company to which I had been posted.

The camp-site was a patch of stony sand and thorn-scrub, part
of a flat plain which stretched for miles in every direction, broken
only by the occasional hill. B Coy occupied part of the camp

perimeter, and everybody had his personal dugout, with a ground-sheet pegged out above it to give a little shade. My orderly soon had one fixed up for me, quite close to the mess, and after I had been issued with a .38 revolver, I was left to take a rest before dinner. A quick look around had been sufficient to establish the essential landmarks: the wire defences, the headquarters of the nearest platoons, the defence points of the adjacent airfield, the abandoned, bullet-ridden lorries of the East Africa Recce Squadron.

The mess consisted of a large rectangular dugout over which was spread the roof-canvas of the only company tent. It contained a trestle table and two benches, but each of us had a camp-chair in which we could take our ease at ground level when time allowed. Supplies of fresh food at all places 'up the line' were meagre and intermittent, as were also deliveries of mail and beer, the cause of constant, and unsuccessful, complaint. We depended, most of the time, on tinned food, much of it South African, together with the traditional army biscuit and potatoes when we could scrounge them. Tinned food was corned beef, sausages, Meat and Vegetable ration, occasionally peaches and perennially guavas. I have no wish ever to taste guavas again. The water in the Wajir area was of appalling quality, being drawn from deep wells through strata which contained potash and other salts. We experimented with every possible brew or admixture, but the water flavour was always horribly dominant and, in the great heat, thirst was a real problem.

Wajir was the main administrative centre for the NFD, and in war-time it was a vital forward base and defence point for the British forces. 'Roads' ran south-west towards Nairobi, and north-west, north-east and south-east towards Italian territory. All the ground in these three latter directions constituted a vast no-man's-land covering thousands of square miles, most of it featureless arid plain or low hills dotted with thorn trees. In this enormous waste, there was a good deal of active patrolling by units from both sides. Initially, the Italians had some success with the Banda, irregular groups of Somalis, led by a few Italians, of whom the most daring was nicknamed Twinkle-toes. A very courageous group of Kenya settlers did much to counter and discourage the Banda by forming and operating the East Africa Reconnaissance Unit. They mounted machine-guns on kit-cars and light lorries, and charged along the main roads and feeder-tracks looking for trouble, which they some-times found in plenty. They inflicted casualties, but also sustained serious losses in men and vehicles. Months (with considerable casualties) were to pass before they received their first armoured car, made in South Africa.

The tasks of 1NR included the defence of the airfield, from which a few South African pilots flew three Gloucester Gladiators which conformed to the general description of the equipment of the East Africa Force: obsolescent or inadequate or both. Gladiators were obsolescent but their fantastic rate of climb and manoeuvrability (they were probably the finest biplanes ever built) enabled them to keep the rather weak-stomached Italian Air Force at bay.

Within a week or so of my arrival in Wajir, South African troops began to concentrate there, and we were ordered south to the Tana river to join a new concentration of the Nigerian Brigade in that area. After a very rough, zig-zagging journey, we camped for the night in a patch of orchard bush around a dry river-bed, and I stretched out in the back of a lorry and slept, deeply. I woke next morning, soon after dawn, amidst a great deal of shouting and general pandemonium. I was told that a herd of elephants had just run through the camp, and that some of the troops had scattered into the thorn-scrub, where they might be lost. We sent out patrols on several compass bearings and managed to find all the fugitives, who were rather badly shaken by their experience. We reached Garissa that evening and found, to our annoyance, that we had been allocated a camp-site in a sun-baked patch of thorn-desert just like the site we had loathed in Wajir. However, water could be drawn easily and in quantity from the river, and we all had much-needed baths. The water, when boiled, had a fairly neutral taste, and we were at last able to enjoy a cup of tea and even a peg of whisky after dinner. I was told that evening that I was being transferred to C Coy, who had a patrol job to do across the river.

The purpose of the patrol was to smooth out the track up to the fifty-mile point, so that a sizeable body of men could be rapidly transported over that distance when the need arose. The surface of the 'road' was a mixture of black cotton soil with patches of clay and sand, all baked hard after the passage of many animals during the brief rainy season. The tracks of the smaller animals caused no problems, but a single elephant left a trail of large deep holes which had to be filled with soil collected from the edge of the road. It was very hard work in the extreme heat, and the troops were somewhat uneasy about the obvious presence of elephants after their experience during the journey from Wajir. However, we managed to shoot some game every day, and the plentiful supply of fresh meat cheered them immensely. Apart from the obvious discomforts, life 'on detachment' had much to recommend it, and I was reminded of the joys of bush-whacking far away from red tape in Katsina. We finished our road-mending by 9 October and returned to the camp at Garissa. Major Fox sent for me to inform me that I was being moved yet again, into Battalion HQ to assist the adjutant, who appeared to be suffering from a nervous break-down. My letters to Jocelyn contain this description: 'I now spend all my working hours "on tap" for any job that has to be done. Counter-order follows order in the most baffling way imaginable. The working environment: picture a couple of dugouts in the red sand, roofed with tarpaulin – the orderly "room" and the signals "room"; before me, a "table" made of petrol-boxes; to my right, the African signaller, sitting by the field telephone (obsolete equipment, often inoperable). In daylight hours, the dugouts are small infernos in which five of us work stripped to the waist, converted into Red Indians by the dust deposited upon us. As the RSM said recently, "This army will never lose its amateur status." Swig is Intelligence Officer, and is one of the few saving graces of this situation. Another is the QM – recently promoted from RQMS – a large, amiable, helpful and most efficient character known, for reasons undisclosed, as "The Baron" or "Mustapha".'

It still seems extraordinary to me that I should have got into such a strange situation, and so quickly, with virtually no warning and no preparation. The adjutant disappeared 'down the line', and forthwith I became acting adjutant, having gained only a hazy idea of what the job involved. The filing was chaotic and weeks in arrears and I burnt much midnight oil trying to sort it out. During daylight hours, I tried to cope with a stream of instructions from Brigade HQ, to extract some decisions from Fox, and to send out the necessary communications: operation orders, instructions, re-ports, returns, ciphers, signals, messages, lectures, demonstrations, rehearsals, reconnaissances, patrols, investigations, trials, punish-ments.

The divisional General decided that the Nigerian Brigade needed a shake-up, following a surprise inspection. The outcome, for 1NR, was that Fox was replaced by a senior major from 3NR; some company commanders were also replaced. The new broom began to sweep; lots of battalion orders were issued, and the new CO was promoted to half-colonel. In those early days, he was all affability and could be very charming. He appeared to be pleased with my command of Hausa and ability to talk to the troops and understand their problems. He, too, had quite good Hausa, and was admired, and feared, by Africans who had served under him. I also began to have some ambivalence of feeling about him. He was helpful, certainly, in getting the office finally sorted out, and in making the arrangements for our move back to base camp to refit at Mitubiri, near Thika, about thirty miles from Nairobi, early in November.

We occupied hutted accommodation at Mitubiri, for which we were thankful, with torrential rain occurring almost every day. There was much to be done to ensure that we were fully equipped with all the items that were available and necessary, such as weapon spares, clothing and footwear. We were all rather cold in this miserable weather, and again I had reason to admire the spirit of the troops, of whom I had written to Jocelyn, some time earlier, 'the men really are magnificent, cheerful under the worst conditions, thousands of miles from their own country, in a desert of thorn scrub, most of them without even the comfort of letters from home'. When the weather permitted, the troops were kept busy on various training ploys, target practice on the rifle-range, route marches, football and 'showing the flag' marches through Thika and Nairobi. The men understood that these activities were in preparation for battle situations, and that some would die or be severely wounded, possibilities that were frequently discussed and accepted with calm resignation. There had been a period when I felt unhappy about the involvement of Africans in this 'war of white faces', but I became convinced that the lot of the African would be slavery and worse under the Nazis, and that we were all in this business together, to win through for the salvation of all. Two years later, as an ADO, I had a furious argument on these lines with a senior colleague.

The CO at last approved my ten days' leave with Jocelyn's missionary brother in the Taita hills near Voi. He told me that Laing, a recently promoted major from 3NR (a close intimate of the CO) would take over as adjutant, and that I should replace Swig as Intelligence Officer.

15

Training with Monkeys and Crocodiles

❧

I RETURNED from leave to Mitubiri on 20 November, refreshed in body and spirit, to cope with the final fortnight of 'fitting out' in torrential rain, with flood water only just below the floorboards of the huts. It was cold and miserable for our poor Africans, but there was some fun for them when the South African Broadcasting Company came to make 'propaganda' recordings for broadcasting from Lagos, Cape Town and London. The troops made excellent recordings of marching songs (translated, and expurgated, in my commentary) and the drum and fife band played the regimental marches ('Old Calabar' and 'The Lincolnshire Poacher'): 'Impossible to describe the glee of the troops on having the records played back to them; the giggling, nudging, and back-chat about the voices of the performers.'

Early in December, we were finally sorted out, refitted, packed and, significantly, reinforced to full establishment by the addition of a number of young officers and sergeants freshly arrived from Britain. We were allocated a company of motor transport, with lively, cheerful drivers from Northern Rhodesia, under the command of a former mining engineer who spoke their language, and set off for the river Tana, glad to be away from the rain and the floods. The heat in the plains to the east of the highlands was intense, and water was tightly rationed. The going was hard for everyone, not least for me, since I had to travel ahead with the RQMS to reconnoitre and mark out the camping area for each night. We soon discovered that the prime requirement for a camp-site was that it should have at least one tree providing a little shade, and room to pitch the CO's tent alongside it!

We made our final perimeter camp in the thorn-scrub about a mile away from the river at Bura, some fifty miles south of Garissa. I went with the CO into the dense forest which formed a belt about 300 yards deep along the course of the river, and we decided that it would be possible to clear the fairly limited undergrowth and establish a camp there. Company commanders agreed with us, and soon had their men hard at work; we moved in two days later. There was much to recommend the new environment, particularly shade and the proximity of the river, but the humidity was high and there were many biting insects, though they diminished in numbers as we steadily removed every vestige of undergrowth. Our presence was greatly resented by a large colony of colobus monkeys whose screeches were echoed by flocks of parrots which shared with them the dense canopy of the trees about eighty feet above our heads. Our groundsheet shelters soon began to sag under the weight of wild figs which were rained upon them by the monkeys and required regular clearance. Colobus are very handsome animals with fine black fur and contrasting white ruff, and we enjoyed their acrobatic performances in the high branches. In time, these creatures became very bold and would descend to steal small articles, particularly the troops' forage-caps which they took off during their working spells. (I never actually saw a monkey wearing one.) The forest yielded two pets which were cherished by our animal-lovers, a bush-baby with large, innocent eyes, and a small mongoose.

I continued with the duties of intelligence officer, assistant adjutant and general dogsbody. One of my main tasks was to recruit and train an intelligence section of six men, who would be capable of carrying out a wide range of tasks; in particular, reconnaissance of ground, positions, distances and reporting thereon. They had to be good soldiers with plenty of endurance, and it was not easy to persuade the company commanders to hand over men with these qualities. However, I got them at last, all men in their early twenties, and was well pleased with them. Corporal Isa Zuru, a Dakkakeri (pagan Hausa from southern Sokoto) was the senior, a tough little professional, strong on discipline and bushcraft, unflappable. Lance Corporal Ibrahim Funtua was a Fulani, a remarkable man and a great personality, one of the finest Africans I ever knew. He had the splendid physique and fine features typical of his race, and his quiet smiling manner concealed a keen intelligence and qualities of leadership which were revealed when the need arose. He told me that his father had felt an irresistible urge to make the pilgrimage to Mecca in 1930, when Ibrahim was twelve. They left their cattle in charge of relatives in southern Katsina, and set off overland, working as they went, taking about two years for the journey. They reached Mecca, but soon after beginning the return journey his father became ill and died. Ibrahim could read, and managed to find a variety of jobs in the course of several years of wandering through the Middle East. His last jobs, before returning to Nigeria, had been with an Italian firm in Eritrea and a French firm in Djibouti.

He learned English after his return to Nigeria, and I was intrigued to hear him improving his knowledge in conversation with Atanas, whose vocabulary and use of idiom constantly amazed and amused us all. (The CO used to draw him out and joke with him during the service of meals in the mess.) The two were very good friends, recognising in each other qualities of intelligence and perception which they could not find elsewhere. I have often wondered about what they did with their lives; Ibrahim later was awarded the MM in Burma, but I heard nothing of Atanas after he said goodbye in Mombasa in August 1941.

English was the last-acquired of Ibrahim's languages; in 1930 he already knew Hausa, Fulani and some Arabic; during his travels in Africa and the Middle East he improved his Arabic, and picked up a useful knowledge of Italian, French, Swahili and Amharic. He reached Katsina in 1938 to discover that nothing was left of his inheritance, the cattle having died, been stolen or misappropriated. Dispossessed and rootless, he decided to join the Nigeria Regiment, and quickly became fully trained and available to serve in East Africa. Surprisingly, no use was made of his linguistic ability until I removed him from the tight hold of A Coy. Perhaps this should be no surprise; the Services at all levels managed to hang on to people who were useful and competent in some relatively routine activity in spite of the urgent need for them elsewhere in some specialist capacity. Ibrahim could have been a valuable operator in intelligence anywhere in the Middle East, but no one asked for him, and I was extremely fortunate to find this man who combined, with all the abilities I have described, the traditional Fulani gifts of bush-craft, direction-finding and tracking. He was my orderly for a time, until promoted, his place being taken by Yaro Peni, a cheerful young Dakkakeri with a great sense of humour, who cared for me wonderfully and really became my shadow; in any tricky situation I could generally find him at my elbow. In quiet moments, Yaro would tell me about the Dakkakeri villages and the way of life in them, dominated by retired soldiers who had cleared away the old haphazard jumble of huts and compounds and rebuilt everything in the style of an army barracks. Lugard recruited many of his soldiers in this area in the early days, establishing a remarkably durable tradition; as Yaro said, 'We are the real old soldiers.'

My final stroke of good fortune was to have Sergeant Frank Lodge, of the Warwickshire Regiment, posted to me as intelligence sergeant. He had been a Bren-carrier driver at Dunkirk, where he was wounded in the leg. 'He's a delightful chap, cheerful and generous, has been married for about a year and seems to be much in love with his wife, to whom he writes long letters – rather a bond!'

I was asked to give lessons in Hausa to the Rhodesians and to the officers and NCOs recently posted to us from the UK. There was some argument that it would be better to teach English to the troops (a policy which was adopted a year or two later) but the CO ruled in favour of Hausa, and I got on with it. Progress was rather slow; we had no grammar books, and the class was large with a wide variation in intellect and capacity for concentration. One of the brightest and keenest was John Rogers, a platoon commander in D Coy, very young, hardly more than a schoolboy. He used to stay on after the lesson and really managed to learn something. Very different, but also very likeable, was his namesake, Captain John Rogers, commanding B Coy, a large, teddy-bearish regular Waff, who became a good friend, valued for his honesty, modesty and lively sense of humour expressed in a deep rumbling chuckle. About this time a regular Waff major, 'Fiery' Fasson (of the Border Regiment) was posted to us as 2 i/c Battalion. He was a tough, wiry little man, very hirsute with crisp, curling grey hair; his only weak spot was his tummy, which revolted strongly against what he called 'South African chop'.

Life in this enclosed environment, working and messing with the same people under the jungle canopy noisy with monkeys, parrots and other birds and with the shooting or scaring of crocodiles at the water point, became monotonous and wearing to the nerves. One day, I had a surprise visit from Bernard Fagg, a contemporary ADO (later archaeologist to the Nigerian government) who had trained in Jos as a sapper and had been given a delightful one-man independent command in charge of the Divisional Field Park Company (the depot for all the divisional engineers' stores) which was located about a mile downstream from our camp. He invited me to dinner, and I found him comfortably established in a tent equipped with all kinds of amenities, including a portable gramophone on which he played the Beethoven 'Pastoral' Symphony.

In mid-January a large group of us were given a specially arranged leave at Malindi, a small resort on the Indian Ocean, about seventy miles north of Mombasa. For some of us, it was a relief to be left alone and simply to enjoy the sea breeze, the surf breaking along the reef and the stroll through the few Arab remains on the low cliffs. The few days which we spent there were certainly restful, and we were well fed, so that we had the feeling of being fattened for imminent slaughter.

On our return to Bura, this impression was strengthened by the surprise arrival one Sunday morning of an ancient C of E clergyman, complete with camp-altar and equipment, to hold a communion service. This was the first time the Church of England had put in an appearance since I had joined 1NR, though the RC padres, perhaps through the influence of the CO who attended Mass whenever possible, had been with us quite frequently.

16

To Mogadishu without Love

ౖౖ

I T seemed a long time since I reported to the regimental depot in Zaria in September 1939. Now, after months of training and preparation, some of it of doubtful value, 1NR was under orders to move, as part of the 11th (African) Division, across the Tana to attack, and take, the port of Kismayu. My recollection is that we crossed the Tana on 13 February. as almost the last of a long column, with divisional HQ a mile or two in the rear.

Thus began one of the side-shows of World War II, now almost forgotten, but at the time an audacious, rapid and far-flung advance into Somaliland and Ethiopia. That it happened at all was due to Wavell's insistence on reinforcing the East African theatre against the urging of Churchill in the autumn of 1940 to reduce to the minimum the forces in Kenya and the Sudan, and to send every available man to Egypt. Wavell was compelled, a few months later, to send troops to Syria, Crete and Greece, and if he had been left with 300,000 undefeated Italian troops in his rear and along the Red Sea and German troops to his front, Egypt might certainly have become untenable. After the initial defeat of the Italians in Cyrenaica, we all had wild dreams of clearing the North African coast, and opening the Mediterranean, but the Vichy French were still there, and the Germans were in France (and soon in Africa) and our communications were overstretched. Wavell was right; we needed to clear our rear and the Red Sea and *then* switch every available unit into North Africa. So, the minor pieces began to move on the vast chessboard in support of the queen, Egypt, the vital centre of our strategy of containment in the year of our 'standing alone'.

Operations began in January 1941 with an attack on the northern front, from recaptured Kassala on the Sudan border through Eritrea towards the mountain fortress of Keren and the Red Sea port of Massawa. The Italians concentrated some of their best regiments in Keren and held out for a month against the heroic assault of the 5th Indian Division, which included battalions of famous British regiments. General Cunningham chose this moment to launch the attack from the south through Somaliland, intending to cross the river Juba before the rains and to draw the Italian reserves away from the Eritrean front. The actuality of events was amazingly to outstrip this programme.

The 12th African Division, comprising Gold Coast, KAR and South African brigades, began the advance by crossing the Tana at Garissa, travelling along the track which we had so painfully repaired, towards Liboi and the Juba. Various Italian positions were outflanked and abandoned including finally Kismayu, and it became obvious that the east bank of the river Juba was to be held as the main line of their defence. The Gold Coast and South African brigades had to find crossings and establish bridgeheads.

On the 12 and 19 February, I wrote brief pencilled notes: 'A good deal of "unnecessary" kit was sent away today [12th] and life is reduced to bare essentials – a bed, a table, a box and a chair. I've just collected my food for the next two days – a tin of maize, one of baked beans, one of bully-beef, and one of the inevitable guavas in syrup. Maps are my chief preoccupation. Books I'm taking are few and probably too serious.'

We crossed the Tana by pontoon bridge, and ploughed into the black cotton soil along the track due east, trying to maintain a little distance from the vehicle in front in order to reduce the amount of dust we swallowed. I was travelling near the head of 1NR with Fiery Fasson, in a Humber staff car, which constituted Advanced Battalion HQ for reconnaissance and local command of 'first contact' action – a concept which never worked properly but was never completely abandoned. Each night, after a journey through the day's heat and dust at an average speed of about 5 mph, we found a bivouac for the battalion in an area allocated by the divisional staff.

Some news of what was happening 'up front' percolated down the dusty trail. Rumours of minefields on and around the track beyond the border had worried us before the advance began, and now we heard that one of the leading armoured cars of the EA recce unit had been blown up with the loss of its crew. A group of brave South African engineers volunteered to go ahead on motorbikes, dragging chains with grappling-hooks behind them. One way or another, the mines were located and cleared, a remarkable achievement. Our other fear had been that our narrow front of advance and its attendant clouds of dust would make us an easily detectable target for the Italian Air Force. Fortunately, a small number of Hurricanes had reached the SAAF in time for them to be used in support of the advance, and bombers had been strafed on the ground at Afmadu and Gobwen, the main Italian airfields on our front. Such planes as the Italians could spare from the Eritrean front were sent out only by moonlight, and 23 (Nigerian) Brigade never suffered any damage.

A river can be an effective defence line when held in strength with modern weapons and good lateral communications (which the Italians had) by determined troops (which they had not). A tropical river in wild country generally has dense vegetation along its banks, obscuring the view of the defenders and providing cover for attackers trying to establish bridgeheads, and these conditions obtained on the Juba, away from the main bridge at Gelib, near the coast, which was held by the Italians in strength. The South Africans formed a bridgehead at Yonte, near Kismayu, and the Gold Coast Regiment at Mabungo, upstream from Gelib, on the 18th and 19th, and held both positions against counter-attacks long enough for the KAR to make a flank march to cut off Gelib. The Italians now began to withdraw towards Mogadishu, followed by the Nigerian Brigade, with 1NR in the van at last.

We crossed the pontoon bridge at Mabungo at dawn on 23 February, then moved south to Gelib to join the road leading north-east towards Mogadishu. A squadron of armoured cars led the way, followed by two companies of 1NR with Fiery Fasson and myself in a staff car sandwiched between them and the two rear companies. By nightfall we had covered some 100 miles uneventfully, and were about twenty miles from the small town of Modun, where there was a road junction for the nearby port of Brava. Modun had been shelled by the navy, and it was hoped that both it and Brava had been evacuated by the Italians. We moved off before dawn on the 24th, and soon passed through Modun, which was empty (Brava was immediately occupied by a detachment of

KAR) and were out into the blue, with our first objective, if we could reach it, the airfield at Vittorio d'Africa, about halfway between Modun and Mogadishu. The country between Mabungo and Modun had been the sort of wild bush and thorn-scrub to which we had been long accustomed, but now the scene was much more open, cultivation and occasional settlements showing that we were entering a colonised area. Soon we were crossing irrigated land with many channels cutting across the line of the road and making it impossible to deviate. About noon, an armoured car struck a land-mine, and came under fire from a small town. Two companies of 1NR debussed, deployed off the road and advanced for about two miles before encountering and clearing the enemy rearguard. Fasson and I were, of course, some long way down the road, and by the time we had caught up (on foot) with our leading troops, it was all over, happily without any serious casualties. The sappers came up and cleared the road of mines (these were the good old days when they were made of metal and could be detected) and by early afternoon we were on our way again.

A few miles further on, there was more serious opposition from high ground and farm buildings on the left of the road, where the Italians were loosing off machine-guns and artillery. B Coy and C Coy were hotly engaged, and we soon had the Nigerian Light Battery blazing away in support, with our own mortar platoon coming up close behind. It was always a remarkable sight to see the battery and the mortars coming into action. All the parts of the weapons were carried at the double on the heads of strong men and assembled swiftly at the chosen firing positions following well-practised drills. The guns were 3.5-inch howitzers, and the officers of the battery, like those of the mortars, sought to locate their pieces under the slope of a hill or a high bank, where they could not be reached by the opposing flat-trajectory weapons. On this occasion, Fiery and I got to the front line just in time to commiserate with B Coy's 2 i/c, a fairly elderly but very determined Rhodesian, wounded in the arm while pursuing the Italians who were withdrawing into the bush beyond the hill.

I went down the road with A Coy for several miles, to make sure that the immediate vicinity was clear, and also to see what were the possibilities for the night's bivouac. The country seemed to alternate between irrigated farmland and hilly stretches, affording limited scope to move away from the road. After some discussion with the CO it was decided to make camp among the hills, as dusk was falling. We were worried about the possibility of air attack in our vulnerable position, strung out along the road in a sort of defile, and were anxious to secure some fighter cover at first light. We had no radio communication with Brigade HQ (nor did we ever have, in my experience) and so Fasson and I were sent off in a staff car in the growing darkness to try to find Brigade and get them to persuade Division to provide the air cover. It was an anxious journey; we were somewhat concerned that we might encounter Italian stragglers who, of course, would know the road pattern, and its scope for withdrawal towards Mogadishu, much better than we did. In fact, the risk of this was greater than we realised, as we were to discover on our return to the battalion. We found Brigade HQ at last, and delivered our message.

On our return, we found Battalion HQ in a state of excitement and some tension. In our absence, C Coy and some armoured cars had been despatched down the Mogadishu road to try to find the airfield at Vittorio D'Africa and to occupy it if possible. I feel that I cannot do better, for an account of this action and of some events at later stages of the campaign, than to quote from the narratives of the war diaries of 11(A) Division and 23(N) Brigade, copies of which were rescued from a waste-paper basket in Nigeria in 1942 and given to me forty years later!

> Darkness fell before the landing-ground was located. While the search for the airfield continued in the dark, two lorries with shining headlights turned on to the main road some four hundred yards behind the column. These lorries approached on the right-hand side of the road and continued their journey side by side until one of our drivers shouted at them, objecting to the double-banking. It was then discovered that the two vehicles with headlights were crowded with Italians in full retreat. From our lorries, rifles and hand-grenades opened up at point-blank range. The Italians were all killed or made prisoners. Later, a third lorry appeared from the same direction, and received similar treatment. At about 1930 hours, the recce party gave up their search for the airfield and returned to the bivouac area.

When Fasson and I were given an account of this incident, I felt at once that it was both bizarre and terrible, and so it still seems to me after this lapse of time. Terrible, because in spite of the account given in the war diary, I have no recollection of any prisoners being taken, and I would certainly have interviewed them if there had been any. At dawn, there was no sign of fighter cover, and fortunately no Italian planes either. We were soon on our way, and after about ten miles or so, the CO and I stopped to examine the scene of the lorry encounter of the previous evening. The lorries, full of bullet-holes, were keeled over into the ditch on the right of the road, and still contained some bodies. The other dead Italians were stretched out on the bank beyond the ditch, young, dark-haired, their pale faces drained of blood. I opened the breast-pocket of one, found his identity papers; he came from Caltanisetta, in central Sicily. My mind went back to the rail journey during my tour of Sicily in 1938, and the wait in the train at Caltanisetta junction, where I watched some soldiers playing pelota on the barrack square. I wondered about the strange providence which had brought us both to this remote place, and him to his sudden, unnecessary death.

I think that this incident had been shocking and probably distressing for the officers of C Coy, who were disinclined to talk about it. The upsetting aspect of the whole thing was that, with everything and everyone in swift motion, there was no safe way of getting the Italians to surrender, which they would probably have wanted to do, and so no alternative to opening fire on them. Obviously, C Coy had used all their weapons, including Bren guns, and the effects had been devastating, but some Italians probably did escape, to join the several hundred stragglers who surrendered to various units (including Div. HQ) whenever their lorries halted on the road during the following day.

We found the airfield, and went on to occupy the small town of Afgoi, about forty miles from Mogadishu, which was undefended. One company of 2NR, with armoured cars, passed through us to ascertain the situation in Mogadishu and, in the absence of enemy forces, to inform the mayor that we should enter the town at 11 a.m. the next day, 26 February. They found the town intact, with its civil administration fully operational and the Mayor willing to meet all demands, including the provision of accommodation for our troops.

We drove through the town, where the streets were lined by the civil police, and took up our quarters in the lavish accommodation vacated a few hours earlier by the Italian Air Force. The CO was

The ADO's House, Katsina.

The Governor's Polo Match, Katsina, 1938.
[RTK second from left]

KANO, NORTH NIGERIA
The Emir and his retinue leaving the palace.

THE OMO RIVER GORGE. The magnificent view across the Omo to Abalti, beside its single, thimble-like, gigantic rock. There, in positions of great natural strength, the Italians stand.

Repairing the demolished road.

THE ITALIAN STAND ON MARDA. Ahead lies Jijiga; beyond, the road winds up the Marda Pass. Observation Hill is on the left, the Breasts and Camel Saddle on the right.

"SURRENDER *NOW*, OR WE ATTACK." An East African armoured car, flying an Italian white flag as big as a bedspread, takes back the envoy who played for time.

The Jubaland Road ; Heavy transport has passed.

FREEDOM ENTERS ADDIS ABABA..One armoured car, flying a home-made Union Jack, "with an attitude of apologetic benevolence," is the only show of force at the ceremony of surrender.

The only tree for 10 miles..

Chiefs and their picked men swear allegiance.

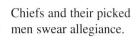
The Coptic Church attends in full regalia.

Dry Juba.

Wet Juba.

appointed Town Major, and I went with him to the fascist HQ building to meet the Mayor, to discover the location of all the military installations and stores and to make sure that we had an adequate guard on each of them. All this took some time, and it was late afternoon before we got back to our quarters, to find that the QM had been on a foraging expedition. He had found the military wine store and removed a substantial quantity of wine only minutes before the Brigade staff captain had arrived to lock the store and place a guard on it. Unfortunately, the Baron had failed to reach the mineral water store in good time, and this was a cause for regret, as the local tap-water was the worst we had tasted since Wajir. Supplies of meat and vegetables in the shops were low in quality and quantity, but there was pasta and some bread. A little later we heard that Division were to take over 'our' air force barracks on the morrow and that Brigade suspected us of looting the wine store and were contemplating disciplinary action; in fact, they did not seem pleased with us at all, and we thought it most unfair.

17

Preparing for Action

ℰℐ

NEXT morning we moved into the insalubrious colonial infantry barracks near the centre of the town, and managed to accommodate the Battalion HQ mess and the company messes in houses nearby. The CO and I then repaired to the Town Hall/fascist HQ to confer with the Mayor, who spoke tolerable English, about various matters ranging from the policing of the town to visiting arrangements for POWs and provisional currency exchange procedures and rates, on which we were still awaiting firm decisions from East Africa Force HQ. The Mayor tried very hard to be cooperative, but the CO maintained an extremely cool demeanour, and it seemed that the more the Mayor agreed to do, the more was demanded of him. I have always had some sympathy with the underdog, and would have felt happier if this defeated enemy had shown some pride and backbone.

Mogadishu was hot, humid, dirty, dusty, and at best seedy and run-down, resembling the poorest sort of Sicilian town, but I was not depressed by it for the first few days, when I was kept very busy. At the end of February, I wrote: 'The Italian lessons are coming in useful now – rather too useful. I'm being called on at all times to straighten out tangles, misunderstandings, and to try to preserve the Italians from being cleaned out completely. Our troops have the makings of first-class looters, and the South Africans are even better at it.'

I had some routine duties in connection with the POW camp, and was constantly on call to help resolve disputes between the troops and members of the public. There seemed to be hardly any free time, and I came to detest Mogadishu and longed to escape to the bush again. The elegant old Etonian G2 at Div. HQ wagged his finger at me, and said, 'You'll be in plenty of time for the battle at the Marda Pass, and perhaps you'll wish you hadn't been in such a hurry.'

The Italians retreated along the Strada Imperiale, which ran northwards for 750 miles out of Mogadishu towards Jigjiga and the mountains which barred the way to Harar and Addis Ababa. After a brief rest and refit, 2NR was despatched at full speed in pursuit on 1 March, using some of the 350,000 gallons of petrol which the Italians had left behind in Mogadishu. They covered an immense distance in spectacular fashion, catching remnants of the enemy at Daghabur (mile 580) on 10 March, and at Jigjiga on 17 March. At this point the Italians evacuated Berbera and British Somaliland and established their first strong defensive position since leaving the river Juba, at the Marda Pass.

On 13 March we were released at last from Mogadishu, and I drove the staff car, with the CO by my side for a change, away from the much-detested barracks in the early morning sunshine, feeling almost elated. The straight tarmac road ran through the flat thorn-scrub for fifty miles or so to the irrigated plantations of the Villagio Degli Abruzzi and then back again to scrub, with ornate markers every ten kilometres at the side of the road commemorating various generals and other heroes of Italian imperialism. We continued in this fashion, day after day, through the changing scene, past the oasis-like Belet Uen, through the waste of white sand to Gabredarré and its impressive mosque, with the road getting rougher all the way now as it followed the lower slopes of the hills lying to the west. Over the 150 or so miles between Gabredarre and Daghabur (mile 580), the road followed the dry valley of the river Tug Fafan, and here there was some vegetation, but my lasting impression of the whole journey is of drought, and again we were on water rations, carrying three days' meagre supply in each vehicle.

A few miles north of the small town of Daghabur, with its airfield and its brackish wells, the road petered out, and vehicles found their own way across a vast plain which stretched for about 150 miles to Jigjiga. For some twenty miles, we were again in deep powdery soil and the passage of the battalion's transport produced a huge cloud of dust which obscured the sun and could be seen for miles. From that, we moved across ground that was only slightly more negotiable and was described in one account of the journey as 'waves of bush-speckled sand-sea'. In the late afternoon of 19

March, after a long day's struggle with this wearisome terrain, we suddenly emerged on to a fully metalled highway for the last twenty miles over the plain looking towards Jigjiga and, beyond it, the fearsome obstacle of the Marda Pass.

2NR were already settled in buildings on the left of the road through the town, and we were quartered in various buildings, including a rather comfortable farmhouse on the right of the road. Swig and I shared a room as usual, and were soon wallowing in our baths. Emerging in clean khaki drill we found the atmosphere fresh and cool (we were at 5000 feet) and felt like new men. For me, there was the added pleasure of getting letters from Jocelyn again, after a gap of over a month. That evening, the CO, John Rogers and I, with some company commanders, walked over to 2NR's HQ to get fully briefed on the state of information and possible schemes for the assault on the pass, which Brigade and Division had proposed should take place on 23 March. There I met 'Knotty' Noble, an ADO somewhat senior to me, who was intelligence officer of 2NR. He gave me his ideas of enemy locations, based on observation of enemy movements, sightings of fires, lights and so on, and we decided to meet the next day to find some cover near the hills to make more observations. We hoped to produce diagrams and panorama drawings, possibly even maps, to help the South African artillery to formulate a fire-plan which could be programmed to fit into the assault plans of our own infantry companies.

March 20th was a lovely bright day, delightfully cool until mid-morning. I set off with Ibrahim Funtua (who had the keenest eyes in the 'I' section) to join Noble in the grassy plain beyond the town. It was now possible, with binoculars, to take a comprehensive view of the situation and to look at some of its detail. The plain seemed to stretch away for ever on our right and also behind the town. On the left, the road climbed steadily towards the col between the cone of Observation Hill to the far left, and the Breasts of Marda to the right. Further to the right and ahead of us rose the long ridge of Camel Saddle Hill, followed by further hills and peaks to the far right. The foothills of this range, which contained three or four small villages, were only a mile or so away, and we felt rather exposed as we moved through the grass, from the cover of one small bush to another, trying to get closer, but always imagining that the Italians might let loose a discouraging

round or two from their artillery. We became bolder in the course
of the day and were able to observe a great deal of movement on
the slopes, around what we took to be gun positions and possibly
mortar positions, which we recorded on our panorama diagrams.
The upper hillsides looked rough and steep, with gullies running
irregularly across them, so there were obvious possibilities for skilful use of the ground in the attack, but also (as events were to
show) to conceal forces to be used in counter-attack. As dusk came
on, lights appeared sporadically in various places, confirming our
daylight observations, and we returned to HQ with a good deal of
information for discussion and planning in the next two days. In
the meantime, small company patrols had been sent widely to the
flanks, using armoured cars as transport, and had confirmed 2NR's
earlier findings that there were no tracks or other approaches which
could be used to outflank the Italian position which appeared to
extend for about four miles, astride the pass, from Observation
Hill on our left to Camel Saddle Hill on our right.

We had a very pleasant dinner in mess that night. John Rogers
had taken over from Fasson (who was in hospital in Nairobi) as
2 i/c Battalion, and his warmth and good nature seemed to evoke
a happy response around the table. The Baron, also, was in genial
form, and had produced a bottle of wine from some private reserve. I, too, must have shown my happiness after getting Jocelyn's
letters, and I remember John referring to me in his developing
Italian, as 'il tenente sorridente'.

18

Marda Pass: an Impromptu Battle

❦

WE were quietly finishing breakfast on the morning of 21 March when the adjutant burst into the mess saying, 'We're off: you'd better get ready.' Questions were flung at him, and we learned that we were ordered to attack the pass at noon. It seemed that Brigade were convinced, by deserters or tribesmen, that the Italians were about to withdraw, and were keen to catch them before they went. In the words of one official account: 'Since it was desired above all things to bring this force to battle, the order was given to attack at once.'

At the time, this seemed to be a strange decision. Today, with more information and more consideration than was available to us in 1NR then, it seems stranger still. If the enemy, with an estimated strength of one brigade and one battalion plus artillery, holding an extremely strong position, chooses to withdraw, why not let him? Why commit our limited resources now, in a hurry, with hardly time to draft the operation order, instead of waiting until 23 March as planned, when 3NR would have returned from Berbera and a second brigade of South African artillery would have been available? The answer, I think, is contained in a paragraph of the same official account: 'It was a real soldier's battle; it took place in the clearest view of all, almost as if it had been a set theatrical piece, and the members of the South African Broadcasting Unit were able to make a unique record of the fight.' In other words, it was unique, dramatic entertainment for the staff and others who were not embroiled in the conflict and were able to stand far enough back to see the whole show, and it was valuable propaganda material for South African consumption.

I remember trying to get some idea of what should be the role of the 'I' section in the coming action, but the CO and adjutant were understandably hard-pressed to get out the operation order, and brief the company commanders who were to bear the brunt of the attack. I was able to give them some of the information which we had gathered the previous day, made a hasty final check of the radio sets and then, as instructed in the last few minutes, moved off with John Rogers in the standard 'advance Bn HQ' order of march. 'We'll get together later when things are sorted out,' said the CO.

The order was to attack and capture Camel Saddle Hill and, from it, the right Breast of Marda. In the meantime, 2NR would keep the Italians occupied in the vicinity of the road by making a move against Observation Hill. John Rogers had B and D companies, who were to tackle the left flank of the hill, while C and A companies attacked in the centre and on the right flank. Soon after leaving the town of Jigjiga we turned off into the grass, bumping and rocking in our lorries over the uneven ground, keeping roughly parallel to the line of the hills, and expecting the Italian batteries to open up on us at any moment. To our surprise, this did not happen, and we supposed that they were holding their fire, and the disclosure of their positions, until we were committed to the ground and line of attack. After what seemed an age, John judged that we had reached our de-bussing point, and the troops got down rapidly and moved into the standard open formation, B Coy on the left and D Coy on the right. John and I with Yaro Peni, who was carrying the Battalion HQ set, walked between the companies, occasionally looking behind us to locate the other companies, who had also de-bussed and were moving off. Through binoculars, I could see that the CO, with Lodge and the rest of the 'I' section, was going with them towards the base of the hill. One of the armoured cars was attacking a village to their front and machine-guns were rattling. I was worried about the way things were developing: we were much more spread out than anyone had expected, with the CO about a mile away, out of contact with me, and without the use of the radio set. It was agreed, after a brief discussion, that I should go and join him, and that John would stay initially in close touch with B Coy HQ, for use of their radio. I felt very unhappy on leaving him, but we both felt that, spread out as we were, the CO needed the help of all his staff as near to the centre of the operation as possible.

Yaro and I moved across quickly. By the time we reached the CO, who seemed glad to see us, machine-guns seemed to be firing from enemy positions all along the length of the hill. The SA battery had established an OP close by Battalion HQ, and I spent some time with the observation officer, pointing out machine-gun positions, which could be spotted as tiny flashes of light as the guns were fired. I found that I was able to locate several of them, which the South Africans had not detected, as a result of the hours of watching on the previous day. The gunners, once shown their targets, were extremely quick and accurate and a number of positions were silenced. Realising what must have happened to the enemy machine-gunners, I felt unhappy but knew only too well that the lives of our own people depended on knocking out these guns.

Then, suddenly, all was confusion, and I am still not clear about exactly what happened in the few minutes that followed. Platoons of C Coy and D Coy came running back down the hill, and there was a lot of machine-gun fire from the slopes to our front, accompanied by mortar or artillery shells bursting around us. The SA battery seemed to stop firing and I heard the observation officer cursing and then dashing away towards the guns. Swig and I mustered the AA platoon and other odds and sods from HQ Coy and joined the platoons of C and D companies who were now firing up the slopes. I remember Swig saying, as we lay alongside the Bren gunners of the AA platoon, 'I don't like these humming-bees around my ears', and I just had to laugh. Then the SA gunners opened up again, and it was soon obvious that the Italians had retired.

We got some idea of what had happened in a brief report from a young Scottish platoon-sergeant of D Coy. It seemed that a group of Italians had emerged from a gulley, firing machine-guns, while our troops were advancing, and that the supporting fire from within the company had not been enough to stop them. Several of our troops had been killed or wounded, and young John Rogers appeared to be dead – this was later confirmed. The sergeant knew nothing of the other John Rogers, who was assumed to be with B Coy on the left, from whence there had also been some heavy firing. Two platoons of C Coy, under its commander John Corbyn, were still making progress up the left centre of the hill.

The battery commander came up to apologise for the temporary loss of their support, owing to a break in their telephone line, probably caused by the enemy shelling. It had happened at a most unfortunate moment, and may have helped the Italian counter-attack on our immediate front and elsewhere. In the meantime, Sergeant Lodge had been trying to make radio contact with the companies, and had success only with D Coy who were now making slow but steady progress. The CO was concerned about A Coy, who had gone far out to the right flank to attack that side of the hill, where they were rather isolated from the rest of the battalion. He asked me to go and investigate.

I set off with Yaro Peni, keeping a respectable distance, as I thought, from the base of the hill. All went well for a few hundred yards, and then machine-guns opened up on us, and seemed to follow us as we tried to move on, crouching in the grass. I remember standing up to try to discover where the fire was coming from, and being pulled down by Yaro, who said in Hausa, 'Don't play with your life.' We lay doggo for a short time, and then noticed two Nigerians approaching from the right, one supporting the other, a corporal wounded in the leg. The Italians, decently, seemed to be leaving them alone, and we joined their path carefully, on our bellies, so as not to stir things up again. From the corporal, Audu Fika, I learned that he was the only casualty in A Coy, that they were beginning to move up the hill and had been helped by our artillery which had silenced two awkward machine-guns. I felt doubtful of getting to A Coy and back in reasonable time, and decided to take this information to Battalion HQ at once. If more was needed, an armoured car might help to shorten the journey.

The CO felt reassured about A Coy, under command of a competent young Scot. He also had excellent news from C Coy (by runner for lack of radio contact) who had reached the right Breast and were consolidating there. It was now late afternoon, and our main concern was that we had heard nothing from John Rogers. B Coy said that he had been with a platoon of D Coy when the counter-attack took place, but we could not get further news from D Coy as radio contact faded.

As darkness fell, the shooting died down, and finally stopped. We all realised that we were desperately hungry, having eaten nothing since breakfast. The Baron (the QM) showed his quality at this time by appearing with most of the motor-transport drivers carrying cooking-pots containing a hot meal for the troops.

Runners came in from the outlying companies, and they were able to guide the food-carriers to the eager consumers who were finding such shelter as they could among the rocks and gulleys and stunted bushes in their sectors of the hillside. I suggested to the CO that I should take the HQ Coy radio (which had been little used) to C Coy HQ, where, closest to the Italians, it would meet the greatest need. This set appeared to be reasonably in tune with the Battalion HQ set, and so, accompanied by the food-carriers, Yaro Peni, Isa Zuru and I started the climb in the darkness. We had a few torches shared among many but, for the most part, it was a matter of feeling rather than seeing one's way. Yaro and Isa shared the heavy burden of the radio very cheerfully, but it did seem a long hard trail, much of it along the bed of a gulley, where we were guided by the men from the company. We reached John Corbyn at last, to find him and his men very cold indeed at about 7000 feet on the exposed hill-top, thankful for the food but envious of the heat we had generated in the climb.

To the right and left along the line of the hills, lights disclosed enemy movement, probably collecting their casualties, which appeared to have been quite heavy (ours were amazingly light). The enemy searchlight continued to shine down the pass, in spite of the South African artillery's earlier attempts to hit it. Lights of lorries appeared to be moving along the road towards Harar, possibly indicating an Italian withdrawal. Apart from the clatter of dishes and a low buzz of conversation in Hausa, all was very quiet; for the present an unofficial truce operated. Later that night, C Coy would patrol towards the left Breast which commanded the road through the pass, and would report (by radio, I hoped) whether it was occupied.

At about 3.15 a.m. the Italian searchlight went out, and at 4 a.m. C Coy reported the left Breast clear of enemy. Having returned from Berbera, 3NR sent a patrol into the pass, and confirmed that the Italians had gone. In the first light of a very cold dawn, Swig and a Rhodesian went to look for Captain John Rogers and found his body lying near the gulley from which the counter-attack had been sprung. It seemed probable that he had drawn the enemy fire upon himself while directing the withdrawal. We buried the two John Rogers later that morning in a small walled enclosure, part of some disused farm, looking out on the hills. I had made the mistake of not seeing John's dead face, and so, in a state of acute tiredness and shock, I was unable to grasp the reality of what had happened in just twenty-four hours. I reproached myself for having left John to cope alone with the left flank sub-command, and then fell to wondering, as often since, how the Italians could have achieved surprise if our standard battle movement drills had been properly carried out. Whatever errors were made, it was doubtful whether I could have corrected them, or would have survived the critical episode.

At the time, I felt angry that we had been rushed into the operation with no proper planning, no possibility of using the information we had gathered, or of concerting the infantry attack with an artillery fire-plan. I would have been angrier still if I had known that a whole brigade of SA artillery was left unused only a few miles down the Mogadishu road. However, the gamble had paid off; our relatively few dead and seriously wounded had paid the price for our over-extended front and communications, and for the failure of the artillery at a critical stage of the Italian counter-attack. Again and again in this campaign, one experienced, or heard of, infantry attacks unsupported, or inadequately supported, by artillery. It seemed as though our regular officers were unused to the cooperation of other arms, or didn't expect them to be available, or wanted to show that they could do it all alone. When, later, we went to look at the Italian positions, we could only wonder that they had not held on much longer, made us pay a far higher price, and we were thankful that no Germans opposed us here.

One supporting arm, the Engineers, were recognised as having an indispensable expertise: the handling of mines. On the morning of 22 March they worked hard on clearing the pass of these in-fernal devices, and on building a diversion around the huge hole which the Italians had blown in the road. It was then the turn of 3NR to go through and tackle the Babile Pass, which was more in the nature of a defile through high crags which lay between Marda and the final approaches to Harar. 3NR did a brilliant job under appalling difficulties, and cleared the way for 1NR to pass through on 25 March. In my view, 3NR was the best of the three battalions, because it was commanded by a man of great ability, dedication and character, Lieutenant Colonel Marshall, who always seemed to be near the centre of action, supplying motivation and con-fidence.

19

Into Ethiopia

ᴄ᷎᷎ᴐ

WILLIE Arkwright was now acting 2 i/c Battalion, and the pair of us, in a staff car, drove on down the road towards Harar with a section of armoured cars in the lead. We did not have the help, on this occasion, of a map produced from air photographs, and knew only that we were likely to run into trouble at the Bisidimo river, a mile or two before Harar. During a brief halt on the way, Willie decided to squeeze into one of the armoured cars. I was joined in the staff car by Tim Harman, a Rhodesian who was now commanding the AA platoon, and we moved up the column to be just behind the armoured cars. Towards the end of the afternoon we had reached the last narrow section of the pass where the road suddenly forked to the right, presenting a wide view of the gently sloping valley of the Bisidimo, with the hills in front of Harar rising beyond it. The armoured cars began to move down the road towards the river but we stopped the staff car in some cover near the fork, and began to survey the ground through binoculars. Then, suddenly, shells began dropping around us and on the road by the armoured cars which returned rapidly. Tim and I dived into a ditch and stayed there until the firing stopped. Later, we extricated the car, which we found to be, like ourselves, amazingly unscathed. It was now nearly sunset, and it was decided that we should make no further move until the following day. We spent a cold uncomfortable night in the vehicles which were strung out along the defile, and were thankful not to be bombed at first light, for which the SAAF, which had raided Diredawa and Harar air-fields, should have the credit.

There was a sizeable hill to the right of the road, forming part of the head of the pass. At first light, the CO and I climbed it, and were joined by Dick Greswell who was looking for an OP for the Light Battery which had sited itself under the slope of the hill, out of sight of the Italians. We found a small hollow in the rock on the crest of the hill, and from there had a splendid view of the river, the hills beyond, and the outskirts of Harar. The CO had ordered two companies to advance to the river and cross it (the water was shallow). The troops first kept to a ditch at the side of the road, and then began to spread out across the slope leading down to the river, finding cover as best they could in the rough ground. Machine-guns and light artillery opened up on them, and they found it impossible to make progress. Our own Light Battery opened up under Greswell's direction, and probably silenced some guns, but they could not reach those higher up the hill which seemed to be of heavier calibre. By this time, shells were passing just above our heads in both directions. The CO reckoned that the Italians were trying to hit the Light Battery (which they could not see, nor were likely to hit with flat trajectory shells); it seemed to me more probable that they were trying to hit us! We stayed put for the moment, and awaited the arrival of the South African Field Brigade and also the SA 6-inch howitzers, which were greatly delayed by the congestion of vehicles in the narrow defile at the head of the pass. The CO was concerned about the halted action, and suggested going down to get the troops out of cover and moving forward again. I could see that this could produce a lot of casualties, but fortunately the SA field guns now arrived and drove down the road towards the river, looking for a firing position. They, too, had some casualties before they found a place with some cover and began an artillery duel which lasted about two hours. The Italians had the advantage (as we knew only too well) of having registered the ranges of all the features on our side of the river, but the South Africans kept their guns firing with great courage, and with remarkable accuracy. Finally, they were able to turn their attention to the Italian machine-guns, and our troops were able to start moving; the CO and I went down to join them.

The forward companies crossed the river, and began to move up the slope on the far side. At this point, an Italian officer appeared, driven slowly down the road, standing in a truck, holding an enormous white flag. This was apparently in response to a message dropped from the air by Division on the Italian HQ in Harar that morning, warning that the town might be shelled if it was not surrendered quickly. The Italians tried to negotiate for more time, but we insisted on immediate capitulation and our armoured cars began to follow the Italian truck into the town. The CO and I perched ourselves somehow on one of the leading cars.

A large number of Italian troops were assembled in a square just off the road at the top of the hill, but I could not see any guns. I suggested to the CO that we should drive down the main road to find them, and within a mile or two we caught up with a whole brigade of heavy artillery, which we had the pleasure of heading off and escorting back into Harar. The senior officer was quite young, and most exquisitely dressed in cavalry breeks and highly polished boots. He surrendered his map-case and maps, which showed the ranges most carefully registered, and his German pistol, which I greatly preferred to the British .38 (as did my brother-in-law, who later used it in Burma).

We spent a week or so in Harar, tidying up, as we had done in Mogadishu, while the South Africans and the East African Brigade pressed on to Diredawa and towards Addis Ababa. I had plenty to do, with 1200 prisoners and much war material to be sorted out, as well as finding accommodation for our troops, writing the War Diary (always an urgent priority), making sketch maps of battle dispositions and getting them copied. (Do they still exist, in some forgotten archive?) There was also the incessant demand from war correspondents for 'colourful personal stories'. The African town was the scene of much noisy rejoicing on liberation from the Italians, and the dirty miserable streets had been decorated for the occasion by festoons of pseudo-balloons – thousands of contraceptives stolen from the Italian military stores!

The effect of the German intervention in the desert war on the situation in East Africa was to cause the Italians to prolong the struggle there by several months, to continue the tying down of about two divisions of useful troops, and the diverting of other resources from the main front. When we heard, on 6 April, that Addis had been surrendered as an open town, many of us felt betrayed, thinking that we should have taken a tougher line and demanded total surrender. Certainly, the Italian command was under strong pressure from Rome to hold out, to help their German allies, but we had a trump card in that the civilian population in Addis and elsewhere were desperately afraid of being massacred by the Abyssinians if we did not provide protection. In the event, we had the worst of all worlds, with many of our troops immobilised on guard duties for several weeks while the remaining Italian forces consolidated their positions in various mountain strongholds to the north, west and south of Addis.

The Governor of Uganda, Sir Philip Mitchell, had been given the additional job of organising OETA (Occupied Enemy Territory Administration) and had scraped together a group of officers from Kenya and elsewhere to cope with the civil administration in the areas which we had occupied. A batch of them arrived in Harar to relieve us, and 1NR moved on to Diredawa, which the South Africans had occupied on 29 March. The distance is only thirty-five miles, but it is an extraordinary journey, like many in that part of Africa. For about twenty miles, the road runs across a tableland at about 7000 ft, and then in the last fifteen miles, winds crazily down a 4000-feet sheer escarpment to Diredawa, on the Addis–Djibouti railway, a town to be remembered for heat, smells, flies and mosquitoes. The road had been blown in many places by the Italians, but 2NR, with Sapper help, had repaired it in a matter of days – a remarkable achievement – so that the South Africans could pass through.

Memories of Diredawa are a few brief flashes in the kaleidoscope; it seemed to contain all the worst aspects of an Italian town. During a brief 'cleaning up' occupation, we found quarters in the town hall, which was infested by myriads of flies. Stacks of official papers, files, pamphlets, admixed with rubbish and filth had to be removed from every room. Outside, in the streets, discarded papers were blown about by the wind, symbolising what was happening to the originators of all this mess. We escaped, for our meals, into the relative order and cleanliness of the Albergo Imperiale, where the CO was so impressed by the competence of the cook, an Italian called Georgio, that he decided to employ him as the Battalion HQ mess cook, in which capacity he served for the rest of the campaign.

For political reasons, South African and East African troops had to be first into Addis Ababa, and so SA troops were passed through us towards the next Italian defence line (weakly held) along the Awash river. After a number of brisk actions, 1SA Brigade and 22EA Brigade entered Addis Ababa on 6 April. In accepting the surrender of the town, the commander of 11th(A) Div. had also accepted a very large security responsibility. There were about 10,000 armed Italian soldiers and police in the town, and nearly every civilian was carrying a weapon. The Italians had fortified the place against possible attack by 'patriot' forces, and its defence consisted of a ring of outer forts on the surrounding hills, together with an inner circle of about fifty concrete blockhouses, connected by barbed-wire fences. Each blockhouse was garrisoned by about forty Italians, armed with several machine-guns, which were often fired at night when they became suspicious of any movement in the vicinity.

Small detachments of South African and East African troops remained in the capital and tried to cope with its many problems while the rest of their troops pursued the retreating Italians along the roads leading north, south and west out of Addis, in the hope of catching some of their tails. However, nearly all the best of the enemy troops managed to escape into mountain strongholds in four main areas: the lakes to the south; along the Jimma road to the south-west; along the Lechemti road to the west; in the Dessie–Amba–Alagi–Gondar region to the north. The main Italian forces in these areas were about 250 to 500 miles from Addis. There was much hard fighting before they surrendered, in piecemeal fashion, and the supply problems for the British forces, along very rough roads in heavy rain, were extremely difficult.

20

Liaising with Italians

✑

T HE Nigerian brigade was pulled into Addis as quickly as
possible to try to sort out the mess there, and 1NR arrived
on 8 April. The security situation was the most serious matter, and the Divisional and Force staffs were anxious to obtain
firm control of all military stores in the capital before they were
looted (as they had been in Harar and Diredawa to some extent)
by the Abyssinians, and even the Italians. These stores were indeed
very substantial, amounting to about a year's supply, covering a
wide range of material, including medical supplies and equipment,
oil and petrol, food, signals equipment and telephones, radio, and
a very modern, efficient air survey and mapping establishment.
When the CO and I drove to Divisional HQ to get our orders, we
found that we had been allocated this survey building and its
grounds as our HQ, with the rest of the battalion deployed north
and south of it; 2NR were similarly deployed over the other half
of the city. The CO took one look at our allocated HQ, decided
that it would not do, and told me to look for somewhere else. Just
a few hundred yards away, I found a residential club for bachelor
civil servants, which appeared to be ideal. Most of the residents
had gone; I told the remainder to clear out, and we moved in, for
a stay which lasted, surprisingly, for six to seven weeks.

The Circolo Funzionari di Governo was really quite palatial,
well furnished and lavishly equipped. It had about ten bedrooms,
a dining-room, lounge and billiard room, and for the first time in
many weeks I was able to enjoy some privacy, having acquired a
bedroom for my sole occupation. The daylight hours were always
very fully occupied, and in the evening I was often, by choice, the
only officer on the premises and so automatically committed to
telephone duty, receiving reports from the companies following the

outbreaks of shooting which occurred, with only brief intermissions, every night.

The first job, for the CO and myself, was to tour the zone of the city for which we were responsible, to position the companies within it, and map out their boundaries. Guards were established on all military installations; we continued to disarm Italian soldiers and to fill the POW cages which were in our charge. These camps were besieged by large numbers of intending visitors, mostly female, and we found it essential to set up a system of limited visiting by pass. Sergeant Lodge and I spent about an hour a day, at first, issuing passes to Italian women of all ages, and a few men (those of military age were sent to Brigade for further interrogation). The women were often tearful, asking for news of 'mio figlio' or 'mio cognato', but there were relatively few wives or fiancées. It was known that many military husbands had removed their uniforms to become civilians and were hiding away, with their wives. Who could blame them? This option was not available to the Italians who had been made responsible for the manning of the forts and blockhouses and who were to be transferred to the POW camps as soon as they could be relieved by our own forces.

One morning, the CO sent for me and introduced me, very formally, to a Colonel Fioretti and a Capitano Nigra, with whom I was ordered to liaise, and to arrange for the replacement of Italian troops by our own in all the forts and blockhouses in the sector of 1NR. The CO's demeanour during this interview was icy and even arrogant. At the end of the meeting, he made it clear that he did not wish to see either of the Italians again, unless serious difficulties should arise, and we were left in no doubt that this contingency was definitely to be avoided.

Colonel Fioretti was a charming elderly gentleman for whom, I imagine, fascism had been an unwelcome but reluctantly accepted aberration in Italy's post-1918 development. He stayed briefly to talk with me, and to assure me that Nigra would be able to handle everything, and we did not meet again.

Luigi Nigra was a lean, lively northern Italian in his early forties who, in civil life, had been Director of Broadcasting in Addis Ababa. Initially, like the CO, I was prejudiced against him because he was wearing Blackshirt uniform, but I soon found that I was dealing with a man of keen intelligence and great sense of humour. He approached our joint task methodically and efficiently, and

1NR's occupation of the blockhouses went ahead as fast as the battalion organisation could cope with it. Each morning, Nigra would arrive in his Fiat 'Ballila', which was even smaller than an Austin 7, salute smartly with a slight bow on entering my room, and present the compliments of Colonel Fioretti. Then we were away in the little Fiat to reconnoitre the next sector of the Italian garrison to be relieved, and to have on-site discussions with company commanders to ensure that the operation ran smoothly. I felt sorry for the Italians whom we put 'into the bag', and would not have been surprised if Nigra had tried to slow down the process, so as to delay his own incarceration, but, to his credit, he did not try to do so. He might have been less cooperative if he had known that it was our intention that Haile Selassie's troops should, as soon as possible, replace our own to enable us to resume active operations against his countrymen. On most days, we managed to find time for an Italian lesson (his English and French, acquired at Milan University, were excellent) and I made some useful progress.

About this time, we had confirmation of the awards which had been recommended after the Marda Pass and Harar battles: MCs for John Corbyn and another officer, the MM for an African sergeant, and the DSO for the CO. Fasson and I, with two companies, spent some days in futile pursuit of Italians who had scattered into the bush between Debra Marcos and Gondar. On our return, I found the CO impatient to send me to the river Omo where 3NR had for several weeks been facing the Italians and probing their defences.

There are three major rivers in Ethiopia, the Juba, the Blue Nile and the Omo, which flows south-west in a great arc into Lake Rudolph. The Italians had withdrawn a sizeable force behind the Omo, so commanding the two roads leading south-west from Addis towards the garrison town of Jimma. Both roads ran through spectacular country and crossed the river in deep gorges lying below escarpments surmounted by high plateaux. The Force commander planned a joint attack, by 2NR and a KAR battalion on the southern road, and by 3NR, 1NR and KAR on the northern road, to be launched on 31 May. The CO told me to go and familiarise myself with 'the ground over which 1NR might be required to operate'. My request for more specific instructions produced only the order to discuss the situation with 3NR, who would be aware of the general plan.

The CO had, for some time, been getting increasingly moody and difficult, and I knew that I had to accept the situation and make the best of it. The abortive mission from which I had just returned had provided an escape from the atmosphere of the HQ mess, and the prospect of a few more days spent away on the Omo was welcome.

I was told that I could get a lift to the Omo with an artillery officer who was returning there from Addis. He was not in either of the hotels, but I found him eventually, in the late evening, in the 'officers' club'. A crowd of hard-drinking types stood around a table at which my quarry was playing poker and apparently winning, judging by the size of a stack of Italian notes on the floor beside his chair. The drinking and gaming appeared to be upsetting the normal business of the establishment, and the 'madame' was wringing her hands and refusing to supply ice or soda (everybody seemed to be carrying a bottle of rationed spirits). With some difficulty, I secured the attention of Major X and arranged to meet him at 9 a.m. next day.

To my amazement, he was there on time, and a few hours later I was reporting to Colonel Marshall, of 3NR, who was, I thought, looking rather grey and tired. He attached me at once to his forward company who were dug in, in fairly thick bush, to the left of the road, about two miles from the bridge, which had been blown. On the far side of the river, one could distinguish the trace of the road which zig-zagged through a tangle of hills to the cutting in the final escarpment along which it climbed to the plateau and the small town of Abalti, about 4000 feet above the river. It was very beautiful, and particularly impressive when seen as a panorama from the artillery OP on the hillside about 1500 feet above the river. There brooded over the place the sinister quiet which belongs to battlefields in the period before action.

I was handed on to a young subaltern, who was instructed to take me next day on patrol in the area to the right of the road which was assumed to be the future responsibility of 1NR.

After dinner, I was invited to join a patrol, in the faint moonlight, down the road towards the bridge, to observe the movement of the Italian ration-lorry. To my amazement, the patrol of about ten men, wearing army boots, walked steadily down the tarmac road, making a very loud and unmistakable sort of noise against the background of complete quiet. When I protested, I was informed that this had been a regular patrol for weeks, and 'nothing ever happened'. We stopped a few hundred yards from the bridge, and heard the lorry descending the hill to provision the forward Italian posts, heard it grinding its way back again, and then we too returned to camp. It was a 'live and let live' situation for the moment, but the Italians must have known, as we did, that it could not last much longer.

Next morning, after an early breakfast, I set off with the platoon officer. We covered about three miles, and agreed that the banks of the river on this, the right, side of the road, were so open, its course so smoothly curved, that it would be very difficult to achieve any surprise in attack across it, while the defenders would have open fields of fire for all their weapons. Colonel Marshall seemed to agree with our findings, on the basis of his own previous observations, and I could not understand why it had ever been proposed that 1NR should make an attack to the right of the bridge. I reported the situation to the CO on my return but was not thanked. In fact, I got the impression that it was my fault that the terrain was so unsuitable.

21

The Omo Gorge

❧

I HAD warned the CO that mosquitoes and other insects had plagued us terribly when we were patrolling near the river, and he arranged for the battalion to camp high on the hillside, two miles or so above 3NR. The weather at first was marvellously sunny and fresh, and the view across the gorge to the plateau was splendidly clear. There was absolute quiet, except for bird sounds, and the occasional exchange of artillery fire.

We wasted much time in further recce of the ground to the right of the road before Brigade were convinced of its disadvantages; I had no help from the CO who never accompanied me. On one of my patrols, I discovered a group of primitive people, quite small, almost pygmies, who were living in huts perched on poles, secure against flooding by rain, which we had begun to experience ourselves. Briefly, I was aware of the presence here of the genuine Africa and its peoples who were the real reason for my being in Africa at all, but there was no time for speculation about them and their way of life.

Suddenly, one morning, there was great urgency. We were under orders to support 3NR the following day in an attack to be launched across the river at dawn. This was to be synchronised with a crossing and attack some fifty miles to the south by the 22nd (East Africa) Brigade, which at present included the 2nd Battalion, Nigeria Regiment. This brigade had been cooperating with 12(A) Div. which had been advancing northwards through the Abyssinian lakes, driving the retreating Italians, after heavy fighting, through the town of Soddu and across the Omo, to defend their garrison town of Jimma.

3NR were to assemble overnight in Mule gulley, a stream which ran down the hillside to Mule crossing, a part of the river deep enough, wide enough, slow enough to enable our assault-boats to operate. I was told to find an assembly area for 1NR from which they could move in support of 3NR, to find sites for KAR machine-guns to cover the initial crossing by 3NR, and to recce a covered route to the assembly area. To avoid confusion in the darkness, we had to keep well clear of 3NR's approach-route to their assembly area. The CO did not offer to accompany me, and I felt the responsibility of the task most acutely. Fortunately, we had an aerial photograph of the area, and I was able to plan a possible approach to a gulley beyond, and roughly parallel to, Mule gulley and to plot the distances and compass-bearings. With the help of my 'I' section, all this worked out well on the ground, and we marked the route on the return journey by slashing bushes and trunks of trees. I reported to the CO and took a few hours' rest before we set off again, with the battalion, at about 9 p.m.

Ominously, the moon was obscured by cloud, and we had to locate our route-markers – the slashed trees and bushes – by torch-light. It began to rain, and we made slow progress in the darkness. The CO became querulous, and added to my anxieties, but I was comforted by the quiet confidence of Ibrahim, who identified and checked every marker. To my intense relief (and that of the CO too), we found our gulley and confirmed that it joined Mule gulley within a hundred yards of the river. It was now raining heavily, the bed of the gulley had become a torrent, and we were all cold, wet and miserable. At about 4 a.m, the operation was cancelled; the river had risen four feet and was seventy feet wider. Three African sappers, fine swimmers, had been drowned in attempting to get a rope across it. We marched wearily back to camp and the hastily organised comfort of a hot breakfast.

In the following days, the Brigade IO found a better crossing-point nearer the bridge, and a new attack was planned for the night of 4–5 June with a KAR battalion in support of 3NR instead of ourselves, which was entirely successful. On 6 June it was decided that 23(N) Brigade would be transferred via Addis to the Didessa river, some 250 miles due west of Addis. As we drove away from the Omo, I was informed by my contacts in 3NR that the river-bank opposite Mule gulley had been thickly sown with mines and that a crossing there by night would have been a disaster.

We spent three days or so on the journey to Lechemti, a small town about 200 miles west of Addis. We bivouacked on the way in the usual fashion, and I travelled ahead to find camp-sites, with shelter if possible, and above the prevalent flood levels. In hilly country, it was often difficult to find much level, or even fairly level, ground and the situation worsened as we moved further west along roads which became narrower, steeper and more tortuous. The CO found some game to shoot, and became more cheerful; the familiar mess routine was re-established

The meal was served by our boys. My own, Atanas, had succumbed to the rigours of campaigning, and was recovering in Addis. The others looked after my needs in mess, the Baron's boy, Utu, being particularly kind and attentive. Utu was a real Kano man, born within smelling-distance of the market, the Hausa equivalent of a Cockney, with all the drollery, shrewdness and 'bounce' of his kind. He complained, amusingly, of the hardness of his duties, wished to enlist as a soldier because life would be so much easier! A great friend and admirer of Alhadji (how sensible of him, after all, to stay in Nigeria, but rather hard on his poor master), he was determined to return me in good order to him, so far as he could manage it. In his eyes, all the soldiery, of whatever rank, were riff-raff (except his own master, to whom he was devoted in his own Jeeves-like fashion), whereas I, a *joji* (judge, or district officer) was someone of true authority and understanding, belonging to the real life of places like Kano market. Furthermore, I was able to understand his derogatory remarks about someone or something, uttered *sotto voce* in his highly colloquial Hausa while handing me a dish at table. Dear Utu, I believe he realised that he helped me to keep sane, and perhaps I helped him, too. After dinner, there was, inevitably, poker. There was simply no escape. Impossible to sit in the darkness in one's tent, or to sit in a corner of the mess-tent to read or write, incurring the displeasure of the CO for whom compliance with mess routines, etiquette and consensus was almost a matter of religion.

The night of 14 June was not one for poker, or for much sleep either. Laing entered the mess saying that we had to move at 6 a.m. next morning and that an operation order was on its way from Brigade; 3NR, who had preceded us into Lechemti, had sent a patrol forward which encountered an enemy force holding a hill position about fourteen miles west of Lechemti commanding the road to Ghimbi, a garrison town which was the brigade's next major objective. We had to remove the enemy from the hill and advance to the river Didessa, some ten miles further on. When the operation order arrived at about 10.30 p.m., it was seen only by the adjutant and the CO, but I now know that it stated that the enemy strength was 'unknown', that the position was surrounded by a 'patriot force approx. 2000 strong' and that, owing to the state of the road, it was unlikely that the Nigerian Light Battery would be available to support us before 1300 hours, or the South African Field Battery before 1500 hours. The CO was to use his discretion as to whether to mount an attack 'before the bulk of the artillery arrives'. This placed an unpleasant burden of decision upon the CO. He called a meeting of company commanders, and issued verbal orders, which were later confirmed in writing. B and D companies were to lead, and we were merely given to understand that artillery support was unlikely to be available.

22

A Blue Nile Tributary

〇

E moved at first light after little sleep. The road to the west of Lechemti was even worse than the bad stretch to the east of it, and it took us over an hour to cover the fourteen miles or so to the Italian position. We had no armoured cars; B Coy was in the lead and had with them a Captain Wyberg, from the Sudan, who was the liaison officer with the patriot force. The CO and I were in one of the leading lorries of D Coy, immediately following B Coy. When we stopped, there was a lot of machine-gun noise ahead, and we found B Coy pinned to the ground by heavy fire from a hill to the left of the road. We soon joined them in the nearest piece of dead ground we could find. There was very little cover, and with bullets swishing overhead, there was not much encouragement to look over the top of our little mound to see what was going on. The patriots appeared to be screaming and yelling everywhere, but Wyberg told us that most of them were positioned behind the hill and across the road, to prevent the Italians from escaping.

D Coy tried to make a flanking movement round the base of the hill to the left, but found little cover, and soon had casualties. The Italians appeared to be well provided with light artillery as well as machine-guns, and after one of their salvoes, the mortar officer flopped down beside us, white-faced and shaken, to report that one of his mortars had received a direct hit, with two men killed. I tried to contact the company commanders, but all I could get, incredibly, from some unknown radio source, was a performance of Beethoven's 5th Symphony! The CO and I agreed that, in the next lull of firing, we should make a dash for it towards D Coy, to see whether we could move them further round the hill, and possibly get some help from the patriots.

At this moment (it was now late morning), there was a roar of guns from behind us, and we knew that the Light Battery must have arrived at last. The bullets stopped swishing over our heads, and, as we moved forward, there were terrific shouts and yells from our own troops and from the patriots, who began swarming up the hill towards where two white flags were waving. The tragic development of the situation now was that the patriots, moving fast with no packs to carry, got ahead of our troops and began killing Italians regardless of the flags of surrender. By the time we had occupied the position and established some control, over two hundred Italians were dead or dying, some of them fearfully mutilated, in a small area on the top of the hill. It was a truly horrifying spectacle, which none of us was ever likely to forget. We called the place Massacre Hill. Some of our own troops made their contribution to the carnage, perhaps in revenge for their own casualties, and some of our officers shot patriots whom they caught engaged in the act of mutilation.

The unscathed Italians were succouring their wounded comrades, and they helped me to sort them into some order of need for MO Garry O'Flynn's attention – they seemed to have no MO of their own. Our own casualties were assembled nearer to the road and included my old friend of Nairobi days, Basil Ledeboer, whose leg was bandaged. We were fortunate that our own casualties were so light: two Africans killed and six wounded, two British sergeants wounded. The Light Battery had arrived in the nick of time, and had been ordered into action by the Brigadier, for which he claimed much credit. In fact, if the action had been properly concerted with the battery from the beginning, we might well have averted many of the Italian casualties – and the attendant horror – as well as our own. I felt desperately sorry for the Italians, who sat around on the stony ground in a state of numbed shock, after all they had seen happen to their dead and badly wounded comrades. We mobilised those who were fit into parties to identify and bury the dead, and the CO told Wyberg to take his filthy patriots away, and never let us see them, or him, again. On 17 June, I reported to Brigade that 231 Italians had been killed on the hill, and 185 prisoners taken, many of them wounded. These men, fine brave soldiers, among the best we encountered, had been uselessly sacrificed by their higher command.

On the far side of the hill, a large section of overhanging cliff had been blown down on to the road, and our companies were set to work in relays to clear it, using pick and shovel. After two days, the way was clear for 3NR to drive through to the river Didessa and we followed two days later. The ten miles or so to the river included a zig-zag stretch down a steep escarpment, accompanied by a startling change of climate, from cool mist to steamy heat. The road surface was extremely rough and uneven; here and there some of our lorries had joined their Italian forerunners, in the ditch if lucky, or down the slope to the next section of road.

Perhaps it should not have amazed me that the situation on the Didessa was almost exactly a repeat of that on the Omo three weeks earlier. We had the same dramatis personae, and the setting was again a river in spate, a blown bridge, and 3NR encamped on the left of the road. The Brigadier ordered 1NR into camp on the right of the road, with instructions to recce the river and find a crossing-place somewhere to the right of the bridge. Once again, I reconnoitred the potential crossing area and found a tributary stream and, in this case, a vertical, unclimbable cliff beyond it. We encountered, amazingly, a patrol from 3NR which should not have been there at all. The CO and the omniscient Brigadier refused to believe our findings, and two further recces (including one by the CO, at last) were required before my initial report was accepted.

Next day, we made a difficult crossing of the Didessa and its tributary the Dabana before the Italians withdrew yet again. I was relieved of my job as Intelligence Officer and told to return to Addis to defend a man being court-martialled for murder. My recollection of the last night 'West of the Didessa' is of playing poker in the mess-tent, with water running in a steady stream under the mess-table and between the little islands on which we placed our feet, while a violent storm raged outside. The CO's concentration was unaffected and was, as usual, reflected in the score.

23

The Regiment Goes Home

ᑲᑐ

M Y 'client' (a Nigerian lance-corporal on guard-duty in
May) had killed an Eritrean POW alleged to be trying to
escape through a window. Garry O'Flynn had examined
the body, and was required to give evidence on the path of the
bullet and other medical details.

In Addis we were comfortably accommodated in the Albergo
Imperiale, along with many other officers who were doing a variety
of A and Q jobs, as well as OETA. One day I found myself face
to face with Michael Gass, a year junior to me at Christ Church
and now ADO, Gold Coast, turned soldier. Michael told me about
the very arduous campaign of 12(A) Division, which split off from
us after crossing the Juba and tackled the Italians in the mountain-
ous lakes area running north and north-east from the Kenya border
towards Addis. This was obviously a vital operation which helped
to ensure the success of 11(A) Division's advance through Somaliland.

In the court-martial, I suppressed my own doubts about the
innocence of my client, and made the most of Garry's evidence
that the Eritrean had been shot from behind and below, supporting
the claim that he had been trying to escape through a window.
The man was acquitted, and I felt glad that the toll of death was
not to be increased by an execution – always a particularly nasty
experience for all concerned. (This was the second time I had
defended against a charge of murder. The first in Addis was unsuccessful.)

At about this time, the news was released that the Nigerian
Brigade was to pull out of East Africa and return to Nigeria 'in

the very near future', and I was advised to await the arrival of
1NR in Addis. This was all welcome news to me: Nigeria was, for
all its faults, the country of my adoption, and it was nearer to
Britain and Jocelyn, whose letters had gone sadly astray during
the Omo and Didessa affairs.

Towards the end of July, I rejoined the battalion in their rain-
soaked camp outside Addis and after a few days began the 'homeward' journey through Diredawa, Harar, Jigjiga, Hargeisa, towards
the embarkation port in once-more-British Somaliland. We passed
all too quickly through Harar and Jigjiga, with hardly time to take
in the view from the Italian positions or, looking back, to remember our own viewpoints and experiences. We looked across
the rolling grassland at the base of the Marda Pass towards the
lonely graves of the two John Rogers, from which one day their
remains would be taken to a cemetery for all their fallen comrades,
in distant Nairobi.

And so, on to our embarkation camp at Hargeisa, an oasis town
in British Somaliland, about a hundred miles from Berbera. The
heat there was worse than anything any of us could remember in
Nigeria. Even the troops, who were jubilant about returning home,
found it hard to bear, and Italian prisoners collapsed from heat-
stroke. We boarded a very crowded ship (one of the old 'Castle'
liners) and found conditions only slightly better as we lay in
harbour for two days before crossing to Aden to pick up a convoy.
We were sorry for the stokers and engineers, who were working in
a temperature of 140 degrees F., and were sometimes carried out
of the engine-room. It was too hot for the troops to stay in their
quarters on the lower (troop) decks, and so they swarmed all over
the upper decks, where the noise was an added discomfort. I almost
wished to be back in Hargeisa, where at least there was quiet, and
even, once, a storm of rain, in which the Baron and I had danced
naked for sheer joy.

Aden, that strange, barren other-Gibraltar, imperial bulwark
against Italians and all comers, was a welcome brief diversion, in
spite of its intense heat and humidity, the little town being set in
an extinct crater, among the great water-tanks contained within its
rocks. The navy was here, and I thought of the vast spread of our
naval resources and installations in so many and so various places
around the world. This was a comforting thought, but also dis-
quieting, at a time when army and RAF resources were spread so

thinly over the Middle East, squandered in Greece and Crete and thrown, unavoidably, against the French in Syria and the pro-Axis elements in Iraq and Iran.

The RWAFF was being pulled out of East Africa, back to West Africa to rest, refit and retrain; for what? Garrison duties in the Middle East? 'Pioneer' operations with the main armies in some campaign? Jungle warfare if the Japanese entered the war? Such little information as we had pointed to this last option, and the contemplation of its possibilities, for me, and my fellow officers and our troops, was not at all cheering. My Intelligence Section, which I had formed, trained and cared for, was handed over to a rotund ex-whisky-salesman with little to commend him. Following the departure of our Rhodesian officers, I became 2 i/c of HQ Coy. The CO, to my surprise, told me officially that I had done a good job as IO, and could look to promotion to captain after some service with a rifle-company.

At Durban, I said goodbye to the Rhodesians whom I had liked but was never to see again; also to Atanas who waved from the quayside at Mombasa with a wide cheerful smile. The ship was now less crowded, and there was space to circulate and fraternise with the officers of the other battalions as we had not been able to do for many months. Lagos at last, and with bands playing on Apapa wharf, the troops were loaded into trains to convey them to various Southern stations up the line through Abeokuta and Ibadan as far as Ilorin. They were, nearly all of them, Northerners, or from French territories even further north or north-east, and complained bitterly about being stationed so far to the south, in thick bush or rainforest. We concluded that we were going to train for jungle warfare, and were soon proved correct.

Sir Bernard and Lady Bourdillon proved to be delightful hosts, as ever. There was some inevitable protocol in the initial reception, but thereafter there was a real party atmosphere which everyone enjoyed, including the Bourdillons themselves who led the dance, as usual, with much liveliness in spite of the heat. Unfortunately, I had not time to see more of my Lagos friends, for we were whisked off to Abeokuta, an Egba (Yoruba) town about sixty miles north of Lagos, where accommodation had been improvised around the area of a former golf course. Quarters were very crude and there was much complaint, loudest of all from the CO, who decided to send me to Kaduna to lay claim to everything which could be identified as 1NR property. It seemed that I was still the obvious choice for any particularly awkward job that had to be done, and I was told to combine this assignment with that of lecturing on the lessons of the campaign to the units based in Kaduna, Zaria and Kano.

The old 1NR mess, and other accommodation in Kaduna was now occupied by one of the new battalions which had been formed during our absence. I was received very coolly by the CO thereof who had been warned of the nature of my mission. I told him that I proposed to remove all the mess silver, and certain chairs and tables which could be identified as items presented to 1NR by former officers. After much argument, I got most of what we wanted.

These frictions did not help to produce a very receptive atmosphere for my 'lecture' on the lessons of the East African campaign. I knew that whatever I said would be reported along the grape-vine to 1NR and so any critical comment was confined to generalities, avoiding analysis of particular operations. I did mention bad radio sets, inadequate cooperation between infantry and artillery, inadequate training in crossing rivers, lack of tents, and dull unappetising food, but said nothing about incompetent and uninspiring leadership. After further lectures in Kano and Zaria, I was glad to be back in Abeokuta with my friends of the campaign. Within a week or two I was travelling north again, on a different errand, to cope with the return, from the railhead near Jos, of the troops (from the whole brigade) who had been sent on leave to their homes in the provinces of north-east Nigeria – Bauchi, Bornu, Benue, Adamawa – and the adjoining French territories. As usual, I was given only very brief instructions, and understood that I was simply to assist, and liaise with, the officer commanding the RE depot at Bukuru (a tin-mining centre about seven miles from Jos) who would be in charge of the operation. On arrival at Bukuru, I reported to the OC, an amiable ex-tin-miner and found that I had two colleagues, from 2NR and 3NR, one of whom was my old friend Williams of the Katsina sleeping-sickness team. It was clear at once that Major X, the OC, and his staff were determined to have nothing to do with the troop movement, and regarded the whole thing as our responsibility. I could understand Major X's attitude, and was grateful that he promised at least to give full support for all our requirements and necessary actions. My colleagues were relieved to find that I was the senior subaltern, and that they could relax (as they thought), leaving the thinking and responsibility to me. However, I made them do some thinking about the allocation of duties, and took them to Bukuru railway station to recce the layout, and to meet the station-master, who proved to be a rather nice old Yoruba on the verge of retirement, with one of the slowest brains I have ever encountered. He had received some kind of warning order from his superiors, but was obviously far from clear about what was required. Eventually, I got it into his head that the operation would extend over two to three weeks and that we should require several special trains during that time. It was soon quite obvious that this old chap had been sent to Bukuru as a quiet place in which to work out his time, and I felt some sympathy for him in his attempts to cope with the problems that were now forced upon him. He was most anxious to know the dates on which the trains were required, and the numbers of soldiers and how they were to be accommodated, and supervised, while waiting for the trains. I had to admit that I had no answers to any of these questions, but assured him that the first lorries from the provincial collecting-points were not expected for two to three days.

There was a piece of flat, open ground adjacent to the station, with some trees and a few sheds. The weather, at 4000 feet, was fairly cool and dry, and the troops could sleep in the open or in the sheds. We relaxed and arranged to play tennis, but I was called to the telephone as I was setting out for the courts. An agitated station-master informed me that troops were rioting at the station and he asked me to come at once. He had called the police.

Williams and I seized a truck and dashed to the station, arriving just in time to prevent the police from intervening in a screaming *mêlée*, mostly of women, but also some troops, who appeared to be fighting for the limited space in the huts. We found a few senior NCOs, and by great good fortune, a bugler with a bugle, whom I ordered to sound the 'Fall in'. Within a few seconds, it seemed, the troops began to assemble, and the NCOs sorted them out and lined them up in their units. I then detached one NCO and a small party from each unit to go and calm the women, and began to take stock of the situation.

No one had told us to expect any women – a horrible complication of a situation already difficult enough. They were a very mixed lot, ranging from shy village maidens to some with rolling eyes and swaying hips, suggesting a professional attitude to the male sex. At first sight, women seemed to outnumber men, due perhaps to the babies which many had slung about their waists. Immediate action was to comfort the station-master and order a special train; second, to ginger up the REs to get cooking facilities and latrines organised; third, to get the women with children into the sheds, while turfing out the rest; fourth, to get nominal rolls prepared, by units, to include the women along with their putative husbands; fifth, to make it clear to the senior NCOs that I held them responsible for the maintenance of order, and that if there was any more trouble, life would be made very unpleasant for them.

I sent an urgent wire to Brigade HQ, with copies to the battalions, informing them about the women, and asking for instructions. The first response was that the women should be sent home, since the Brigade might be ordered overseas again at short notice. I kept this to myself, and had a talk with the NCOs. They said that they had accepted their deprivation of women in East Africa and the degradation of brothels, but now that they were 'home', they wanted their own women to sleep with them and cook for them, no matter how short the time. I could sense the intensity of feeling, and knew that there was no need to prolong the discussion. After further telegrams, I obtained agreement for wives to accompany husbands on a one-to-one basis. This required some local adjustment, since a number of men appeared to have brought more than one woman. Most of the surplus were re-allocated to new husbands and the balance were sent home, tucked tearfully into the corners of the returning lorries.

The next fortnight was a stressful time for the station-master and for me and my 'staff'. The troops were short of money, and had returned from leave faster than expected. Fortunately, the weather was dry, but there were problems of accommodation and food. There was much acrimonious communication with the railway bureaucracy, who seemed to have no sense of urgency or understanding of practical issues. (This was a useful rehearsal for another battle with the Nigerian Railway two years later.) Finally came the happy day when the last special train departed only half full, and we left the remaining trickle of late arrivals to be dispatched by the REs by warrant on the regular train services. I returned to Abeokuta to find myself posted as 2 i/c to Swig Swainson, now commanding D Coy.

Area Command in Nigeria had set out a strenuous schedule of field-training, involving much manoeuvring in thick bush, and 'realistic' battle-training at all formation levels, which occupied, with weapon-training, several hours of each day. D Coy, with two Hausa speakers (Swig and myself), was given the task of developing a new training scheme for tactical movement in thick bush. Appropriate commands in Hausa, and English equivalents, were devised and were drilled into the heads of the troops, even the thickest ones, so that they could understand, and react quickly to, a limited range of orders given in English. This was for the benefit of British officers and NCOs brought in to staff the new battalions and reinforce the old ones.

On 20 December I was posted next on the list for leave. I could hardly believe it, but sent a carefully worded cable to Jocelyn. Soon I was back in Lagos and driving to Apapa to join the MV *Accra*, the ship on which I had travelled out in 1937. In Freetown, we waited for a convoy to assemble. One week merged into two, and we began to wonder whether we should ever move, or whether the war in the Far East had caused such a shipping crisis that the *Accra* would have to be diverted elsewhere. (In the midst of my preoccupations with D Coy training and uncertainties about leave and so on, I had been thinking of the much greater problems and anxieties facing Jocelyn's sister, Alison, and her husband, Stephen Kemp, who was in the army in Malaya.)

We left Freetown at last, some time in the last week of January, as the commodore's ship of a large convoy, but still leaving many ships at anchor, awaiting their turn to move south or north in the circumnavigation of Africa to which so much shipping was committed in the weary years from 1940 to 1944. Our course took a wide sweep out into the Atlantic, to reduce the risk of German air-attacks from N. Africa and France. Gun-nests, fitted with anti-aircraft guns, had been constructed on both sides of the ship and passengers from the armed services were on a rota to keep them manned on a twenty-four-hour basis. Twice we had escort-vessels dashing around dropping depth-charges which produced rather alarming noises, like massive hammer-blows against the sides of the ship.

The radio news, during the last week or so of the voyage, was most disturbing and tragic. The Japanese attack on Singapore began on 8 February and the island was surrendered on the 15th. I was to learn later that those who were surrendered with it, to a cruel enemy, included Stephen Kemp and an old schoolfriend, but at the time we knew only that our losses were appallingly heavy, and included two divisions which were landed during the final days into chaos, another pointless sacrifice to be added to that of the *Prince of Wales* and the *Repulse* in December. Many of us in the *Accra* boiled with anger at the incompetence of our leadership, and my own anger still simmers whenever I think of it. The Commodore was a dedicated man who spent much time on the bridge, and many of us came to recognise him and exchanged smiles with him as he paced to and fro. It was therefore with a sense of almost personal tragedy that we heard of the loss of his son, a Swordfish pilot, during the attack on the *Scharnhorst* and *Gneisenau* as they ran through the Channel, by daylight, on 12 February. Once again, we, and the public generally, sensed incompetence among those in authority, as a subsequent Board of Enquiry was to establish.

24

Farewell to Arms

❦

JOCELYN, from her sources of information in Bletchley, was able to follow the progress of our convoy, and to plan accordingly to make the most of the short time we expected to have together. When at last we were reunited, on 17 February, the frustrations of many weary months became as nothing in the warmth of a welcome that was also more of a homecoming than I had imagined possible. In spite of all the uncertainty of timing, and the wartime shortages of nearly all the things needed for the staging of a wedding, Jo and her parents had completed nearly all the arrangements for our marriage at Hampstead Parish Church, on 21 February. A surprisingly large number of our friends materialised, and the parents somehow managed to seat and feed them in their home after the ceremony, from which we emerged into snow flurries with breaks of sunshine. In the midst of so much austerity, this gathering was a happy moment of reunion for many friends and relatives before dispersing to their varied ploys at 'home' and overseas.

The authorities in Bletchley were very understanding and kind in allowing Jocelyn to extend her leave to stay with me when my freedom came to an end after 21 March. Thereafter, my time was monopolised by the army for the remainder of my stay in England. I was told to report for duty at Warley Barracks, the depot of the Essex Regiment on the edge of the town of Brentwood.

I seemed to be the only supernumerary officer at Warley, where I was 'attached for Infantry Training'. Fortunately, and most agreeably, this was not interpreted as square-bashing or weapon-training, and I was handed over to a very pleasant young sergeant for a fortnight's instruction in the handling and use of a Bren gun carrier. This was the smallest of the army's tracked vehicles, as yet unknown in West Africa, and unlikely to be of use in jungle conditions. Somehow, the sergeant and I managed to fill in the time: we imbibed vast quantities of tea in various roadside cafés. I learned to manoeuvre the carrier over many kinds of terrain, and the open road, consuming horrifying quantities of petrol in the process. Impossible to imagine, then or now, the tortuous channels of decision within the army bureaucracy which produced this particular and rather conspicuous waste of time, effort and scarce resources. While I was thus employed, Jocelyn was left to her own devices in the local environment, a small commuter town known only for its barracks and a minor public school.

The Bren-carrier course came to an end, and there was no sign of my onward movement. My sergeant (to whom I appeared to be delegated by the adjutant) suggested that I should learn all about despatch-riding, and to that end produced two very powerful and noisy BSA motor-cycles. I survived the first hour or so without accident and with some exhilaration, and thereafter we covered many miles on main roads, side roads, bridle-paths, footpaths, uphill, downhill, in delightful weather, and consumed large quantities of petrol (and also of tea in roadside cafés). This idyll also came to an end, and the adjutant, now in a state of near-despair, passed me on to a sergeant of signals. This was a man with a feeling for history and a belief in fundamentals which took us back to the Crimea and semaphore. After a few sessions of flag-waving, we moved into the electrical age, and I was introduced to the mystique of running a cable from a rear position to a forward position. We then connected the Morse keys and a battery and started to send simple messages. The sergeant was a very resourceful man and could doubtless have continued 'the course' indefinitely, to include coded messages, field telephony and ultimately the wide new world of radio, but just as I was getting the hang of reading Morse, my movement order came to report to a transit camp in, of all places, Birmingham. A month later, there came a day, about 20 June, when I was told to report that night to entrain for an undisclosed destination. Jocelyn received the news stoically, and we spent the day happily, rounding off the evening with a very good concert by the City Orchestra. I left her to return to the hotel alone, as I ran to catch a bus to the transit camp. Like many couples at that time, we were parting with very little idea of when and how we would be reunited. I had hoped to be allowed to work on military operational research, but it seemed that I was returning to 1NR and a regime which I found oppressive. News from the war fronts was bad, even appalling. In recent months, several friends had been killed and others had become prisoners of the Japanese. After an overnight journey to Greenock, I boarded the *Batory*, a Polish troopship, in sombre mood. Fortunately, we had a relatively rapid voyage (without alcohol – all troopships were now 'dry') of about three weeks to Lagos, and I had the company of some pleasant people, including several 'Northern' ADOs with cheerful dispositions.

Enquiries in Lagos revealed that the Governor had applied for my release from the army, along with that of a dozen or so of my colleagues, to avert what he had described as 'an imminent collapse of the administration'. Certainly, administrative officers were now very thin on the ground, there being no recruitment of cadets, while the natural wastage of senior officers through invaliding and retirement continued and the work-load had, for various reasons, greatly increased.

For the present, it seemed, I was still in the army, and soon I was back in Abeokuta, sharing a room with old comrades, who were cheerful and friendly as ever, and charged, like myself, with some special aspects of training. Looking through battalion orders, I found that I was officially 'released for civil duties as from April 1st 1942' and 'mentioned in despatches, February–July 1941'. In a letter to Jocelyn in mid-July, I wrote that my 'release' seemed to have very little bearing on the situation, which was surrounded by an air of mystery: 'No one can tell me, or will tell me, why I am here, or what is my present status, which is still under consideration by the GOC in C. On 25 July, I was posted, and moved, to 13NR, the Lagos garrison battalion, pending a final decision on my future; I assumed that this implied that I would either become an 'army scientist' or be returned to the North as an ADO, but that my service with the RWAFF was about to be ended.

In Lagos, I was sent to the airfield at Apapa to join the security company (A Coy, on detachment from 13NR) there. This airfield was one of the vital links in the air-supply route across Africa to our forces in the Middle East. It seemed unlikely that it would be attacked or sabotaged in any way, but no chances were taken, and A Coy patrolled the field perimeter closely at all times. The planes passing through were either Dakotas carrying freight or personnel, or fighter planes which had been uncrated and assembled on the spot or flown in from Takoradi (Ghana) after assembly. From Apapa, the planes were flown to Kano, Maiduguri, El Geneina, El Fasher, Khartoum, Cairo and beyond.

I found that the detachment was commanded by Ronnie Lane, whom I had last encountered on the river Didessa after avoiding shooting up the 3NR patrol which he was leading. The platoon commanders included Rusin, a young Polish officer (one of many who were sent as reinforcements to West Africa).

On 19 August, I heard from Jocelyn that a much-loved Oxford friend had been killed. The sense of futile loss was increased by the outcome of the Dieppe raid. We had allowed ourselves wild hopes when the news of the operation was released, and Rusin was rejoicing that we were back on mainland Europe at last. Then came the disillusion, and the news of the terrible losses of fine Canadian troops.

From Apapa we moved to Lagos and the daily training routine at Ikoyi Barracks, in which Rusin was most valuable. He had been a regular officer in the Polish army and was the best 'practical' soldier I ever met. There was nothing in the infantry martial arts that he did not do well, but his demonstration of grenade-throwing was quite memorable for its cool, professional competence. He managed to train some of the troops to handle grenades fairly well, but I had to agree with Lane that, on the whole, the troops of 13NR would be more dangerous to their comrades (or themselves) than to the enemy. But Rusin tried hard. I found him an intriguing person, 'an original. He has the mind of a wayward, attractive child, with a kind of wistful cheerfulness and strangely British teasing humour, which just keeps the upper hand of his Slav melancholy. Asked about his father, he said, "He was bloody fool, like me. He die in last war. Bloody Germans."'

The CO of 13NR was a decent, amiable man, who was particularly kind to his half dozen or so Polish officers, trying to make them feel welcome within the battalion and within the context of Lagos colonial society. A dance was arranged, and was a great success, with the Poles gallantly teaching the ladies how to dance a true polka or mazurka, and showing very good form in a Viennese waltz. When it was all over, Rusin and I sat listening to Chopin most beautifully played by the senior Pole, and then went our separate ways, leaving him alone, still playing.

Perhaps it was out of kindness that the CO decided to give me another change of scene, and sent me to join a detachment at Badagry, on the Dahomey border, which I had visited five years earlier when I was in the Audit Department. I was met by Captain Field, a Yorkshireman and promoted 'ranker' who commanded the detachment, and was shown to my hut on the water's edge about thirty yards from his own.

Nigeria was surrounded by French territories. On the west, the colony of Dahomey was loyal to the Vichy government, as was Niger Colony, on the north, which was in a state of near-war with its neighbour, Chad, in French Equatorial Africa, which had declared for De Gaulle. The French Cameroons was also Gaulliste, and this fortunate circumstance enabled us to maintain a clear, friendly air-route all the way from Lagos to Khartoum – a factor of crucial strategic importance. We were not at war with Vichy, but we had no diplomatic relations, and the border had been 'sealed' by the erection of a boom barrier across the creek. It seemed unlikely that the Dahomey authorities would launch any kind of sabotage effort along the creek, but the operations at Apapa were deemed so vital that the Nigerian government decided to take no chances. The elimination of trade with Nigeria also increased the economic pressure on Dahomey, and these considerations were deemed to justify the maintenance of the border guard.

These were my last days of army life, spent quietly and rather pleasantly in the company of a good representative of that element in the British Army which I liked and respected: those who had progressed through the ranks by hard service to NCO and beyond. My experience of regular officers – those seconded to the Waff – may have been unfortunate. Too many of them were disagreeable by my standards; the few that I really liked seemed to share my view of the army, as I had known it. On 5 October arrived a telegram stating that I was 'released to civil employment' and that the CO would take me back to Lagos after his inspection visit on 9 October. I spent the intervening days trying to come to terms with the changed situation and planning a new attempt to get myself transferred to a scientific job of some kind; best of all, one that gave me a chance of living with, or near, my wife, whom I was missing dreadfully. I left 13NR on 11 October, removed my uniform for the last time, and returned again to Bridge House to enjoy once again the warm welcome and hospitality of Ruthven

Wright, most generous and understanding of friends. On my arrival, I found to my delight and surprise that he had under his wing Frank Lodge, who had been my Intelligence sergeant and was now on his way to a posting in Freetown. We spent a happy weekend together before my return to 'civil employment' in the remote 'bush'.

PART III

Muslims, Tribes and the Secretariat

ଏଡ

Bornu District Head to District Officer: 'Something must be done about it, or we shall all be disgraced' (Maiduguri, Northern Nigeria 1943)

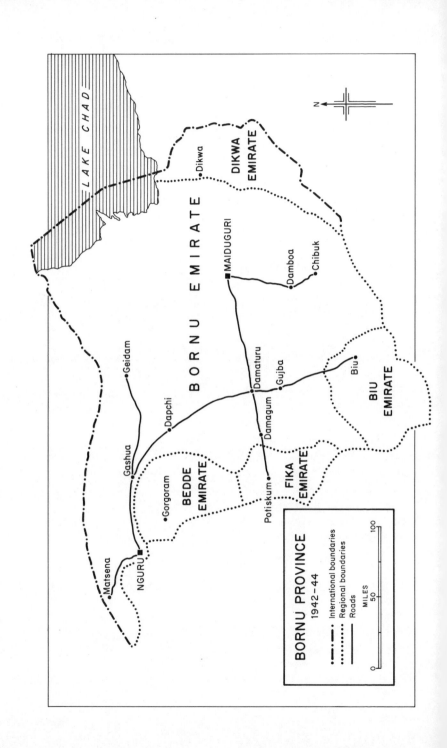

LAKE CHAD

DIKWA
EMIRATE

Dikwa

BORNU EMIRATE

MAIDUGURI

Damboa
Chibuk

Geidam

Dapchi

Damaturu

Gujba

BIU
EMIRATE

Biu

Gashua

Damagum

Gorgoram

BEDDE
EMIRATE

FIKA
EMIRATE

Potiskum

Matsena

NGURU

BORNU PROVINCE
1942–44

International boundaries
Regional boundaries
Roads

MILES

0   50   100

25

Quick March to Bornu

❧

IN the course of three crowded days of new-found freedom from 'bull' and 'brass', I assembled my kit and purchased a great deal more, including saddlery, after being informed by the Secretariat that I was posted to Maiduguri, in Bornu Province, near Lake Chad, and about 1000 miles from Lagos. During one shopping expedition, I was hailed by a cheerful-looking chap whom I recognised as Tanko, who had been Macfarlane's horse-boy (and briefly mine) in Katsina. He said that Alhadji had heard that the ADO reservists (including myself) were returning to their old jobs, and that Alhadji was looking forward to rejoining me very soon. Tanko had Alhadji's address, and I wired, asking him to meet me at Kaduna Junction on 15 October. Another brief encounter was with 'Dennis' Wheatley, that great survivor from the submarines of World War I, and the early days with 1NR in Kaduna and Nairobi, who inevitably became the overlord of all the East African POW camps, with the rank of Lieutenant Colonel. Irrepressible as ever, he regaled me with a salty account of his successful one-up-manship and told me of the very fair and humane treatment of Italian prisoners in Kenya, in contrast to the cruel regimes imposed by the Japanese and Germans in their camps. I was glad to hear this for the sake of my old 'friend' Luigi Nigra.

Ruthven's boys helped me through the usual chaos at Iddo station, and I found myself sharing a compartment with a surveyor who was also en route for Maiduguri. I was concerned to find no Alhadji awaiting me at Kaduna, but there was much rejoicing on being reunited with him at Jos and finding him accompanied by a broadly smiling Francis who had decided to rejoin the team. I was deeply touched that these tried and trusted servants had decided to leave the comforts of town life to go with me into what they knew to be the relative hardship of life in a remote province, involving much bush-whacking. The surveyor and I spent a few days in Jos securing suitable transport (a large, reliably maintained lorry) and used the time in purchasing stores and buying at auction some of the kit of an official who had died while touring in the bush. I obtained some urgently needed wooden boxes with hinged, padlocked lids, indispensable for making up headloads while on tour. Jos was always a meeting-place for old acquaintances, and on this occasion I found Bernard Fagg, very comfortably housed, 'looking after' labour in the tin-mines. This job was to open the way for his epoch-making discoveries of terracotta and other arte-facts of the Nok culture – the ultimate example of his capacity and flair for being in the right place at the right time.

The surveyor and I left Jos at 2 p.m. on 19 October, sitting in the front of the lorry with the driver. Our boys snuggled down as best they could between the softer items of our kit and theirs, and wrapped up their heads against the onslaught of the dust thrown up from the road. We drove through the night for 360 miles over the heavily corrugated surface and reached Maiduguri in a thoroughly exhausted state at 7 a.m. The surveyor went to set up camp near the airfield, where he was to work, and I was set down at the Residency rest-house, a pleasant, thatched building in the Residency compound.

The rest-house, simple but unusually comfortable, had been built to the design of the Resident, Rex Niven, and was somehow typical of his sensible, no-nonsense approach to the solution of any prob-lem. I had met him, and come to respect him, on the voyage out in 1937, since when he had mellowed slightly under the heat and burden of responsibility. He was still unwilling, perhaps constitu-tionally unable, to suffer fools gladly, however senior, and he made enemies more easily than friends. His wife, Dorothy, adored him, and was always happy to talk about Rex's thoughts, plans and achievements, even in his presence, without creating any noticeable embarrassment. They were both extremely kind and generous to me, for whom Rex's virtues far outweighed his alleged faults. He was knighted towards the end of his service, but never achieved the governor's status which he deserved.

Bornu was, and perhaps still is, a remote and somehow separate part of what was known as 'The Holy North'. Its people, the Kanuri, had successfully resisted attempts by the Fulani vassals of the Sultan of Sokoto to subjugate them, and the paramount chief, the Shehu of Bornu, had retained an Islamic independence, being regarded as 'leader of the faithful' by Muslims to the east as far as the borders of the Sudan. In comparison with the northernmost emirates of Hausaland, Kano, Katsina and Sokoto, Bornu seemed dull, flat, harsh in climate, and its people rather heavy and sullen, lacking the humour and liveliness of the Hausa. Even its rivers were sluggish and contrary, flowing away from the sea towards Lake Chad. However, it seemed to exert a subtle attraction for many of the British who served there, and had been the training-ground for some of the most capable and forceful administrative officers of the past. It was the largest province (much of it was sparsely populated) and had five divisions: Bornu Emirate, the largest, with headquarters at Maiduguri, Dikwa Emirate in the Northern Cameroons (mandated territory containing some pagans), Biu Emirate, in the south, Fika Emirate (HQ Potiskum) in the west, Bedde Division (HQ Nguru) in the north-west. Most of this large area (about 50,000 square miles – the size of England) had been little affected by the war, but the impact of war on conservative, traditional Maiduguri had been sudden and considerable.

The African town, known as Yerwa to the Kanuri, had much in common with the other major towns of the North such as Katsina. It had mud buildings, narrow walled lanes, the Shehu's palace in a walled enclosure, offices, courts, mosques, workshops, markets. Its most striking feature was the 'dandal', a large roughly rectangular open space about half a mile long, entered through the main gate in the town wall, opening a wide view to the palace at the far end. This space was used for ceremonial gatherings, particularly at the Muhammadan festivals, when hundreds of horsemen would be assembled from all the districts of the Emirate.

The government 'station' lay on a low ridge about two miles from the African town, and consisted of twenty or so houses, including the Residency and the old Residency (well built of mud and still habitable), together with golf course, tennis courts and even a squash court. The Provincial and Divisional Offices, newly built of concrete, lay in a shallow valley between the town and the station and became infernally hot by midday. Until 1940, this whole complex, known as Maiduguri, remained remote, separate, worlds away from Lagos and even from Kaduna. At any one time, perhaps ten British officials and one or two traders would be 'at home', and a roughly equal number away 'in the bush' on tour, dealing with the perennial departmental problems: roads, water, health, crops, cattle, schools, tax, law and order. The collapse of France, the entry of Italy into the war, and the closure of the Mediterranean changed all that, and Maiduguri became one of the vital links in the air supply route from the USA via Brazil, Accra, Lagos, Kano, Maiduguri, El Geneina, El Fasher and Khartoum to the Middle East, India and beyond. This was made possible by the courage and vision of the black governor of neighbouring French Chad territory, Félix Eboué, who declared for De Gaulle (and influenced some others to do likewise). He died a few years later and was laid to rest in the Pantheon in Paris. (This remarkable episode, which had a vital influence on the war, is little known, and received no mention from Churchill.)

The new Entente Cordiale was soon manifest in the appearance of a squadron of the Free French air force who occupied the old Residency for several months, to be followed by the RAF, who were there much longer. The major invasion, however, occurred a few months later, when an American party (ostensibly from Pan American Airways) arrived to set up, under lend-lease arrangements, a full-scale staging-post. Niven, who was Resident at the time, wisely decided to accommodate these newcomers in the station, where they would be under his eye, rather than at the airfield some five miles away. Vast quantities of material were transported to Maiduguri by road and air, and a large hutted camp was constructed, providing new amenities such as piped water and electric power, and able to accommodate a permanent staff of 500 as well as 1000 overnight transit personnel. When the United States entered the war, the staff removed their PAA badges and replaced them with US Army badges of rank.

By the time I arrived in Bornu, the American presence was thoroughly established. My feelings about the invasion were somewhat mixed: 'They cause amusement and exasperation, with their wise-cracking and bragging, noise and utter disregard for any way of living but their own imported brand. The lads ride ponies about the station all day long, regardless of the heat, at full gallop, chewing gum the while. I find them down in the native town at all hours, absorbing the local colour, driving great buses through the narrow streets, buying and bartering. Dollar bills have become a secondary currency in the town – the traders can quote a rate very accurately. On the whole, though, they're a dull crowd, perhaps because this just isn't their milieu – one could hardly imagine an atmosphere more foreign to the American ideal.'

I took over the job of ADO Emirate from my contemporary Dick Peel whom Niven had married to Alison, the station nursing-sister (her successor married another ADO, Owen Strong, a year or so later!). The job had a very strong dogsbody element owing to the varied nature of the new tasks and responsibilities which had arisen as a result of the war and its enlarged American dimension. In Maiduguri alone, the extension of the airfield runways produced an enormous demand for labour, and the American presence gave rise to a variety of problems which were time-consuming. There was a never-ending flow of VIPs to be met, refreshed, accommodated and cared for. The strain on the Resident and the DO was unremitting and it was a great help (they said) to have a competent junior around to assist generally and fill gaps at short notice.

In the south-west of Bornu Division (Bornu Emirate) there were three large districts with a total area of about 10,000 square miles, which had been under-toured for years, owing to lack of staff, and I was asked to spend ten to fourteen days per month in the area to 'sort it out', and also to coordinate the effort to recruit labour for the tin-mines from that area and from the neighbouring divisions of Potiskum and Biu. Corn to feed these labourers was to be purchased and stored at Damaturu, about eighty miles from Maiduguri, and this was an added task.

I was despatched to Damaturu within a few days of my arrival in Bornu, and set up my touring HQ in the rest-house, a large building with three sets of 'quarters', sited on the junction of the main Jos–Maiduguri road and the road leading south through Biu to the province of Adamawa and its capital, Yola. The town, and its district HQ, lay about a quarter of a mile away to the north, in a slight hollow; otherwise the terrain was flat and sandy with a few trees around the rest-house and on the edge of the town. There was a post office and a small trading store (in the charge of an African clerk), both well constructed to resist robbers, whereas the rest-house was open to the four winds and to the local, and expert, population of thieves.

The District Head (Ajiya in Kanuri), who called himself Hadji Sudani, had been appointed a few months earlier, on the firm and insistent recommendation of the Shehu. Before that, he had been an overseer in the Native Administration Works Department, in charge of several gangs of road-maintenance labourers, and had contrived, in the course of a decade or so, to accumulate considerable wealth. It was well understood throughout Northern Nigeria that nearly all NA (Native Administration) appointments were obtained or solicited by making payments to the paramount chiefs and their influential subordinates, but in Bornu the ramifications of the system were so extensive as to be the cause of open cynicism among the educated and very competent younger NA staff. It was widely rumoured, and believed, that Hadji Sudani's appointment had cost him £600, and that he was determined to recoup this expenditure without delay from tax and other sources.

The Ajiya had been warned of my impending visit but was away in the bush when I arrived. I sent for him and received a reply implying that he would return in his own time. I sent a further message by a fast horseman (he was twenty miles away), giving him twelve hours to report, failing which I would come and fetch him. He arrived in time, and we had a preliminary meeting which was distinctly lacking in cordiality. He was a slim, active man of about fifty, affecting an Arabic style of dress and deportment, obviously intelligent and wily, speaking Hausa and some English as well as Kanuri. A self-made man, an opportunist using the system to the full for his own ends, he seemed to me to exemplify the shape of things to come when the British might have departed. I told him that I wanted a report, by the following day, on the apparent shortfall in the district *jangali* (cattle tax), and the slow progress in recruiting labour for the tin-mines and constructing corn-pits to hold the grain reserve; I would also inspect Damaturu town and expected to find it clean. All this was conveyed, following the rules, through the Shehu's representative, Abba Mallam, a young sprig of the 'royal' house, who was quite well educated and spoke English. Hausa, however, was spoken throughout, for the better understanding of everyone, but particularly Sambo, the Fulani messenger from Maiduguri, who was travelling with me, a man of great dignity and long service who knew the province and its personalities very thoroughly. After the meeting, I found that Sambo had taken careful note of the points which had been raised. He was staying with an old friend in the town, and would collect information from his various contacts, including any Fulani who were still around.

During the next ten days, I visited the other two district HQs. Damagum, about forty miles west of Damaturu on the Jos road, was a sleepy, undeveloped village with a district head to match. He was an amiable, easy-going chap of about forty, ineffectual in most things except, apparently, the production of children, who swarmed in large numbers around his compound. He always received me with courtesy, but I had the impression, more than once, of having disturbed his connubial bliss. His tax records and other paper-work were rather messy, but appeared to be reasonably honest, and I agreed with the chief scribe in the Waziri's office that this man needed advice and stimulus rather than admonition. I found later that he would, when sufficiently goaded, produce results. I must mention one example of his courtesy and kindness. One day, I hitched a lift by lorry from Damaturu to Damagum (having no transport of my own except a bicycle and a horse), expecting to hitch a lift back later in the day. On completion of our business, I told the Ajiya that I would walk along the road, for exercise, until a lorry came along, and set off. After about half an hour, a servant of the Ajiya caught up with me, leading a spare horse. He had been told to see me safely aboard a lorry, or to ride with me to Damaturu – an exhausting possibility, which fortunately did not materialise.

Gujba, the third of the district HQs, lay about twenty miles to the south of Damaturu, on the road to Biu (the main road, in the rainy season, to distant Yola, on the river Benue). It was sometimes possible to synchronise one's visit with the movements of the mail-lorry and get a lift, in preference to the dull hard slog along the road by horse or bicycle. On my first visit, I found the district head of Gujba (a rather pleasant small town) waiting for me: 'I must tell you of the pleasantness of my reception here. The Ajiya (a brother of the Shehu) is a man of dignity and his village heads a most venerable collection of bearded ancients. We sat in the shade of a tree for an hour and a quarter, with Sambo translating Hausa into Kanuri and vice versa with much expressive gesture. I can't help feeling that one achieves more thus than in many days of paper-transactions in a stuffy office, where tempers get ragged, and one sometimes sees the worst side of the African (and of oneself!). There's a nice little rest-house here, of the old-fashioned round thatched type, which I like best, set among trees, and withal delightfully quiet, just outside the town. The usual "presents" arrived: from the town head, about twenty pounds of onions, and from the Ajiya, a large bowl of rice and a large pot of honey.' (Such 'presents' often added a welcome variety to one's diet, and were always 'paid for' by an appropriate 'dash' to the messenger.)

I enjoyed my visits to Gujba district, and the horseback touring to its villages in the bush. The district head seemed to be efficient and competent, and there was no very obvious corruption – remarkable, considering that he was the Shehu's brother! There was an interesting situation in Gujba town itself, producing a sort of balance of power which probably helped to keep the administration clean. The village/town head was a lively, impressive, youngish man, with a decisive, independent manner. I was told that he was a descendant of one of Usuman dan Fodio's lieutenants, and that his family had retained a foothold here, on the boundary of the old Fulani Empire, before and since the coming of the British. His village area was very large, extending almost to the Bornu–Fika border, and he was obviously regarded as *primus inter pares* by the other village heads, and with particular respect by the Ajiya. The town was impressively clean, and well supplied with trees, in spite of the very deep water-level. My bath water was drawn from a well 160 feet deep, and the weight of the rope was greater than the weight of water in the bucket.

In Damaturu, my first concern was to try to elucidate the cattle-tax situation. The season was really almost over, the grass was drying up, and the Fulani were moving south, and also into the few local marshy areas, which were drying out and beginning to grass over. I managed to locate, and count, a few herds, and found, as expected, that they appeared to be under-assessed. Hadji Sudani put forward various explanations for the shortfall in collection of tax, including, brazenly enough, his own previous inexperience of the extreme cunning of the Fulani. I found that there were no satisfactory records of the previous season's collection, and so no attempt had been made to check the movements and sizes of herds and the names of their owners.

The rate of progress in the construction of corn-pits was most unsatisfactory, and the cost much in excess of similar bins being built in Maiduguri. I examined the time-sheets which indicated that more labourers had been employed in the weeks before my arrival. The number had been reduced, I was told, to prevent them getting in each other's way! It seemed only too obvious that the time-sheets

included people who did not exist, the amount paid out for them
having gone into the pocket of Hadji Sudani. I warned him that
he would be debited with any excess in cost of the bins, compared
with those in Maiduguri, and he began to show a marked interest
in the progress of the work.

I had instructions to organise the recruitment of labour for the
tin-mines from the three districts, to assist the DO at Potiskum
(about sixty miles west of Damaturu) to recruit labourers in his
division, and to coordinate the movements of all labourers to the
mines on receipt of instructions from Jos. I was never really clear
about the basis of this recruitment operation, whether the men
were supposed to be volunteers (actually, or in the well-known
army sense) or whether their employment was authorised under
the Forced Labour Ordinance. I was not happy about 'persuading'
men (and a few women as cooks) to leave their homes for a span
of four months to live in the artificial camp environment of the
mines, but had, at this time, a clear conscience about it. The consequences of a German victory, for black Africa, and for the British
territories in particular, would have been appalling: the widespread
introduction of a new kind of slavery, the ruthless, ultimate
enforcement of the South African system of racial exploitation.
Compared with the sacrifices of the British people, the early deaths,
torture and imprisonment of friends, the mines-labourers were
required to give relatively little, and were supposed to be properly
paid for it. My own attitude was, perhaps, influenced by the news
of the death of an Oxford friend in an accident during an army
training exercise. The sense of personal loss was acute, and there
was the added feeling that the war was removing the leavening
from the lump, leaving an unhealthy proportion of I'm-all-right-
Jacks.

Bornu province was required to produce, in the first instance,
about 1000 men to dig and carry the ore in the open-cast mines of
the Plateau. A quota had been calculated, in proportion to population, for each district, and the district heads had agreed, with the
village heads, the numbers of men which each had to muster. (I
had checked the numbers, and had been present at meetings with
the village-heads.) Captain Guy Money, MC, the DO i/c Fika Emirate at Potiskum, had received his instructions from the Resident,
and during my first Damaturu 'tour', I called at Potiskum to make
sure that all was proceeding according to plan.

Money had joined the Nigerian Service from the army around 1920. He regarded himself as a 'real bush DO', did not seek, or expect, exceptional promotion, and never got it. Some people, including Rex Niven, described him as a fat man, but my own impression of him was 'extremely tubby, resembling a Phiz cartoon of Mr Pickwick or Toby Weller'. He had very bright eyes, set in a pink face, which could beam with benevolence or blaze with anger, changing in a twinkling. He may have possessed some other wardrobe, but to me he appeared to be eternally clad in a white tennis shirt (plus tie for formal occasions) and grey flannel trousers girdled equatorially by an old leather belt, now notched to its limit, but showing evidence of progressive expansionary notchings over the years. He perspired profusely and continuously, to match his intake of fluid which was considerable, though I never knew him to be inebriated. He had a very kind and generous spirit, combined with some obstinacy, and an extremely hot temper. We were all fond of him, particularly the swarms of small children from the local school, who would come and 'help' him to grease his car and do a little gardening. Like many bulky people, he was amazingly light on his feet, moving rapidly over short distances, and he had competent hands, swift and deft. His car, a large ancient Vauxhall saloon, trundled about the roads of Bornu loaded with his servants and himself and towing a trailer containing his camp kit. His journey from Biu (for which he was also responsible) to Potiskum took him through Damaturu, and occasionally I travelled with him, marvelling that the car survived the additional load, and Money's driving style, taking the engine through all the gears with rapid flicks of the fingers to a speed of about 15 mph. Once, he stopped the car with a jerk and leapt out towards a man who was driving a donkey with a stick along the side of the road. He seized the stick from the astonished peasant, and belaboured him with it most vigorously, castigating him also in incomprehensible Hausa. Then, with blazing eyes and purple face, he returned to the car, and drove on saying, 'That'll teach him.'

Money's attitude to the mines labour operation could only be described as non-cooperative. He would not attend any of the meetings with his village heads and delegated the matter entirely to his assistant, a young cadet just out from England. Everyone sensed his attitude, and so progress was very slow. Money and I now had our first row. He said that he simply did not agree with the policy of taking people from their villages and sending them to work in the mines; it ran counter to the ideals of the service, and to what we were fighting for. I said that I had much sympathy with his views, but he must surely realise that we were faced with a desperate situation, and were asking little of these people, compared with what was at stake. Since the loss of Malaya, Nigerian tin had become absolutely vital, and production had somehow to be increased. He must realise that his attitude was making my task impossible. I found it most unpleasant to be arguing in this way with a man who was very much my senior, and discovered, as others had done before me, that any serious discussion with Money generated heat. However, I think we both recognised that we had to settle this matter between ourselves. Money's solution was to opt out and leave me to cope. Whenever I visited Potiskum, Money was at Biu, and vice-versa. I dealt directly with his people in his absence, and there was no further trouble, except for my experience of the authorities in Jos, who were perhaps more preoccupied with archaeology than with mining tin. Twice I arranged the transport of 1000 men, only to have everything cancelled at the last minute, and I had great difficulty in convincing everyone that the third occasion was for real. Money laughed and laughed, but for once (or twice) my sense of humour deserted me.

It was sometimes rather too active in my dealings with Hadji Sudani at Damaturu. This man was an accomplished rogue but not really a villain (there is a distinction!) and he had a way of looking at me when trying to put across some tall story which made it hard not to burst out laughing. It was a help to find some light relief at Damaturu which was, in most respects, a detestable HQ. One dark night, a thief tried to enter Alhadji's hut, and was not caught, in spite of the hue and cry and the presence of the police patrol. Apparently, the man followed the local custom of operating stark naked and covered with grease; hard to see, hard to catch, and hard to hold. I slept with an Italian pistol under my pillow, but never felt quite safe anywhere in Bornu. It was, perhaps, not surprising that every household in the town seemed to keep a dog, and the nights were made hideous with howling and barking. In addition, there was, all too often, some occasion for drumming and dancing going on into the small hours. Wakefulness at night added to the loneliness one experienced in the heat of the afternoon. Letter-writing was difficult, with mail taking two months or more to arrive from England, and my 'replies' to Jocelyn's letters must have seemed to have little relevance by the time they reached her.

I had the occasional letter from my army friends, but already that part of my life seemed to be receding rapidly into the store of memory. Then, one day in Potiskum, I was saluted by a man with a wooden leg. It was Corporal Audu Fika, whom I had last seen being helped off the battlefield at the Marda Pass. He was a local hero, and I achieved some useful kudos by association.

26

Worthwhile Work and
Agreeable Associates

ぐ

FOR about three months, I divided my time roughly equally
between touring the western districts and assisting the DO in
Maiduguri who was, in fact and appropriately to the job, a
Senior District Officer (SDO), Captain H. D. Tupper-Carey. He was
an Old Etonian of the best kind, a clergyman's son, a Christian
with many of the qualities I admired in Ruthven Wright including
honesty and straightforwardness, which made him a splendid man
to work with. He was not a large man but, even when clad in his
'office' clothes, he gave an immediate impression of tough, rugged
strength, intriguingly combined with a soft voice, blue eyes and
warm smile in a weather-beaten face. I worked harder for him than
for any 'boss' before or since, and the work at times indeed seemed
never-ending. Throughout the war, office work was always increasing, and inevitably there was a tendency (which had to be strongly
resisted) to spend less time on tour. In the bush, owing to shortage
of staff, there was less work going on of the kind which I had
found so interesting, and time-consuming, in Katsina. Tupper hated
office work, but stuck at it dutifully. He gave me a glad, warm
welcome whenever I returned to Maiduguri, and handed over a
random selection of problems to 'get my teeth into' and to discuss
with him. Together, we got through a vast amount of work with
great harmony, and I enjoyed it immensely. My only problem was
hunger. Tupper would call for me at 6.30, and it was often 9.30 by
the time we returned for a quick breakfast. We were rarely home
for lunch before three. I was reminded of pre-breakfast tactical
excercises with Colonel Owen (whom Tupper resembled in some

respects) and again found comfort in tobacco, in this case following Tupper's example by smoking a Nigerian cheroot.

The Nivens did their best to help the work along. Dorothy was functioning as ADO Provincial Office, and Rex worked on the spot, instead of being detached in the Residency. He called me in to discuss, with Tupper, the report which I had written after my first tour of the western districts. It was very critical of some aspects of district administration as I had found it, particularly the lacka-daisical attitudes of some district and village heads, and the serious inadequacy of district records. I had found it almost impossible to check the work done by district heads (no properly kept diaries) and the tax-recording, particularly of the cattle tax, was incom-plete, slipshod and inaccurate. I accompanied Niven and Tupper on their visit to the Shehu-in-council at which the report was raised and discussed, and it was obvious to me from that moment that I shared with Tupper the animosity of the Shehu and the Waziri. The Shehu, in spite of a bent and rather shrivelled appearance, and eyes apparently developing cataracts, was a figure of consider-able dignity. His replies to questions, and his comments, always quite brief, appeared to be well considered, even when evasive (as they often were), and Tupper and I put this down to his feigned ignorance of Hausa. We reckoned that he understood our Hausa perfectly well, and thought out the answers while the questions were being translated into Kanuri. He had lived through the battles with the war-lord adventurer Rabeh, who had killed his father before his eyes, and he continued to be a great survivor throughout the period of British rule and after it, somehow avoiding the fate – exposure, disgrace, even imprisonment – of some of his underlings.

I saw something of the Waziri in the course of my work around the town, and particularly when visiting the prison, for which he was responsible. He was a large man, carrying the weight of sixty years or so of good feeding, his bulging stomach accentuated by a large collection of leather-bound Koranic charms suspended about his neck and hidden beneath his gown. His rather prominent eyes were usually expressionless unless I was investigating some com-plaint which might concern him, when they would light up with wariness and suspicion, but never with any evidence of guilt. I had dealings with three other members of the Council: the Chief Alkali, a shifty character who was a tool of the Waziri, and two younger men, the Wali and the Mukaddam, both products of

Katsina College, with an excellent command of English. The Wali was a very good Arabist, and a considerable legal authority, far outclassing the Alkali. He was supposed to keep the Shehu's court on the correct procedural lines, and was sometimes obviously under considerable pressure from his senior colleagues to help to satisfy their interests, if they were involved. He produced a transcript in English or Hausa of all the cases heard in the Shehu's court, and it was my job to go through the details of any case which had not been discussed with the DO. The Wali was also a bulky person, with an honest face, generally wearing an anxious expression, as of a man walking a very difficult and dangerous tightrope. His colleague, the Mukaddam, had a very different personality, lively and cheerful, with a great sense of humour

Corn-pits were under construction at Maiduguri and Geidam (in the north of the division) as well as at Damaturu. They were intended to store grain to be held in reserve to feed the labourers recruited from Bornu and elsewhere to work in the tin-mines in the Jos area. The slow and expensive progress at Damaturu caused much trouble and some worry, but the construction of similar pits at Maiduguri was managed with speed and efficiency by the Wali. Strictly, I felt, this should have been the job of the Mukaddam, who was in charge of the town and surrounding district, but the Waziri was jealous of his influence and outspokenness, and added this burden to the Wali, who was the willing work-horse of the Council.

Storage of corn on this scale had never been attempted before in Bornu and, prior to my arrival, there had been much discussion as to how it was to be done. Over most of Northern Nigeria corn for domestic use was stored in bins made of sun-baked earth or basket-work, lined with grass matting, topped off with thatch domes; the whole structure was supported on legs above ground-level. In Bornu, because the water-table nearly everywhere was so low, the custom was to store grain in pits lined with grass mats, with a layer of corn-chaff between the earth wall and the mat lining, which formed a barrier against penetration by termites (white ants). It was decided to store the corn reserve in this way in pits many times the domestic size holding about twenty tons each, and to locate them on the empty ground between the Provincial Office and the edge of the town. Every morning, I would meet the Wali on site, and we would check progress with the headman, beginning with the digging of the pits, the making and sun-baking of the bricks for the walls, below and above ground, and ending with the lining, thatching and filling with corn. The scene was one of tremendous activity and considerable noise, including the braying of the many donkeys which were delivering corn-chaff from distant farms, as well as matting, rough wooden stakes, rope and thatching-materials, then water to make the bricks and, finally, corn. The whole thing was a triumph of organisation by the Wali, who was to become a major political figure in Northern Nigeria some ten years later.

The Mukaddam had been given the highly unpopular job of recruiting mines labour in the Maiduguri area. The work brought him closely into touch with the other local district heads, and he learned a great deal about their relationships with the Waziri and the Shehu of which I was to hear later. He was very capable and efficient, saving me much time and energy which I was able to devote to other tasks, the chief of which was, inevitably, the supervision of the Native Treasury. This was a larger and more responsible task than the routine monthly check of the accounts which had been a boring chore in Katsina. Tupper delegated to me the charge of the Treasury, and I simply reported progress, or lack of it.

We did, in fact, make good progress. The Treasurer, Umar Yakub, was half Arab, a charming, smallish man of handsome appearance with a pointed beard and a rather shy smile. He spoke good English, and was very competent technically, though keen always to improve. He was an enthusiastic gardener and had a pleasant house of sun-baked brick set in a sort of oasis of palms and other greenery outside the town near the river Alo. He and his two young principal lieutenants, Tukur and Talib, became my good friends, and the Bornu Treasury remains for me the happiest of experiences of collaboration with Africans. I was to find corruption and malpractice in plenty in Bornu, but within the walls of the Treasury Umar Yakub maintained standards of probity and reliability which were respected (perhaps out of fear) even by the Shehu and the Waziri. Occasionally, Umar Yakub would come to me, voucher in hand, with clouded brow, to inform me, warn me, that he was about to reject some dubious transaction, and that someone might appeal or complain. They never did.

One of my regular jobs, when in the station, was to maintain 'a

personal friendly relationship' (Tupper's words) with the staff of
the American Army Air Force camp. The CO was a colonel in his
early thirties, competent and brisk in manner, considerate and
friendly, fortunately without the heavy heartiness which characterised some of his seniors whom we met *en passant*. My main
contacts were with his adjutant, twenty-five-year-old Dougie Jorn,
the son of a Colorado rancher, and with Tex, the quartermaster.
These two were delightful people to deal with, combining a real
sense of responsibility with cheerfulness and humour. I can recall
several occasions when these qualities were manifest and valuable.
There was the afternoon when Jorn came to my house in a state
of some agitation to report that one of his men had shot and
killed a woman at Lake Alo, about fifteen miles from Maiduguri.
We drove to the place, and found that the dead woman was the
senior wife of a fairly ancient Shuwa Arab, who showed no signs
of grief but clearly required some compensation. With the Shuwa
in the back of the car, we returned over the very rough road to
Maiduguri, wondering all the way whether the Shuwa, or his
homespun gown, had ever been washed in their joint lifetime, and
whether our stomachs could stand the strain. I held an inquest,
finding a verdict of accidental death, but also reprimanding the
shooting-party for firing at sitting ducks, or geese, with service
rifles and ball ammunition, without regard to possible ricochets
from the surface of the water. The old man claimed the original
bride-price of five cows, and was paid £15. Lake Alo was placed
out of bounds to American personnel, on Jorn's initiative.

We would have liked to place the whole of Maiduguri town out
of bounds, but agreed that it simply was not possible, or enforce-
able. We decided instead that I should try to clean up the town,
and in particular break the association of illegal beer-shops and
brothels which had developed in the ward nearest to the government station. I never discovered how or why this disgraceful state
of affairs had been allowed to occur in what was supposed to be a
mainly Muslim town. The Mukaddam, with whom Jorn and I
toured the area, said that undesirables had swarmed in, attracted
by American money. The leading 'madame' was a renegade Fulani
called Fatima Mbula, from a town near Numan in Adamawa
Province (where Jocelyn and I were stationed in 1945). She kept a
bevy of Fulani girls who were particularly popular with the Americans, and one girl at least seemed terribly young to be involved in

this business. One sensed a whiff of slavery, and a need for a thorough investigation of what was going on and who was behind it. However, with so many other matters urgently demanding attention, we decided to limit the immediate action to the restriction of the drink abuse. Jorn managed to prevent the export of drink from the camp, and the Mukaddam closed the illegal 'breweries'. (New ones, however, sprang up daily.)

The Americans were very hospitable. I enjoyed their company, but found their food, processed, canned or dehydrated, desperately boring. Fortunately, they seemed to enjoy greatly the dishes which Francis produced from local materials and so I was able to invite them to meals with our departmental officials, including some very likeable and capable people. Andrae, the engineer, had an enormous amount of work to supervise, including the aerodrome development, but found time to help me occasionally with my corn-pits problems. We both became good friends with Russell, the Forestry Officer, who shared our love of music. I returned from one of my trips to Damaturu to find that Russell had died of blackwater fever in my absence. Life in Nigeria had these sudden sadnesses, and one had to become hardened to death, and also to the sudden transfer of friends to remote stations; one simply hoped for some future reunion. Happily, in my time in Maiduguri, I was reunited with both Len Wileman, the foreman-mechanic, and Guy Gilbert, an MO from Katsina days. Guy had great warmth and friendliness, combined with reliable, honest common sense, and he was a tower of strength in times of difficulty. I owe him a great deal for the support he gave me after the departure of Tupper, my other guide and mentor.

We all had ambivalent feelings about the war and our remoteness from it, and from those who were enduring it 'at the sharp end'. Jocelyn's letters kept me in touch with her way of life, but there was little she could tell me about her activities at Bletchley Park, though I could guess something of their general nature. All this seemed much more to the point than was the chivvying of district and village heads in the Bornu bush. However, when I was finally informed that the Governor was unable to support my transfer to a technical corps of the army, on the grounds that I could not be spared from the job I was doing, I decided to accept the situation and make the best of it. On the day I received the ruling, 'the best of it' took the form of entertaining a party of

Free French officers at Damaturu. They were on their way from
Fort Lamy to Zinder and other towns in French Niger, where they
were to take over the administration from the Vichyssoise, as we
called them. This happy event resulted from the changed state of
affairs in North Africa to which all who were working in little-
known Maiduguri felt that they had made some contribution. Men
and material continued to stream through the airfield to support
the advance beyond Alamein, and the Americans could now feel
that they were helping to support their own people after the 'Torch'
landings in Morocco and Algeria. For the handful of British administrators, the need to boost the output of Nigerian tin and
groundnuts was seen as likely to endure for years, rather than
months. I had to admit that the Governor was right, and I had to
stay where I was most needed.

Tupper felt that it would be dull and miserable for me to spend
Christmas at Damaturu and insisted that I should return to
Maiduguri for a spell; there was always plenty to do. He was
equally insistent that he needed a rest from station life and that
the ideal change, for him, would be a camel-trek into Marte district, on the sandy trail towards Lake Chad. This addiction to
camel-trekking as a form of refreshment after a surfeit of office
work was a kind of nostalgia which Tupper shared with Robert
Coulthard, the vet, who sometimes accompanied him. They had
both served in Kenya's Northern Frontier District and loved its
open, arid spaces where this form of travel was customary. Robert
was seldom on the station, and so it took some time to get to
know him. Physically rugged and tough, like Tupper, he had a
surprisingly imaginative sympathy for people, often simply conveyed by a quick glance from his very expressive eyes. He was a
very generous person in every way, hospitable, and most undemanding as a companion. I became very fond of him, and of the pet
camel foals which he kept in his compound, but I never had much
liking for their mothers.

Christmas and the Scottish New Year in any Nigerian station
was always a sustained, demanding round of entertainment, and,
with the American contribution thrown in for good measure, I
could see that Tupper had been wise to make his escape. The
saving grace, as in Katsina in 1938, was the early Harmattan
weather, bringing cool evenings and the welcome blaze of a log
fire round which we would sit and chat after dinner. Lunch, in the

heat of the day, was always harder work, long-drawn-out and offering no means of escape until it was time for late-afternoon exercise:
tennis, squash or riding. Tupper returned from Marte to report
that the thieving and general lawlessness for which the district was
notorious were as bad as ever. He was also concerned about the
state of the road to Mongonu along which the groundnut crop
had somehow to be transported by lorry, and he asked me to go
and deal with it.

There were a number of strange anomalies in the administration
of Northern Nigeria which appeared to have survived, and even
been fostered, since Lugard's time. The provincial allocation of
government expenditure (from central funds) included provision for
the maintenance of 'Temporary Buildings' and 'Temporary or Dry-
season Roads' and Residents made miserly sub-allocations of these
funds to their divisions. The amount of the allocations was, in
everyone's experience, notoriously inadequate, and officers (as I
shall relate in due course) had to exercise their ingenuity to make
roads passable, and keep roofs over people's heads. All Residents,
even those who were on good terms with their provincial engineers,
seemed determined to maintain administrative control of this
expenditure, and engineers were not allowed to touch it, or even to
advise. Some cynics declared that this was symptomatic of an
attitude of temporary presence, here today but probably gone tomorrow, which did not go unnoticed by the African hierarchy. In
Katsina, even Margery Perham commented on the ramshackle state
of the government station, where there was not, in my time, a
single permanent building. Most provinces had one, sometimes
two, all-season roads (linking provincial headquarters with the
outer world during the rainy season), maintained to professional
standards by the provincial engineer. The real die-hards regretted
the passing of the old days when the only access to some headquarters, such as Yola, in the rains, was by river, so ensuring the
absence, for several months, of too many visiting big-wigs.

Bornu had two all-season roads, one running west to the Bauchi
border (for Jos) and one running south from Damaturu through
Biu to the Adamawa border (for Yola, which was 520 miles from
Jos by this route). There were, in addition, five or six fairly important dry-season roads, and all the district headquarters were
accessible by some kind of road or track. The chief problem of
road maintenance in Bornu was the almost complete absence of

'metalling' – hard material such as rock or stone – and the prevalence of sand over most of its area. Here and there, patches of clay or black cotton-soil could be found which, mixed with the sand into a sort of mud-pie and baked hard by the sun, formed quite a good surface crust, suitable for light traffic in the dry season but soon broken up by heavy lorries. For many weary miles of these roads it was a matter of ploughing through sand or sandy soil, hoping not to get stuck in the worst patches. Repairs were carried out after the rains, by local labour, recalling the words of Isaiah: 'Prepare ye the way of the Lord, make straight in the desert a highway for our God. Every valley shall be exalted, and every mountain and hill shall be made low: and the crooked shall be made straight, and the rough places plain.' Humming or whistling the music of Handel to these lively and forthright words was sometimes an encouragement when planning operations in the midday sun, and making straight the crooked was certainly a full-time occupation in the land of Bornu. I spent a few days on the Mongonu road, visiting the worst places with the headmen and deciding what had to be done. The most important tasks were to moderate the gradients into the beds of the streams, where the old road-surfaces had been scoured away by the rains, and to fill in ruts and potholes. It was all very rough, but better than nothing at all, as I was to realise later when travelling in northern Bornu.

27

Prematurely a DO

❦

NIVEN was granted leave at last, on the insistence of the MO, and Tupper, equally overdue, was instructed to act as Resident until the arrival of his relief, a senior Resident. To my surprise, Tupper told me that I would take over the Bornu division from him until some senior DO was posted to the province. Derek Wright, with whom I was sharing a house, was a year senior to me but had not had time to get to know the division, and was needed to cope with the Provincial Office.

For a day or two, I consulted Tupper about almost everything of any importance, and then he told me firmly that I should get on with the job and (with a smile) if I made a really serious error I should probably get the sack. This caused us both to laugh because some weeks earlier I had tried to resign, following frustration of my attempts to transfer to a scientific job, and exasperation over frequent moves from house to house in the overcrowded station. I was 'calmed down' and told that there was no hope of my resignation being accepted!

Tupper moved into the Residency and I moved into the DO's house, to have the use of the telephone which was really essential with so much happening out of office hours. I found that I could cope with the general demands of the job, but could not, simultaneously, discharge my old responsibilities for touring the Western Districts, mines labour, and corn storage. Derek Wright intended to take over these tasks but had much to do in the Provincial Office, following the departure of Dorothy Niven, who had done a remarkably good job, but latterly had been very tired. The Provincial Office was also the Divisional Office, using the same staff and the same files (as in Katsina), resulting in much frustration, confusion and near-chaos. The staff had become slack under Dorothy's kindly rule, and I complained bitterly in a letter to Jocelyn: 'The African staff are pretty hopeless, and one has to watch them like a hawk, to ensure that important action doesn't get overlooked.' At the same time, I felt much sympathy with those clerks who were stranded in a strange environment about a thousand miles from their homelands in the South. 'If only one had the time, there are all the makings of a crusade to be waged among "literate" Africans whose education is really bounded by the three R's, the Bible and a dictionary. They have no other background against which to set their acquisition of an English vocabulary ... I would like to start clubs and libraries for Africans, some kind of social activity which would make them think and break out of their preoccupation with status, salary scales and tribal separateness.' I found it surprising that some Education Officers, who were not exactly hard-pressed during the war, did little or nothing to help in this way.

I now spent much of my time in the NA offices in the town, and with the senior NA officials. Once a week, in the late afternoon, I rode around the town with the Mukaddam, a jovial character whom we all liked and respected. He had been headmaster of the Middle School for about ten years and had given it a deservedly high reputation. The old town was full of tortuous alleys, its problems of overcrowding and sanitation made worse by the influx of strangers and undesirables. Niven, with his usual energy, had started the construction of a new town, a little detached from the old one, to accommodate the immigrants, and this was growing fast, to a well-designed plan.

The one area in which little or no progress seemed to be made was the incidence of corruption and extortion, as evidenced by the complaints which Tupper and I heard every day for an hour or so after breakfast, and whenever we went on tour. Many of them were directed against the Waziri, or one of his henchmen, but we were never able to assemble enough evidence to make the allegations 'stick'. Niven's attitude to this situation was somewhat *laissez-faire* (he had so many other urgent problems to deal with) and I found a similar attitude in Guy Money who once told me, with some heat, 'the African doesn't want justice; he doesn't understand it'. Tupper and I held the completely opposite view that corruption was something we could never tolerate, though we admitted the necessity of living with some degree of it; we could not expect, few as we were, to change completely the ethos of a long-established society. I saw little of the Waziri himself, except on visits to the prison or to quiz him about complaints against him (mostly of extortion or bribery without delivery of the expected favour). On most of my visits to his office, I saw one of the senior staff, a very tall, well-educated and competent Kanuri in his early thirties. He had a manner which seemed to disguise a certain insolence, a near-contempt, beneath a subservient behaviour. His eyes (like the Waziri's) had a kind of impermeability, and one felt one had no knowledge of the real man. However, I had no doubt that he was fully in the Waziri's confidence and knew all about his misdeeds and perhaps those of the Shehu and his council. I am sure that he regarded most of the British as idealistic fools, tied to the rigid formula of Indirect Rule, content to have the wool pulled over their eyes day after day, year after year.

One day, before one of our rides through the town, I asked the Mukaddam to come and have tea with me. As we sat together on the veranda, he asked me whether he might 'speak his mind'. He then went on to tell me the most amazing story, that the Waziri master-minded the activities of several groups of thieves in Maiduguri and in the infamous Marte district. He said that he had informed the DO and the Resident, but, and here he chuckled characteristically, nobody would believe him. 'Something must be done about it,' he said, 'or we shall all be disgraced.' I spoke to Tupper about the Mukaddam's allegations. He said that he believed they were true, but dared not say so because he would have been expected to take some action, and this seemed impossible while we were so short-staffed. In his view, the situation required the full-time attention of an experienced officer, preferably a Kanuri-speaker. We both agreed to sit on our hands and try to contain our frustration.

In fact, not the least amazing feature of this story is that it took another ten years to get 'something done about it', to get the Waziri dismissed from the Council and finally convicted and jailed. The dramatic resolution of this affair in 1952 by the Governor, Sharwood-Smith, is described in his book *But Always as Friends*. He mentions only briefly that this situation had worsened over the years while the province had been in the charge of some people who knew it well.

Niven, who was again Resident, Bornu, from 1948 to 1950, published in 1983 a book of reminiscences, *Nigerian Kaleidoscope*, in which he recalls his Bornu experience as the most important and significant of his career. He speaks of the Shehu with a sort of affection as 'my Shehu' and does not refer to the events of 1952. There is a reference, however, in the autobiography of the Sardauna of Sokoto, the first Prime Minister of Northern Nigeria. In it, the Sardauna appears to comment rather sourly on the Bornu scandals (including one in which his old schoolfriend, the Wali, became involved when he, in turn, became Waziri) and opines that Sharwood-Smith did not understand Bornu, never having served there. The latter, in a footnote in his book, says that the Sardauna was fully informed of, and in agreement with, the action in Bornu. One should perhaps mention that Sharwood-Smith had a deep attachment to Sokoto, where he spent some of the formative years of *his* career! Behind these versions of Bornu affairs, one can discern differences of attitude towards the tolerance of corruption as part of the system, and also perhaps the strong affection which even senior officers developed for places in which they served, and people with whom they worked.

These first few months in Bornu, after three years away from the job, caused me to question, more sharply than before, what the colonial administration was trying to do, and what was my role in it. From my early days in Nigeria, I had shared the view of most of my contemporaries and of many thoughtful seniors that the Nigerians must have an increasing say in the management of their own affairs, and that the time would come when we should withdraw completely. In 1942–43, it was obvious that one effect of the war had been to contract considerably the probable time-scale of these events. Ideally, we should therefore have devoted increased time and resources to the development of the individuals and institutions which would have to carry new and enlarged responsibilities. The sad irony of the situation was that we now had fewer officials, and less available time, than in 1939 when the need had seemed less urgent. In this dilemma, I decided that my own priorities would be the war-essential tasks, however boring and frustrating, the maintenance of law and order and fair government and the training of promising officials (particularly the younger ones). The second and third priorities were linked in that one tried to establish standards and examples and I always made clear my own attitude to corruption. Tupper and I, and many like us, were convinced that corruption was the most destructive influence in

African society as we knew it and could ruin the development of an independent and progressive Nigeria.

This view of the effects of corruption was confirmed by the events following the military coup in 1984. The Western press was full of denunciations of the regime for its series of in-camera trials of leading politicians and officials charged with corruption and misappropriation. It was all very regrettable, but also inevitable. We, the British, did not have time enough to clean up the system and probably were not sufficiently firm, hard or determined. Whether the Nigerians themselves can succeed where we failed (and failed, too, in India over a longer period) remains to be seen. It took centuries to bring this particular evil under control in Britain, and there are some who would argue that it still exists, in modified forms, and that the poor, as ever, are the chief victims.

Law and order, and its associated machinery, soon became my chief preoccupation after I took over Tupper's desk. He told me not to bother too much about some of the long-standing matters in his 'pending' tray, but I found that, constituted as I am, I could not avoid sifting through the mass of papers it contained. This job occupied my 'spare time' for several days and resulted in a division of the material into three categories. There were a number of files and papers dealing with long-term problems and other intractables, most of which Tupper had inherited from his predecessor. These I grouped roughly by subject and tied into a bundle to be brought up to his successor! There was also a collection of what Tupper described as 'bits of paper', some of which he regularly passed over to me on my returns from bush, including all kinds of matters requiring non-urgent attention, some of which were becoming urgent through lapse of time. The third category contained the subjects requiring (as I saw it) urgent action, chiefly the fourteen cases of homicide which were pending before the Shehu's court.

Transcripts, in Hausa or English, of the court proceedings, had been prepared by the Wali and passed to the DO. I found time to read them before the scheduled visit to the prison, when the wretched accused, who were on remand, were brought before me for interview. Most of them were quite resigned, even fatalistic, about their situation, but a few were, understandably, incensed about the very long time taken in deciding their cases. It is true that the court did not display any great sense of urgency, but one had to admit that long delays between hearings were often unavoidable. Bornu covered a very large area, and some districts were two hundred miles or more from Maiduguri. The need for certain witnesses would arise as the presentation of the case before the court took place. They had to be summoned, found and brought, often on foot, from great distances. In the dry season, a man might leave his home village for several months, to visit distant relatives or friends, or just to wander and explore, perhaps never to return. One unfortunate accused had been on remand for over a year, awaiting the arrival of witnesses who could not be found, and I wonder if they ever appeared.

Investigation of these cases was very time-consuming; the most tiresome and frustrating of them all was a clear and most unpleasant case of murder, in which the court had insisted on awarding a Koranic substitute of *diya* (blood-money with imprisonment) in place of the capital sentence. The accused was a man of some substance from an influential family, and the argument was that it would be far better for the relatively poor family of the murdered man to accept this form of retribution than to have the murderer killed. My argument, expressed forcibly to the Wali, was that the proposed sentence was inconsistent with the Nigerian Criminal Code Ordinance and therefore, under Section 10 of the Native Courts Ordinance, was not allowable. I brought the matter to Tupper, who agreed with me, but still the Shehu's court, as represented by the Wali, was obdurate. I began to suspect that there was some dark dealing behind the scenes, and informed the Wali that I intended to transfer the case to the High Court for the attention of the visiting judge. Judge Ames, whom I had known in Ibadan, arrived a few days later and disposed of this case, and also of another in which the Shehu's court had imposed the death sentence where there was some evidence of insanity. I was disappointed by the attitude of the Wali; he was an intelligent man, and must have been fully aware of the issues involved. I made my peace with him over tea and sweet cakes, but never gave him the same degree of trust again.

The streams of planes passing through the airfield in both directions brought large numbers of visitors and birds-of-passage requiring attention over and above the 'local' demand. In a letter to Jocelyn, I said: 'One has the feeling of being deprived of private life. Outside office hours, one has to make contact with Europeans, Africans, Americans, and a fair amount of entertaining and invitation-accepting is unavoidable. Tupper is mentally weary after his long tour and frequently calls for help in looking after the never-ending stream of guests. The housing situation here is acute, and every rest-house (with which we were once well provided) has been taken over for some war-time establishment or other. All the big-wigs passing through are billeted on the Resident or DO, as a matter of course, ranging from Ministers of State to generals, air-marshals, and hypochondriac maharajahs, from Persian potentates to voluble Free Frenchmen.'

We used to try to guess who or what would be the next most improbable creature to drop out of the skies but, on one occasion at least, reality outstretched our imaginings. One evening, the Post Office messenger arrived hotfoot with a priority telegram from the Resident, Kano: 'Colonel Holman-Jones, leading authority on the STOCK-WHIP arriving yours shortly. His exhibitions of first-class propaganda value.' I wrote, on 10 February: 'The stock-whip merchant arrived two days ago, and moved on today, leaving Tupper, who had been putting him up, in a state bordering on desperation, something unusual in that equable soul. Apparently, the first person figured largely in his conversation, mainly of how he had whipped himself around the world I don't know how many times, of the celebrities he'd met, and what he'd said to them and what they'd said about him. His one-man show was certainly pretty good. We assembled the Shehu and a multitude down in the town, and then he proceeded to do his stuff whilst their eyes nearly popped out to see this mad white man doing unbelievable things with a 25-foot whip. He cut a piece of paper two inches long neatly in two halves while two fearful Africans held it between their fingers. Greatest feat of all was his tying a knot about a man's neck without causing him to wince. To have such an eye at sixty is extraordinary, but one was left jittering with nerves in case the old man should make a mistake.'

Not to be outdone, the Americans materialised a whole concert-party by air across the Atlantic. It was led by Jack Benny, who did most of the talking and was supported in song, dance and repartee by a glamorous troupe from Hollywood, of whom I can remember only the beautiful Veronica Lake. Tex, the QM, had cleared the main warehouse store of the camp for the show, and had engineered a stage and a good deal of strong lighting. I arrived, as invited, a few minutes before the show was due to begin, and found the camp in a state of flap. 'Come and look,' said Jorn. Inside the warehouse, amidst a good deal of shouting and cursing, the Americans were conducting a highly mechanised war against the adversities of the Bornu climate. Several large air-conditioning units were blasting cold air towards the stage, while squads of men were pumping insecticide into the remaining air-space. Myriads of insects, attracted by the lighting, were being slaughtered by the insecticide or being cooked on the floodlights. The smell was indescribable.

I shall never forget the sheer professionalism with which that concert-party carried on the show that night. Somehow, they, and we, avoided asphyxiation, and we could only sense, not hear, the crunching of the insects under their feet. Jack Benny made the most of the occasion, wise-cracking and ad-libbing about the warmth of their reception and the sweet smell of success. He and the rest of his group were in great form at a party after the show.

All this rather hectic and sometimes sophisticated station life was in marked contrast to the daily round in the office, in Maiduguri town, and in brief forays into the districts, which was intense and wearing, rather than hectic. I became very much aware that the DO was always 'the man in the middle' in any dispute or awkward situation, the first person to be called upon to sort out any mess. Tupper showed his true and remarkable kindness by relieving me of some of the most unpleasant duties, including the supervision of hangings in Maiduguri prison – a responsibility shared with the Medical Officer, and an experience which quite removed any subsequent appetite for breakfast. There was, inevitably, a file on the subject, which covered all the grisly details of the procedure, the most important of which was the calculation of the length of the rope (and consequent drop) in relation to the height and weight of the convict, which were always checked most carefully, to avoid the ghastly consequences of error.

28

Personalities and
Problems

ஒ

M Y two-month spell as DO, Emirate, officially responsible
for the administration of about a million people, came
to an end soon after the arrival of the new Resident, and
I reverted to assisting Tupper in a range of tasks, some old, some
new.

I moved out of the DO's house back into all the frustrations of
the station's housing shortage. Everyone seemed to have a higher
priority than Derek Wright and myself, and we were moved around,
often together, to occupy, very temporarily, some vacant house or
other. This was uncomfortable for us, and became unbearably so
for our servants, who did not get on well together, and had quite
inadequate quarters. It was a relief to escape to bush, even to
Damaturu, where the corn-pits were filling with corn, and Hadji
Sudani had been evicted, leaving behind a trail of roguery and
inefficiency. I had further experience of the awful quality of Bornu
roads when I was sent to tour the Geidam district, north-west of
Maiduguri and reached by a long dog-leg journey via Damaturu.
After six months of the dry season, I found the town of Geidam
in the midst of a fiendishly hot sandy waste dotted with thorn-
scrub and doum palms, with only a trickle of water in the bed of
the river (the Komadogu) which was the sole redeeming feature of
the place. On the far bank, away from the town, was the rest-
house, set amidst the remains of the old barracks of the Mounted
Infantry, which had been stationed in this border area for a decade
or so in Lugard's time. I was fortunate in having with me as government messenger a remarkable old soldier called Mohammadu
Masu, who had served with the Mounted Infantry, and had been

stationed in Geidam before his World War I service in the Cameroons and Tanganyika.

Mohammadu was the DO's chief messenger, and I had greatly enjoyed his company, his repertoire of stories of his long and varied service, and his delightful dry sense of humour, during my spell as DO, Emirate. He gave me, quite frankly, his impressions of the DOs and ADOs he'd worked with, of district heads and other common acquaintance, and I was amazed by the shrewdness of his judgement. He was deeply attached to Tupper-Carey, described him, in Hausa, as 'makera wandon-karfe' ('the smith who makes iron trousers') a tribute to his driving-power and tenacity of purpose. Mohammadu looked forward to *jangali*-touring with me in the approaching rainy season. 'The Fulani here are like a real enemy; they shoot poisoned arrows at you. It's quite exciting – you'd like it as a change from the office!' With Mohammadu Masu, it might have been quite an experience, but, sadly, we missed it.

The district head at Geidam was an old battle-scarred warrior, a survivor from the tribal wars, a trusted lieutenant of the Shehu, who carried the title of Kaigamma. He was a capable chief and reasonably honest, being sufficiently remote and inaccessible from Maiduguri to operate with a certain measure of independence. During his long headship, Geidam had developed into an important trade-centre and the big trading firms were represented there by senior African clerks and the odd British manager, one of whom I found spending a nostalgic local leave under canvas near the river. I invited him to dinner, and we sampled the surprising wealth of vegetables produced in the river-bed while he regaled me with stories of his service with the Border Intelligence Unit during the days of Vichy power in French Niger, a few miles to the north.

The brief for my visit was to make a rapid survey of the supply and transport situation for some of the main products of the region, including grain, groundnuts, hides and skins, Fulani butter, smoked fish and gum arabic. The roads were really punishing for motor transport, and also exacted a high consumption of scarce petrol. Camels were available, but their Touareg owners could not always be mustered in the required numbers and they knew how to drive a hard bargain. There were 900 tons of grain to be moved to railhead at Nguru, as well as thousands of tons of hoped-for groundnuts. I was surprised to find that the tonnages of the other products, particularly of skins and smoked fish (from Lake Chad and the river) were so substantial. The fish was in great demand in Kano and other large towns, and commanded a good price in spite of (or because of?) its malodorous nature. Fulani butter was packed in the ubiquitous petrol-tins, in which it apparently did not easily become rancid as it did when used as a hair-dressing by Fulani and Shuwa-Arab women. It was rumoured that this stuff was exported to the UK, processed and retailed as 'Empire Butter'. Gum arabic was purchased and graded by representatives of Rowntrees in Nguru. They used buying agents scattered throughout Bornu and adjacent provinces, wherever the thorn-acacia was found. As a crop, it was so easy and remunerative that it depressed the production of other cash crops such as groundnuts which were so urgently needed. The groundnut campaign staff deplored the low level of production in Bornu, but we informed them that they could not have everything, and that the sucking of Rowntrees Gums must have calmed many war-jangled nerves.

I made detailed arrangements for the urgent movement of grain by camel from the Geidam storage-pits, to be completed before the rains, only to have the whole thing cancelled by Jos, who found they didn't need it after all. Once again, in exasperation, I totted up the time I had wasted, or allotted to activities alien to my instincts, training or better nature since 1939, and felt that I would have been better employed doing almost anything elsewhere.

This feeling was intensified after my next foray into the bush. One morning Tupper tossed 'a bit of paper' across the desk. It was a letter from one Ira S. Petre, an American missionary living among the pagan folk in Marghi district, the southernmost part of Bornu bordering on the hills of Adamawa Province, complaining of extortion, bribery and corruption in relation to the recruitment of mines labour and the supply of corn for the reserve. Tupper told me that the district head had been under suspicion for some time, and was being moved to Nguru (290 miles away to the northwest) where he would be under the eye of the DO stationed there. It seemed no one had toured the area for several years, and the most recent report of any merit was written in 1930.

I travelled to Damboa, the district HQ of Marghi, in one of the long-suffering Albion lorries which Len Wileman somehow maintained in working order, taking about five hours to cover the sixty-odd miles of sand, ruts, bumps and dry stream-beds. I found that the district head had departed for Nguru (on hearing of my impending visit, no doubt) and his replacement was not expected for some weeks. The rest-house was agreeably located outside the pleasant little town, and to it I summoned village heads and others, to try to assess the situation. There seemed to be no great complaint in Damboa and the surrounding area, but the story was quite different when I moved to Chibbuk for two days' stay in a hut in the village (there being no rest-house). It seemed fairly clear that an unfair share of the burden of mines-labour and corn-quota had been imposed upon the pagan villages to the benefit of their Muhammadan (Kanuri) neighbours. I found that things were still much as reported twelve years earlier and wrote, in a letter to Jocelyn: 'It's all wrong that a pagan area should be administered through a Muslim potentate who puts his own favourites into positions of authority, so that the wretched pagans have no chance of developing along their own lines and forming their own authority. We are allowing to flourish, here, the kind of oppression which we are fighting to eliminate in Europe.' Margery Perham had also commented adversely on this type of situation when she travelled through Bornu and Adamawa in 1932.

At Chibbuk I noted: 'The Petres are charming. They come from Maryland and belong to the "Church of the Brethren", which is similar to our Plymouth Brethren. They have three small children, and another missionary and wife from a neighbouring station who are staying with them have no less than five. They are all young, thirty-ish, and seem to thrive on family-raising, looking very well after three years without leave. They live very simply on a small salary, their only concession to American ways being the inevitable refrigerator and Coca-Cola ... Petre is working very hard to establish something which might be of great benefit here, but he is up against great difficulties. All his efforts are being sabotaged by the local chiefs, and I imagine that they are inspired to do so from Maiduguri. My impression is that Muhammadanism is gaining on the people faster than any influence he can provide, and all the weight of native authority is thrown on that side. It seems an awful pity, when one considers how little the pagans stand to gain by being more closely bound to the Shehu with his grasping ways, and how much they might benefit from the formation of a Christian community.'

April is notoriously the worst month for heat and humidity in any part of Nigeria, and I wrote to Jocelyn on 5 April after a week of horse-trekking through villages to the east of Chibbuk and Damboa: 'I've been unutterably weary for the last few days, but the long trek is over at last, and I'm back in Damboa in comparative luxury and ease. The distance was rather more than I'd bargained for, and even the peerless Alhadji was showing signs of strain towards the end. The lesson is clear; in the climate of Bornu, one cannot cover eighteen miles or so before breakfast and then face the heat of this season. Perhaps I'm not as fit as I used to be ... The last two days of the trek took me through some pleasant hill-country, and twice I found camps under big shady trees, with a view over scattered pagan hamlets that was a reward for the trials of the journey. In other ways, the trip has been worthwhile. One gets practically no idea of how people are living by operating from a headquarters established in the district rest-house, and this kind of tour brings one closely into touch with the real people of Africa and the way the great majority of them live, in little villages far from the amenities that our administration is supposed to offer. If possible, I am more critical than ever ... Most of these people get *nothing* in exchange for the tax they have to pay each year, except Pax Britannica, and, if they are very lucky, the use of a Government-built well. Hospitals, dispensaries, schools, agriculture and forestry departments serve the towns and the larger villages, and the folk in the remote bush foot the bill.'

In spite of my misgivings, I always hoped for a better future for the peasantry, and everything one hoped for depended on winning the war. We had to try to persuade the farmers to grow more groundnuts and more grain, while they complained of lack of scrap-iron from which to make hoes, and lack of the popular consumer goods, such as cotton fabrics, enamelware, knives, hurricane-lamps, at reasonable prices. It was remarkable that the various production-drives were so successful in spite of the many difficulties and obstacles.

Those of us who were grappling with these problems at first hand received no help or encouragement from the new Resident: 'The man is something of an enigma. He's apparently well thought of, professionally, but I don't see, in what he has done in the last two months, any sign of the direction of a master-mind. He's imperturbable, in the way that goes with large, well-fleshed men. In two months, he has not invited Derek or myself even to a drink, the most commonplace of Nigerian civilities. The burden of hospitality and of keeping people happy and motivated is borne, as ever, by Tupper, on a much smaller salary.'

The Resident had assumed responsibility for the allocation of accommodation in the station, and in this matter, as in others, seemed to show no concern or consideration for the comfort of his own junior staff. My letters show that I was in a state of near-rebellion after several moves at short notice from one set of discomforts to another. The breaking-point came one morning, before breakfast, when I was told by Tupper that I would have to go out to bush that day because the Resident had allocated my house to a rather unpleasant and self-important engineer who had recently arrived. I replied that after six years of inadequate housing or no housing at all, I intended to claim my rights, and was returning to 'my' house and would occupy it until some suitable alternative was found. After an hour or two, I was moved to the forestry house, which had been vacant for weeks, and with the current shortage of forestry staff, seemed likely to remain so. Two weeks later, miraculously, a Forestry Officer was posted to us, and although we all believed that he would never arrive (he didn't!) I seized the offer of secure tenure of a mud-and-thatch bungalow vacated that morning. This modest dwelling consisted of a small sitting-room-cum-dining-room and a bedroom, and the servants' quarters were of a matching standard, but, after so many moves, we were thankful for any place of our own, and for the peace and quiet of relative isolation on the edge of the station. The 'compound' extended for two or three acres, and Alhadji and Co. planted groundnuts – a happy farming cooperative.

Hardly a week passed without some administrative officer being posted to us, including several putative reliefs for Tupper. Most of them did not arrive, being 'dropped off' along the thousand miles from Lagos, or sucked into the bureaucratic maw of Lagos itself. Finally, it was agreed that Money would relieve Tupper, who departed expressing the hope that we might work together again, a hope that, sadly, was never fulfilled.

Money arrived early in the morning after Tupper's departure, and by two o'clock, everyone who had dealings with him was exhausted. 'Most people around here declare quite frankly that he is slightly mad, but I suspect the trouble is due to change of life, glands, and the energy of frustrated purpose.' He had no intention of keeping the place warm for Tupper, and began a new-broom sweep at once. After some skirmishing, he decided to leave the Treasury in my hands, and we achieved an uneasy *modus vivendi* in other matters. Out of office hours, he was remarkably friendly, and I used these times to broach with him some problems of the departmental officers which they had been disinclined to raise with him officially, for fear of an explosive response.

It was not an easy life, but I respected Money for his honesty of purpose and his courage. He was not afraid to tackle anyone, including the Resident, when roused, and I have good reason to remember one such occasion, a week or two after my move into the 'thatched cottage'. Apart from being small and dark, its main disadvantage was its floor, of beaten earth, a sort of clay and sand mixture which was never really clean and produced new dust at every sweeping. One day, I bought some woven rush mats from a Hausa trader, and was delighted by their bright cheerful appearance when spread on the floor. The next morning, Alhadji reported, with concern and indignation, that the mats had been largely consumed by white ants. He was indignant because he thought it was quite wrong, and unfair, after all our housing problems, that this house did not even have a concrete floor, something one expected to find even in a bush rest-house. I asked for a concrete floor to be laid, and was told that most of the 'temporary buildings' money had already been spent or allocated, and the balance had to be held against real emergencies. Further enquiries revealed that some of the money had been, or would be, spent on extending the servants' quarters at the Residency, which were not temporary buildings at all. I mentioned the matter to Money, whose face reddened as he listened. 'Leave this to me,' he said. I never knew how he managed it, but I did, quite soon, get the concrete floor and, for good measure, fresh whitewash on the walls.

When the rains came at last, Maiduguri seemed more bearable, and it was cool enough to play tennis or squash. On the warmer afternoons, I liked to ride along the river-bed towards Lake Alo, exchanging greetings with the Shuwa Arabs returning from Maiduguri market, or moving camp with all their belongings loaded on the backs of their cattle. Horse and rider revelled in the sight and texture of fresh green grass, and the moist air moving across the valley. By June of 1943, the war situation seemed more hopeful, with the North African coast in our hands, and the mail situation was slightly improved – a boost to the morale of the many grass-widowers. It seemed almost impossible to secure a passage for a British wife from the UK, but the French did much better. One Sunday morning, Money burst into my house like a cannon-ball, having covered all of the hundred yards between our houses by car and, breathing heavily, asked me whether I spoke French. He then introduced Lieutenant Caltucci, who was in a great hurry to proceed to Jos 'pour ramener ma famille', and return with them to Fort Lamy.

A week or so later, I had another opportunity to exercise my schoolboy French and try to prevent it from lapsing into Hausa in mid-sentence. The impulsive and inconsiderate authorities in Fort Lamy this time launched upon us seventy-three hungry and demanding Frenchmen, ex-Vichy in sympathy, en route for Dakar. It seemed that these people – soldiers, sailors, airmen, minor governors and so on – had been sent from Dakar to Fort Lamy in 1940, to put over the Vichy point of view, and after three years under house arrest were being returned to Dakar to be welcomed by wives, sweethearts and General Giraud, and to receive three years' arrears of salary. 'I spent all of yesterday and most of this morning acting as mâitre d'hotel in the rambling old Residency where we housed them, and doing most things required, short of cleaning their teeth and clipping their beards, which, believe me, needed some clipping. The party left today at noon, under escort of Money for Potiskum (where they will sleep tonight in the school) after presenting a long address of thanks to the Resident who, in his customary fashion, had done precisely nothing. Right now, I'm enjoying imagining Money's dealings with the party at his old HQ tonight.'

The following day I wrote: 'Appeals in two murder cases are due to be heard in Jos and the papers have to be posted at once. It's an anomalous position for an administrative officer. The Shehu's court tries murder cases by Muhammadan law, and has powers to pass sentence of death. My own powers as a magistrate are limited to three months' imprisonment, yet here I am, responsible for vetting capital proceedings and trying to ensure that justice is done. In reviewing a native court case, I can increase the sentence arbitrarily, say from two years to five years, or reduce it, as the case may require. Not much logic in the arrangement, though all cases are subject to appeal to the Supreme Court.'

On 27 June: 'Tomorrow, I'm off to Potiskum for two days,

followed by two days in Damaturu. Jobs to do: mines labour, groundnuts, and sanitation. Money is disturbed about the floating population at Damaturu (mines labour en route to Jos), and how they're to be housed and so on. His concern is justified, but other bees in his bonnet are the office flag-staff, which doesn't conform to Colonial Office pattern No. N/32/5B/Mk11, and the local egg supply, which was fine until he started to improve it. Potiskum is not in this division, but Money has a watching brief over it, and also Biu (he seems to be running the province!) and I'm to help out a young ADO who is holding the baby there pending the arrival of Maiden, the new DO.' Later: 'Travelled with the African assistant MO, a nice fellow. Enlightening to spend a few days with an African of the professional class. He has become almost entirely Europeanised, spends hours humming snatches of Romberg, Lehar and Strauss, and complains that there are so few amenities, domestic or social, in Maiduguri. It's rather disturbing to find in him, and in others of comparable education, an apparent lack of the spirit of public service. Equipped to practise medicine, and competent, he now regrets that he did not take up engineering, because he thinks that it pays better. I suppose it's our fault, in some way, that this attitude has developed.'

I tore myself away from the pleasant ambience of Potiskum to make what would prove to be my last descent on Damaturu, and managed to clean the place up so that it looked reasonably tidy, at least as seen from the road. Returning to Maiduguri: 'I found Money having a fight with someone over the telephone, and the precincts of the office littered with complainants who had apparently been told to await my return. One in particular, whose case was investigated and declared sound by Tupper, has been trying to get justice for over three months now, against the vested interest of the Waziri. Money adopts an attitude of indifference to complaints and won't help me to get them settled, so I've now taken the only course open to me, of washing my hands of the whole business. It's sad that we have so little in common, and often no common ground of approach to subjects that matter.'

Fortunately, Money and I did have one thing in common which helped us, to some extent, to work together. We both enjoyed working with, and encouraging, the young educated Kanuri who were making their careers in Native Administration jobs. He revived the Bornu Literary Society and transformed it into something like a club, serving a number of activities. We coerced visiting departmental big-wigs into addressing it, and sometimes even the more amenable of our transient VIPs. A surprising number of members of the society became senior civil servants after Independence.

About two months after Tupper's departure, I found to my dismay that Money had made no social contact with the American camp, and the Resident seemed to cultivate the RAF in preference to the Americans. The turnover of British personnel in the station had been so rapid that I was the only person left who knew Jorn, Tex and the other 'permanent' staff at all well. Money was very shy of making new contacts, but he agreed to attend a party I gave for Jorn and Co. to meet most of the recent arrivals. All concerned behaved rather well, and I was amused to hear the comments of both sides afterwards. Money: 'They're rather difficult to understand, aren't they? Very loud voices.' Jorn: 'He seems to be a very quiet person, but he must have been tough to survive the trenches of the last war.'

I had been invited to spend local leave in Lagos and Money and the Resident readily agreed to release me, pleased, I imagine, to have me out of the way for a time. August in Lagos can be quite cool, with fresh sea breezes, and I looked forward keenly to the change, and to seeing some old friends. The problem of transport was happily solved when Jorn arranged for me to travel overnight to Jos in a comfortable staff car with two visiting American doctors. On the day before our departure, Money returned from a conference with the Resident and told me that, provided I was passed fit, I would be posted on my return to Nguru, in the remote north-west corner of the province, to relieve the DO i/c Bedde Division. The issue of fitness arose because Guy Gilbert (and Money, too, apparently) had been concerned about my loss of weight and occasional attacks of low fever. I told Gilbert that I would benefit enormously from a change of scene, and the absence of Money, and it was left that a final decision would be made after my return from Lagos.

29

Relieving an Outpost: Nguru

೮ಾ

I SLEPT during most of the journey to Jos, but the two Americans shared the driving, and whenever I woke up seemed always to be discussing the same subject: their loss of income since joining the army, which appeared to be considerable, but much less than that suffered by their plastic surgeon colleagues. This latter category included men whose skill in cosmetic surgery had earned them vast wealth in Hollywood and other centres of glamour and affluence. This was my first introduction to American professional attitudes to medicine as a career, and I was to contrast it later with the dedication shown by the American missionary doctors serving in leper settlements and elsewhere in Nigeria.

Lagos was windy, cool and damp, recalling my experience of Apapa a year earlier. Sailing was a particular pleasure and, once again, I enjoyed the company of the naval officers who were based on Lagos, and had the generous loan of boats from members of the club. I dined one night aboard a corvette, and spent the whole evening discussing Nigeria, its administration, and life in the far North, so remote and so different from Lagos harbour, which was almost all the crew had seen of the country. I walked along the corridors of the Secretariat, chatting with old acquaintances through the open windows until I came to Louis Bain, established at last in the Finance Section, for which he was always destined since his transfer from the old Treasurer's Department. He found the work interesting and even satisfying, but complained bitterly of the careerism and selfishness that regulated the behaviour of some of his colleagues, and advised me to stay in the bush (to which I was now due to return) in spite of all its discomforts.

One of my RAF sailing companions got me a lift, at very short notice, on a plane to Kano, where I stayed the night. Next morning, I was called in the middle of breakfast and deposited into a USAF Dakota, along with the pilot, co-pilot and a good deal of freight. The flight-time should have been two hours, and so, after two and a half hours, I went up front to learn that we had overshot (on the automatic pilot) and were about to reverse direction. We found Maiduguri and landed safely, with a little fuel to spare. I reckoned that the RAF were preferable as flying-mates; they seemed to pay more attention to detail.

It was agreed that I was fit enough to go to Nguru, and the first working day spent with Money after my return from leave was sufficient to convince me of the wisdom of making the move, much as I hated the prospect of leaving my Maiduguri friends, particularly Guy Gilbert, who was so kind, tolerant and unselfish. The DO in Nguru had not been visited for many months, and was thought to be having a nervous breakdown. His last letter to Money contained this remark: 'I hope my relief arrives soon, before the arrears of work assume impossible proportions', so I was urged to pack up and leave at once. I had the choice, in the middle of the rainy season, of making the long, safe, detour via Jos, Kaduna, Kano, about 800 miles, or chancing the 230-mile slog via Damaturu with some 100 miles of road which could be impassable after rain. I opted for the shorter journey, and then found that there was no available lorry large enough to carry all my belongings and staff. After much trouble, I managed to hire a lorry from Jos, only to run into further bureaucratic problems in supplying it with petrol, which took three days to resolve. Guy Gilbert and Robert Coulthard gave me a valedictory breakfast, and I set off for Damaturu, where I had one last day's work to do. On Saturday 28 August we took the road (it was little more than a track) leading north from Damaturu and did very well until about sixty miles from Nguru when the sandy surface petered out and the lorry sank to its axles in the middle of a marsh. I cycled to a village to get help, and then twenty miles on to Gashua, where I was given cold drinks and food by two Canadian lady missionaries of the Sudan United Mission who were stationed there in strange and anomalous isolation.

They talked a great deal, but I was still far from clear about the objectives and methodology of their work among the Bedde pagans when the lorry rolled in at last and we moved into the rest-house and settled thankfully to sleep. I was to see much of Gashua in the coming months, but on the following day my urgent priority was to get to Nguru where we arrived in time for breakfast in a very pleasant, well-built rest-house close by the DO's house and office.

Nguru was an untidy and necessary anomaly in the administrative set-up in Bornu Province. It was the headquarters of one of the five divisions of the Province and the officer in charge was styled 'DO i/c Bedde Division'. In fact, the affairs of Bedde Emirate (for which he was responsible to the Resident) occupied about a quarter of his working time, the remaining three-quarters being devoted to the care of the four north-western districts of Bornu Emirate; Nguru, Matsena, Gashua and Borsari, for which he was responsible to the DO i/c Bornu. Occasional visits to Geidam (100 miles to the east) were also required, involving some arduous and time-consuming travelling.

The DO Bornu would have preferred to forget that Nguru existed. Even Tupper, that conscientious soul, left it well alone, concentrating on the plenitude of problems on his own doorstep in Maiduguri. Ideally, it was felt, the place should be left in the charge of some competent unflappable chap who would implement the general policy (if any) determined in Maiduguri and let sleeping dogs lie, at least for the duration of the war. I think it unlikely that I was regarded as measuring up to this specification, but was perhaps the best thing to hand, and in any case, Money wanted me out of his hair.

The DO was tall, thin, pale, tense and harassed-looking. He was all for making a start on the office hand-over, but I insisted that we should make a rapid tour of the local area in the only available transport, a clapped-out Ford kitcar belonging to the Bedde NA, but commandeered by the DO for the duration. As expected, the general environment of Nguru was much like the rest of the Bornu plain but possibly sandier and flatter – thorn-scrub bush dotted with doum palms. Through this featureless terrain, the single-track railway ran south-west for mile after mile, 170 of them, to Kano City, crossing the Bornu border a few miles out of Nguru. A dry-season road, or track, ran roughly parallel to the railway westwards towards Kano and, in an easterly direction, from the railway station and post office as a service road, past the Rowntree Company's compound, through the trading area with its shops, trading-posts, warehouses (known generically as canteens;

Kanti in Hausa), past a branch into the African town, then becoming the main road to Gashua. From the middle of the trading
area, another service road ran south, for about a quarter of a mile,
to the so-called Government Station, consisting of the DO's house,
with the rest-house, the Divisional Office and the divisional clerk's
quarters clustered around it. The road leading to the trading area
was lined with neem trees and drought-resistant shrubs forming a
straggly hedge. The whole area had an unkempt appearance, which
was not improved by the tattered thatch of the clerk's house and
the adjacent ruin of the former mud-built rest-house.

The DO was anxious to be helpful, and wished to make a
thorough hand-over, lasting a fortnight or so, but I managed to
persuade him to leave quite soon so that I could unpack and have
the place to myself, and have also the undivided attention of the
clerk, Mallam Hassan, a Fulani and the only true Northerner I
ever found holding such a government post. The head messenger
was also a Fulani, and this racial set-up served to emphasise the
unusual nature of this outpost of Kanuri Bornu. Hassan was a
slender, mild-mannered man of about thirty, moderately intelligent,
very hard-working and cheerful under a heavy work-load. The
arrears of office work were truly horrifying, and we tackled them
together, working long hours, without comment on the situation,
and with expressed agreement not to allow it to deteriorate again.

The total work-load of the job was certainly heavy, and I could
well imagine that my predecessor, having been ill, had found the
arrears of work increasingly worrying. I was reminded of the time
when I took over the adjutancy of 1NR , but, fortunately, on this
occasion, I had a better idea of the scope of the job, which seemed
to divide into three main areas. First, the four districts of Bornu
which constituted a responsibility not unlike that which I had held
previously, based on Damaturu, with the difference that Nguru was
a large and growing town, containing a sub-treasury, prison, school,
dispensary and an important court. It was also very remote from
Maiduguri, and was visited by the Shehu and Waziri at most once
a year. Second, Bedde Emirate, which was a small, separate administration, and, as yet, an unknown quantity to me. Its headquarters
town, Gorgoram, lay about thirty miles south of Nguru and was
separated from it in the rains by two substantial rivers and a large
swamp. It had not been visited for several months. Third, the
Nguru 'Government Station' area (for want of a better term),

comprising the railway terminus, the trading plots, the post office, and my own office and surroundings. The divisional office jobs were a familiar time-consuming list including the magistrate's court, and the local (government) Treasury, but to it there had been added the war-time extras of mines labour, corn-requisition and storage, the groundnut campaign, and a fast-growing local industry – the production of dried salt meat. The departing DO complained bitterly that he had been left to cope with all these problems without help or advice while two senior DOs (one senior to Money) had recently been posted, one to a quiet easy job in Potiskum, and the other to a similar assignment in the delightful hilly surroundings of Biu.

By the end of September, the arrears of office work had been cleared, the office cleaned and rearranged, files reorganised. A fairly new typewriter was obtained by repeated telegrams to Maiduguri (there was no telephone link) threatening to cease rendering returns. A start was made on repairing buildings, including Mallam Hassan's house, with noticeable effect on his morale. I began to have more time to spare for the Bornu districts and for Nguru in particular.

The Shehu had a representative permanently stationed in Nguru, a rather worn, dignified man in his fifties, of gentle demeanour and seeming honesty, who bore the courtly title of Wuroma. He came to my office every morning at ten o'clock to report any news and to discuss any necessary action, and I soon discovered that he was worried about the general slackness (he even hinted at corruption) of the local NA officials and the district administration. He arranged for me to inspect Nguru town in the company of the Boguma, the district head who had recently been transferred from the Marghi district, which I had toured from Maiduguri in April, finding evidence of extortion and other malpractices. I have always had a soft spot for a rogue with a sense of humour (some dogs come into this category) and I found it necessary to keep reminding myself that the Boguma was a villain who had been sent to Nguru for close supervision. I made it clear to him at once that I had first-hand experience of his activities in his former position and would not tolerate any similar nonsense in Nguru. It is unlikely that he reformed completely, but he managed somehow to keep his crimes under cover, and we became quite good friends. 'He's a giant of a man, some twenty stones or more of solid bone and muscle, with a great sense of humour and a laugh that reverberates through his huge frame, giving me an uncontrollable desire to laugh just as merrily. He wears a vast robe of dark brown silk, set off with a brilliant yellow turban and a blue cloak on cold days, rides a massive stallion which carries him with difficulty and which has developed spinal curvature from doing so.'

The landing-ground at Wajagal, about seven miles south of Nguru, was intended to form part of the air-communication network of Nigeria, looking towards a future when air-transport would be used to compensate for some of the deficiencies in the road system which were such a hindrance to development and good administration. The place was in the charge of a young Kanuri, a former middle-school boy who spoke very good English and was intelligent, but seemed shy and rather withdrawn. He supervised the work of about twenty labourers who kept the ground in good condition and helped in the operations of landing and take-off. The airstrip was only sufficient for light aircraft, but was being gradually extended to take larger planes so as to be available as an emergency landing-ground between Kano and Maiduguri. I went there frequently, to monitor progress, to pay the labour, and also to try to cheer up the young overseer who was quite isolated from people of his own educational standard and who was, I feared, in a state of mental and moral decline.

The 'road' continued south from Wajagal for some miles, before petering out into the wetlands of Bedde Emirate, which I was anxious to visit, but was advised against doing so before the end of October, when the floods would begin to recede. On 22 October after leaving the airfield, my staff and I pushed on to a village on the edge of the marsh where we spent the night. Next morning, we plunged into the waters and took some five and a half hours, by horse and raft, to cover the remaining seventeen miles to Gorgoram. We crossed the three rivers without untoward incident, and I received only one ducking when my horse lost his footing. We were led by one of the Emir of Bedde's retainers on a horse which seemed to know the way, and which our horses were willing to follow. I removed shoes and socks, since for much of the time the water was washing round our knees. The carriers made a strange sight, with only head and shoulders (and, of course, their loads) showing above the water, and fortunately my precious book-box, on the head of the strongest and tallest, did not suffer immersion.

In a letter, I mentioned the odd coincidence of reading Macaulay's account of the floods in southern England in 1680 when 'it was necessary to ride to the saddle-skirts in water, and none but the strongest horses could get through the bog, in which, at every step, they sank deep'. There were compensations for the tediousness of any journey in Nigeria: 'One of the rivers made a delightful picture in the early morning, with sunlight dancing on the water, and butterflies and kingfishers skimming in and out of the shaded banks. Water-lilies were everywhere, and the very large yellow variety was just bursting into bloom.

'Gorgoram is an old walled and moated town, which had its value as a stronghold in the times of tribal war, but is now the worst kind of anachronism. Surrounded by hundreds of square miles of marshland, infested by tsetse and myriads of mosquitoes, it's not surprising that the population has fallen steadily until the town is little more than a palace-community, just courtiers and hangers-on. There are no markets, no trade, no outside contacts; a most unhealthy atmosphere for any administration however small. Every DO reports adversely on this state of affairs and suggests improvements which would involve some boundary adjustments with Bornu, but nothing ever happens.'

I saw little of Mai-Bedde, the Emir, a rather sad and withdrawn figure, and spent most of my time with the son and heir-apparent, a charming young man who spoke good English and was in charge of the Native Treasury. He seemed to get very little exercise, and so I suggested that we should go for a walk along the only dry path leading out of the town. He seemed reluctant, and I realised that he considered it *infra dig* to go anywhere except on horseback. Then suddenly his face lit up, and he agreed. 'It will be like the scouting we used to do when I was at school,' he said.

Resident and Chief Commissioner appeared to show sublime indifference to the watery stagnation of Bedde for most of the year, until the annual ritual of the submission of the Native Treasury Estimates for their approval, when there was no lack of criticism of pernickety detail. I ran into trouble because I could see little justification for 'creative development' proposals in the decaying environment of Gorgoram. Later, I was able to hit back in the Annual Report on the Emirate, when I commented on the incidence of sleeping-sickness and other diseases and the lack of interest shown by the Medical Department. All this waspishness may have had some effect, because Money informed me, some months later, that the Shehu had agreed to a boundary change which would give Bedde an outlet on the main road at Gashua.

With the onset of the dry season, travel to Gorgoram became easier, and I made a visit each month, without ever feeling convinced that the journey had been justified in relation to the time it required, and the pressures of my other responsibilities. Of these, the most worrying and time-consuming arose out of the considerable, and growing, trading activities in the area. Several of the big trading companies, including the United Africa Company (UAC), had branches at Nguru and in feeder-towns such as Geidam, and there were several small independent traders, including Cypriots and Lebanese, who sometimes collaborated with the larger firms, but usually competed, in buying and selling. The largest trade, by far, was in hides and skins, of which the UAC seemed to get the major share, as also of groundnuts. I was never able to determine the size of the gum arabic trade as the Rowntrees agents were very tight-lipped, but it must have been considerable to support the size of their establishment.

The most troublesome of the traders should not have been a trader at all, since he was a full-time salaried employee of the railway, the clerk in charge of its motor transport. He was a large Yoruba with a bullying manner who dominated the older, milder, amiable stationmaster (to whom he was officially subordinate) and exploited the locally recruited labourers. He was always ready to poach on the preserves of the legitimate traders (who, unlike him, paid rent for their trading-plots), provoking violent outbursts from the rough-tongued manager of the UAC, and more polite ones from the others. He was much involved in the trade in dried salt meat and dried fish, for which there was a ready and profitable market in Kano and towns further south.

Meat and fish were relatively cheap in the sparsely populated districts of northern Bornu where there were vast stretches of empty bush for grazing and the rivers of Bedde, Gashua and Geidam were well stocked with fish. Immigrant entrepreneurs, Yoruba, Ibo and Hausa, had put up some very primitive meat-drying establishments, and were exporting large and increasing quantities of goat-meat and mutton, salted and dried, by rail to Kano and beyond. The clerk meddled in all this, and producers of dried meat and fish found it advisable to be on good terms with him if they wished to ensure prompt despatch of their produce from Gashua and Geidam, the clerk claiming that his lorries were exempt from the restrictions imposed on the use of the road during rain. In my first month at Nguru, there were bitter complaints from the NA roadmen that the railway lorries had by-passed the control gates and had seriously damaged the wet clay-sand surface of the road. When I remonstrated with the clerk, he was complacent to the point of insolence, and warned me that the NA could not prosecute the railway for a breach of NA regulations (this was, in fact, the legal position). I had to agree, but informed him that the situation was quite unacceptable, and that I was determined to find some way of ensuring that he respected the regulations like any other road-user.

The clerk chose to interpret this as a threat of physical restraint of some kind, and complained to the railway HQ in Zaria from whence I received a letter more or less advising me not to interfere with their operations. I replied, informing them that the NA had evidence of independent trading by the railway clerk, and that they were proposing to sue him personally for the cost of damage to their road. This produced, very quickly, a visit from a Zaria-based official (a rare event, indeed) and an understanding that the road regulations would be observed in future.

The health problem associated with the meat-drying trade had been largely ignored by the Medical Department, in spite of reports and appeals from my predecessor. A visit from the MO in Maiduguri seemed to be out of the question, and so I appealed to the MO in Hadejia (a neighbouring division in Kano Province) to come and look at the situation and make recommendations. Dr Pearse, an Ibo, arrived after much delay, and produced a report condemning the whole operation as primitive and grossly unhygienic. During the rainy season, much of the meat was not properly dried and became putrid. The slaughtering conditions were quite horrifying, and the arrangements for disposal of blood and entrails most unsatisfactory, producing much pollution and breeding myriads of flies. It took several months to obtain noticeable improvement, and my efforts to improve the slaughtering arrangements ran into the usual problem of lack of money. Fortunately, I had help from Arthur Pretious of Rowntrees (out of sheer good nature on his part), a useful gang of prisoners, and some cut-price cement from the UAC. The final outcome was a slaughter-slab of approved design and a long rail with hooks from which the animals could be suspended while being skinned (this led to improved quality of skins, free from knife-scars). All this took much time and effort and on completion gave me some satisfaction, if only because it had been done in spite of the indifference and non-cooperation of those who should have given me their help and advice. At this time, there were no less than four engineers in Maiduguri, but none of them ever came to Nguru, and I was left to cope with roads, buildings, wells, corn-pits and the airfield as best I could. With the rainy season coming to an end, I made a rapid tour of Nguru and Gashua districts to check the cattle-tax situation and to organise an immunisation camp for cattle in Gashua district, where there was good and lasting grazing. Back in Nguru, the major tasks were a repetition of those of Damaturu a year earlier – corn storage and mines labour – plus the removal of corn from Geidam and the groundnut production campaign. If one could keep up with the work, it was good to have plenty to do.

30

Sand and Swamp

☙

I T was possible, indeed all too easy, in a place like Nguru, to
become so immersed in its problems and the way of life they
imposed, that the outside world lost some of its reality. Fortunately, I now had the use of a good radio set supplied by the
Information Office in Lagos (Rex Niven's latest assignment) which
helped to keep me informed about the progress of the war, and
the world in which Jocelyn and my family were living. All too
often, I was joined at the time of the evening news by one of the
three British residents or one of the surprisingly numerous visitors
arriving by train from Kano or by car from neighbouring Hadejia.
The autumn and winter of 1943 and the spring of 1944 saw rapid
changes in the war situation in Italy and Russia, so it was not
surprising that my radio (and my limited supplies of whisky!)
brought visitors to my door. Frequently they stayed too long, and
I was frustrated again and again in my attempts to use my scant
leisure and spare energy to write to my wife and those friends
who still kept in touch.

Nguru was, for me, a lonely place, in spite of my meeting many
people, because I had so little in common with most of them, and
there was no one whom I could call a close friend. Tommy Spiers,
the Rowntrees manager and his assistant, Arthur Pretious, were
both kind, generous and helpful, but lived very separately, even
from each other. Tommy (known always as TS) was a retired bank
manager (BBWA) and spent most of his time in Nguru running
the headquarters operation and supervising the warehouse in which
a dozen old Hausa ladies spent their day cleaning and grading the
crude intake of gum arabic. He was a man of about sixty, somewhat asthmatic, of gentle demeanour and firm character, with
social charm but limited sociability. He and Pretious dined with

me occasionally, and I met them fairly often, even called on them, when riding or walking in the late afternoon, when Spiers would be taking his daily stroll and Pretious working in his 'workshop'. They lived in separate small houses built of mud in a compound behind a high mud wall (I could just look over it, when riding, by standing in the stirrups). Spiers maintained a very neat, formal establishment, into which one might, very occasionally, be invited to a drink, but never to a meal.

Arthur Pretious (known always as AP) was a tough, wiry little man with a soft voice and a warm smile, who had been a sergeant in the RAMC in World War I. He had always been interested in things mechanical and was in charge of all the more strenuous operations in the Rowntree set-up. His special responsibility was the supervision of the collecting and buying centres, many of them in remote villages in the bush, to which he travelled in an ancient Chevrolet kitcar. He collected information as well as gum arabic and was, for me, a valued source of intelligence on many subjects. Much of our conversational exchange took place across the Rowntree compound wall, during my evening ride, after I had summoned AP by ringing an old shop-bell which was fixed to the main gate. From the saddle, I would see him emerge from his little veranda and walk towards the gate followed by a flock of doves which he would feed from a supply of food in his pocket. There was a large dovecote near his house and it was popularly supposed that he lived entirely on the eggs. 'Nice creatures,' he said to me, 'but they do breed so fast.'

I was occasionally admitted through the gate, but never penetrated beyond the edge of AP's veranda. It was said, by those who knew him well, that he had a bed, a table and a chair just inside the door, and that the rest of the house was full of racks and shelves containing his 'collection', together with a small lathe and other tools. The 'collection' (catalogued amazingly fully in his memory) consisted of an extraordinary assembly of motor spare parts, light engineering and electrical equipment and spares, nuts, bolts and screws. He had a small forge, and a supply of iron, steel, brass, aluminium, from which he would fashion all kinds of things, including (at no cost) the hooks and rails we had erected for skinning animals after slaughter. His Hausa nickname was 'Mai-taimako', the helpful one, and he certainly lived up to it, frequently supplying someone (even the Public Works Department) with a spare part unobtainable elsewhere. He collected anything and everything he could fairly lay his hands on, and I remember the light of battle in his eyes one afternoon when I encountered him driving off, apparently in a great hurry. 'I've just heard that a Dakota has crashed near Damaturu,' he said. 'There might be something worth having.' I wondered how he knew, and supposed that one of his agents must have wired him from Damaturu, proving once again that his intelligence network was better than ours.

The only other permanent British resident in the station was the United Africa Company manager, a Lancastrian, eager for friendship on the personal plane, but often critical and difficult when I had to deal with him officially. UAC were the appointed agents for the purchase of corn for storage at Nguru and Geidam, and it was essential, if not always easy, to maintain good relations with their people. The other traders, particularly the Cypriots, were pleasant, but always embarrassingly keen to offer hospitality, which I managed to limit to the occasional cup of coffee. In this rather strange parish, which contained so many competing and variously entangled interests, the DO, so often the arbiter of disputes, had to be and to be seen to be utterly impartial. Debts and other claims between Africans and non-natives could not be pursued in the native courts but were proper subject-matter for my own (magistrate's) court. Litigation wasted my time (in my view) and increased the clerical workload, which was already too heavy, and so I tried hard to persuade parties to settle their differences informally, often with success. The UAC manager was more difficult than the rest, but he improved after a visit from the Kano UAC area manager with whom I had a good relationship.

Perhaps there is time yet, before the Reaper takes us all, for some latterday Kipling to emerge to sing the praises of those who entered the Colonial Service to serve by rolling up their sleeves to do hard physical work in great heat and in conditions which no British trade union would ever have tolerated. Carpenters, fitters, welders, electricians, linesmen, miners, tunnellers, plate-layers, engine-drivers all sailed from Britain in their second-class cabins and emerged in Lagos, Mombasa, Singapore and dozens of lesser ports as Foremen of Works, or some equivalent, with emphasis on the Works. These people made things tick, and without their service and dedication the administration of a vast territory like

Nigeria would have reverted to the situation of Lugard's time, when even Residents sometimes took months to reach their primitive headquarters. I have already recorded my respect and admiration for the foremen whom I knew in Katsina, including Len Wileman who moved from that frying-pan into the fire of Maiduguri. In Nguru, I counted Arthur Pretious as an honorary member of the fraternity, and there were two regular visiting members who drove trains once or twice a week between Kano and Nguru where they stayed overnight.

Taffy Glover and Jim Maynard belonged to the small group of British engine-drivers who spent most of their time in Nigeria driving the passenger trains which ran thrice weekly between Lagos and Kano, and also the special trains which made the same journey to meet the mail-boats. As they approached the retirement age of fifty-five, they were transferred to shorter runs on the branch lines, of which the most desirable was Kaduna–Jos, and the most detested Kano–Nguru. Taffy was a large, shambling sort of man, warm-hearted, good-humoured and talkative, with a very loud voice. ('My name is Taffy, but most people call me Noisy.') Jim was small, but in most other respects resembled Taffy and was, if possible, even more talkative. I tried always to be patiently receptive to the flood of words, remembering that the drivers had just completed an eight-hour stint on the footplate, limited to a few monosyllabic exchanges with an African fireman. The heat and general discomfort of the job must have been hard to bear at times, and I was amazed and impressed by their cheerfulness and resilience. I joined them on the footplate during my two trips to Kano for medical treatment, and found that a two-hour spell was about as much as I could tolerate of the hard conditions and the monotonous landscape.

The trains brought a surprising number of visitors, mostly officials on inspection duty from various departments, but only once (on my initiative) from the railway. A hides and skins inspector from the Agricultural Department came to complain about the quality of skins from the area, and was horrified when shown the primitive slaughtering arrangements, before improvement. He arrived with a small suitcase, under the impression that Nguru had a fully equipped catering rest-house, and I had to feed him and supply linen and drinking water. A few days later, in the midst of having my hair cut by Arthur Pretious of the many skills, I was told of the arrival of an RAF corporal who had no baggage whatsoever. 'He asked, blushfully, whether I could put him up for the night. Appears that he walked twenty miles up the line from Kano, and then found that there was no train to take him back. He spent the night in a wayside station and then took the train on to Nguru. He's a regular, only twenty, joined up at fifteen, been to a decent school, has moved all over the globe, written some poetry. I suppose he just got fed up and felt he had to break away from the Kano camp atmosphere or go crackers.' He, the UAC manager and Noisy greatly reduced my stock of whisky overnight, and the next morning: 'I gave Walker his breakfast and decanted him on to the train in the custody of Noisy, who was grumbling about "these bloody brake-pistons" and other picturesque technicalities.' Dear Taffy Glover loved his arduous job, was 'entirely devoid of imagination, complexes or any modern ills', and, for all his garrulousness, was a refreshing change from the neurotics and egotists who so often came my way. These latter included Commander John Carrow, RN (retired) who was generally considered to have an outsize ego, as well as being physically very tall, and was cordially disliked by some who had served under him in Kano (where he was Senior Resident) and elsewhere, including Money who hated him. The job of Resident Kano was supposed to be the most demanding in Nigeria, but an extra outlet for Carrow's abundant energy and ability had been found by putting him in charge of the groundnut production drive, for which task he had the priority use of a small plane in which he proposed to land at Wajagal airfield. Money arrived on a Wednesday for an impromptu visit, and disappeared to Gashua next day to avoid meeting him.

The arrival of a plane at the airfield was a great event, and the whole population turned out to welcome Carrow. We had met previously on a train journey, and again I found him charming and we got along famously. He held forth in very fluent Hausa to the district and village heads assembled by the Wuroma, who translated into Kanuri with much dramatic emphasis. A good time was had by all. Perhaps it helped that the DO's groundnut farm, planted by station labour on my predecessor's initiative, had yielded three-quarters of a ton of nuts. I hired four Hausa women to do the last process, separating the kernels from the shells, and they did a splendid job as well as providing much amusement. They sat on a patch of cement in the garden under a tree, and bashed away at the nuts with sticks, singing and chattering the while in broad Kano dialect, and would insist on favouring me with all the gossip of the town whenever I went along to observe progress. Since every village had to produce its quota of corn and labour for the mines, it was perhaps too much to expect a record production of nuts as well. However, persuasion and a good price had some effect and wagons were loaded and shunted around the goods yard well into the hot and sleepless night, or so it seemed to me.

Money returned to Nguru for two more days and was kind and helpful in settling several problems. We had a couple of squabbles about nothing much, but got along rather well, although I found his company as enervating as ever. Apparently he disapproved of the engagement of Owen Strong (ADO) to Miriam Duxbury (nursing sister), the second such event in Maiduguri within two years. After some probing, he revealed that Miriam had declined to run a baby-clinic in just the way that he had wanted it done, and he had taken umbrage. This was the most extreme and ridiculous example, of the many that came to my notice, of Money's treatment of departmental officials, and after hearing of it I was again thankful that there was no likelihood of my returning to Maiduguri. However, I felt grateful to him for having made the long and arduous journey and for his obvious concern for my well-being. I had the impression once again that this hyper-active DO was relieving a rather lazy Resident of some tiresome travelling, and that I was unlikely to have a visit from the latter for some time, if ever.

We were well clear of the rains, and even the swamps of Bedde were beginning to shrink in the intense heat of the post-harvest season which the Hausa call *bazara*. About three miles down the railway line and a little way into the bush there was a small lake which, as other ponds dried up, became surprisingly well stocked with the common species of geese and duck, namely spurwing and knob-nosed geese, pygmy geese and whistling teal. These birds provided a welcome change of diet from stringy chicken and tough beef, the so-called 'teal' (actually fulvous tree duck) being the slowest flier and easiest to shoot. The best eating were pygmy geese, which swerved and dived in the air at great speed and so were hard to hit, as the UAC manager found, blazing off boxes of cartridges without success. Around the lake and the dried-out ponds, the tall grass used for thatching ripened rapidly in the hot sun, and my mind turned towards repairing and improving the station buildings.

Needless to say, there was hardly any money, and there was even a shortage of prisoners for labour. About this time, I received a petulant telegram from the Resident, relaying a complaint from Jos that a recent contingent of mines labourers had included a considerable number of well-known thieves, and that they were being returned forthwith. I taxed the Wuroma and the Boguma with this situation, and they smiled in a guilty fashion and spread out their hands, palms uppermost, an eloquent gesture. Within a week or so, the jail was fairly full again, and I drew my own conclusions. My anger with everyone concerned but particularly with the Resident and the Mines Office was softened by the satisfaction of being able to employ the labour which Jos had rejected!

The most urgent task was to renovate the house of Mallam Hassan, my long-suffering clerk. Emergency repairs to the thatch had been done soon after my arrival, but it was clear that the building needed a new roof and some protection against termites. With so many visitors, there was a need for more rest-house accommodation, and I decided to rehabilitate the old rest-house and use it to accommodate Hassan while his house was being re-roofed. We also needed more servants' quarters and a stable. All this called for men, materials and, above all, a headman to take charge and drive the work along. Fortunately, I found the right man in Maina Kobbam who took charge of the 'regular' station labour whenever there was money available to pay them. I paid tribute to him, and some of my other helpers in a letter to Jocelyn: 'Thank Heaven for my African pals, who keep alive one's faith in human nature, and one's sense of humour, too. There's Maina Kobbam, the headman, who does everything at the double and who derives immense prestige from the possession of a 50-foot measuring tape with which he makes all kinds of wonderful calculations by a process beyond my comprehension. In colder weather, he turns up wearing an ancient pair of puttees and a venerable army greatcoat. His latest brainwave is to use the spent liquor from the UAC arsenication tank (used for dipping hides, to preserve them) as "medicine" against white ants. For some reason, he refers to this vile concoction as "No. 1" (pronounced 'lumbarwan'). Maina has two inseparable mates or cronies, an old Fulani man and a deaf-mute boy whom he adopted in infancy. The Fulani acts

as a kind of liaison officer between the other two, and the panto-
mime of giving instructions and asking questions is something
beyond my powers of description. Then there is Abba Kichi, the
charming old carpenter, who stutters, and smiles a heart-warming
smile whenever you make a special effort to understand him. All
these, and Usuman, the good-natured UAC headman, are my true
friends, and cooperate marvellously to do jobs that couldn't be
done with money alone in these days of scarcity. Life would be
dull and hopeless without such as these, and old AP, who is always
longing to do something for one, from mending a car to giving a
haircut.'

There were never enough prisoners. I suspect that the news of
the hard regime spread far and wide and kept down the crime
rate. For those committed to long days of hard work, there was
the inducement of extra rations provided the work targets were
achieved. Vast quantities of thatching-grass were brought in, ropes
were woven, doum palms were felled and split to produce termite-
resistant rafters, and all this was done with much good-humoured
banter and even singing. Maina Kobbam was here, there and everywhere, pulling down termite-infested walls, mixing mud with the
poisonous 'lumberwan', measuring rafters and window-openings
with Abba Kichi, instructing prisoners and warders in preparing
the grass to lay on the mats which formed the base of the thatch.
I enjoyed visiting this scene of lively activity two or three times a
day, and saw the new rest-house gradually emerging from the ruins
of the old one.

Three hundred yards away, in the empty space between the
station and the trading-plots, I planned to dig corn-pits. They
would be easily accessible from the UAC store where the grain
could be weighed and paid for before being deposited into the pits.
I agreed with the manager that we would start on this operation
after our return from Maiduguri where we were invited to spend
Christmas.

A jeep would perhaps have been the best vehicle for coping with
the roads and tracks of Bornu, but the UAC's nearly new Chevrolet
light truck was probably the next best thing. Nevertheless, it was a
desperately tiring journey on Christmas Eve, with the worst of the
230 miles to Maiduguri lying in the sandy stretches between
Gashua and Damaturu. In the rains, the sand was fairly firm, and
the worst hazard was getting stuck in the marshy patches. In the

dry season, the hazard was exactly reversed, and so it was always a losing battle. The warmth of welcome from my friends was most refreshing, and the hospitality overwhelming. I was just in time to say goodbye to Jorn and other Americans who were returning to the USA. Guy Gilbert had gone to Adamawa, and I felt the absence of Tupper, now acting Resident in Ilorin and doomed, by his seniority, to move through a succession of such jobs. Derek Wright was wildly jubilant, about to go on leave, and there was an official view that I, too, might escape in April or May if only people could be got back from leave on time and did not get 'reposted' somewhere between Lagos and Bornu. I spent much of 27 December 'in close session with the Resident, having found him in mellow and communicative mood, and really made the most of it. He's even promised to come to Nguru next month ...'

Back in Nguru, 31 December was the end of a month, a quarter, a calendar year, with all that that implied in terms of returns, statements, statistics, estimates, cash checks and stock checks. At the end of all this, and a visit to Bedde, I felt desperately tired, and the Hadejia MO, on a brief visit, insisted that I should go to Kano for a check-up. In Kano hospital they found me full of malarial parasites, and kept me there for four days while they jabbed quinine most painfully into my behind. The MO reckoned that I was a stone underweight, and saw no hope of improvement while I was in Nigeria because of the climate and the wear and tear of the job, or on leave in the UK where food was more strictly rationed than ever. Thus comforted, I returned with Noisy to Nguru and toured the Bornu districts of Gashua, Borsari and Matsena to examine the progress made in assessment and payment of tax and to exhort people to sell part of their harvest of groundnuts.

The recently appointed district head of Gashua, Abba Kyari, was a Kanuri 'aristocrat', one of several heads involved in a 'general post' as a result of incompetence or corruption, or both. He was a very smooth talker with a great deal of surface charm, which he had exercised to considerable effect on the two missionary ladies, with whom I had supper. When I returned to the rest-house to sleep, I found that the floors had been covered completely with Persian rugs, and a retainer of the district head was waiting to ensure that I was comfortable. All this, of course, caused me to examine his work and his tax records very thoroughly, but I could find nothing seriously wrong. Gashua, where there was always a supply of fresh vegetables and fish (combined rather well in mission meals) would have been a convenient and tempting place from which to carry out 'hit and run' touring of neighbouring Borsari district (HQ at Dapchi on the Damaturu road), Bedde (along a dry-season bush-path to Gorgoram) and Geidam (by the infamous sand 'road'). However, I resisted the temptation and joined the UAC manager for a two-night stay in Geidam to stir up the groundnut trade. Geidam, equally inaccessible from Maiduguri and Nguru, was a no-man's-land of shared and ill-defined responsibility. I was supposed to visit it 'when time allowed', and when specially requested to do so by the DO Bornu. In fact, time never really did allow, and visits became a matter of conscience, or rather conscientiousness.

Experience had convinced me that one should spend at least one night in a district HQ when touring, and, ideally, one should also horse-trek to each of the main villages in the district, to get the flavour of it, to assess its needs, and to give people the opportunity to bring their complaints, if any. During my spell in Nguru, there was no time to spare for village touring, but I tried to visit the district HQs regularly, in spite of the road conditions. Dapchi, some forty miles of sand to the south of Gashua, had quite a pleasant rest-house, which I found to be occupied by 'Pop' Bowler, the Senior Education Officer, when I arrived there late one afternoon. We spent a pleasant evening together, and made a joint inspection of the school the next morning. Bowler was a bachelor with a comfortable salary and some private means, which enabled him to maintain a life-style and domestic standards which were quite beyond the reach of most of his colleagues. He had a flair for good housekeeping in every sense of that word, and his dinner parties were renowned for the quality of the food and elegance of service. He toured in his own car, accompanied by a NA lorry which carried all that was required to furnish a rest-house to his standard of comfort. He limited his touring to the better rest-houses, and I was astonished to find, at Dapchi, rugs on the floor, curtains at the windows, cushions in the chairs, and a kerosene-operated refrigerator producing ice. When he retired, he found what was probably his true *métier*, as a sort of hotelier, running the very pleasant Hill Station at Jos, set in delightful gardens, with the best climate in Nigeria.

31

A Remote Work-station

❧

I RETURNED to Nguru for a brief rest before tackling the journey to Matsena, about forty-five miles to the north which, I had been warned, was worse than any other journey of that distance. I found this hard to believe, but in fact it proved to be so. The environment showed increasing signs of desiccation as one approached the French border, and I was reminded of a similar experience when travelling to Kaita district in northern Katsina in 1939 and Zinder in French Niger in 1940. This was the Sahel, the band of desiccation which runs across Central Africa south of the Sahara. It was spreading then, and is now, together with the comparable phenomenon in East Africa, one of the world's great problems. It requires skilled agricultural and forestry management and planning to bring it under control, and there seems to be little hope that these skills will be made available, or usefully applied by the African regimes in most of the areas concerned. In Katsina protection and management of the forest in the west of the province was effective, and there were useful beginnings of afforestation elsewhere, but in Bornu I was not aware of a forestry policy, and we appeared to be short of a forestry officer for most of the time while I was there. Without an official policy of establishing reserves by legal process and providing means for their protection there was little that the individual DO could do, apart from encouraging villagers to plant trees for shade, and as windbreaks. It can be argued, and I would not deny it, that the wartime drive for increased production of groundnuts and corn led to the clearing of large areas of bush, and I found this worrying at the time. The trade in meat and hides and skins undoubtedly led to much over-grazing. I do not know what, if anything, was done to try to correct this situation in the post-war years, but Nigeria was certainly well supplied, in the universities in Ibadan and Zaria, with the knowledge and skills required.

To return to Matsena. The district head had been given some days' notice of my visit and probable time of arrival, and so I was rather surprised to find no village heads alerted to meet me on the way. Within a mile or two of Matsena itself, after forty miles and three-and-a-half hours of jolts, jars, grinding gears, boiling radiator, sticking in sand, pushing and pulling, the Bedde NA Ford settled into a deep bed of sand and refused to move. There was no sign of the district head or any of his retainers, as one would normally expect, and I set off, on foot, in the mid-morning heat, with the Wuroma who had travelled with me. By the time we had reached the little town, we were hot, tired, disgruntled, and prepared to vent our feelings on the district head. The town, or rather village, was set in a waste of sand and was about the most miserable, ramshackle collection of dwellings I had ever encountered. On its very edge, on a ridiculous little tumulus of sand tufted with withered stalks of coarse grass, sat a small round hut – the resthouse. From somewhere close by, there emerged a little old man with a bundle of grass-stalks in one hand and a tattered sheaf of papers in the other. He handed the papers to me and entered the hut to drive out chickens, and remove dust, cobwebs and fallen thatch by vigorous application of his little 'besom'. I looked at the papers, which proved to be the remains of the rest-house register, and my anger died within me. The last entry was dated 1937!

After fifty years, I still have prickings of conscience about doing so little to try to improve the situation in Matsena. The district head was a man in his fifties, passive, unresponsive, quite incapable of producing the energy and drive required to make any sort of impression on a neglected and intractable environment. Sadly, I had to admit that my own energy would not be equal to the demands of this difficult area, in addition to all those which existed more accessibly elsewhere. I reported to Money that Matsena, in its impoverished state, was probably over-taxed, and that its many problems required the full-time attention of a touring officer whenever one became available.

That night my staff and I ate our meal, and slept, under the stars. We did not dig holes for ourselves in the sand, but in other respects I was reminded of the 1NR camp outside Wajir, and, in recent years, the setting of a Samuel Beckett play stirred this memory. There is a tail-piece to this story. In the 1960s, Jocelyn and I used to entertain African students at our house in Kew, and on one occasion we had, as guests for the day, the first Nigerian cadets to be admitted to Sandhurst. There were two of them, both Northerners, and one was called Umaru Matsena, a son of the district head, and probably a babe-in-arms at the time of my visit. His manners left much to be desired and he already had the arrogance which affected so many of his generation in Nigeria, but perhaps Sandhurst cured some of that.

Back in Nguru, I found Miss Baxter, one of the missionaries from Gashua, occupying the rest-house and, supported as usual by my splendid staff, I laid on a dinner-party for her to which Spiers, the UAC manager, his visiting boss from Kano and Noisy were invited. It was a very civilised occasion with a smiling Alhadji wearing a fez and red cummerbund, and Miss Baxter was quite charming. She told me something of her nursing career in Canada and at the Katsina leper colony of the Sudan Interior Mission where she was going to spend some leave. It was there that she had been engaged to a young doctor who died of meningitis, one of many such tragedies evidenced in the scattered cemeteries of Nigeria. In Gashua, she and her fellow worker ran a small dispensary, and visited a number of villages within a few miles of the town, where they had made a few converts among the pagans. This seemed to be a sensible activity, and I felt reassured.

My move from Maiduguri to Nguru in August 1943 followed the ending of the Sicily campaign, and my stay there continued through the desperate fighting and heroism of the campaign in Italy. For those of us living and working in Africa, there was at least the satisfaction that the Axis powers had been removed from the continent and that the Mediterranean had been freed for the movement of our ships. Some of us who had been hoping for improved postal communication with the UK suffered a sorry disillusionment. Letters from Jocelyn in January and March 1944 took seventy and seventy-one days to reach me. In January, there was the first mention of Nigerian troops in action in Burma, and I thought of my old comrades with whom, to my shame, I was out of touch, hacking their way through the jungle of some remote hillside, as we had done, three years earlier, on the Didessa. It was some comfort that their mail might reach them quicker than it did in those East African days. Those who, like myself, were now out of the firing line felt ashamed of complaining about their lot, but the feeling grew, month by month, that the Colonial Office knew very little about our difficulties, and cared less. Even I, with limited responsibilities and living cheaply, noticed the apparent 'shrinkage' of my salary, unadjusted for wartime inflation, and for my seniors, with wives and children and homes in the UK, the financial situation was serious. It was not until the summer of 1946 that payment on revised scales was actually made to the long-suffering Colonial Service in Nigeria and elsewhere in West Africa.

Most of us had an anodyne for our ills ready to hand in the shape of hard work and plenty of it. Following consultation with Money, it was decided that the corn-pits to be dug in Nguru should be similar to those in Geidam, which were about to be emptied. I wrote to Jocelyn on 28 January: 'The digging of the pits for storing corn is a vast labour and requires constant supervision with only one person – RTK – apparently able to provide it. We dug one pit, 26 feet in diameter and 11 feet deep, to hold 100 tons, and it looked fine for about three hours, when it suddenly caved in, luckily when nobody was inside it. Three of the others are still standing up, or standing down, but I shan't be happy until corn is inside them to hold up the walls. The mines labour agony begins again on February 7th and with good management should prove short and sharp. Unfortunately, the labourers have to be carried on the Railway, and the wheels of that organisation grind small and slow in ruts about twenty years deep.' (This remark was not for the ears of Jocelyn's uncle, Wilfred Bostock who, strangely enough, as deputy general manager of the railway, had been in charge of the construction of the Nguru line in the 1920s.)

Another strange circumstance was the arrival, on transfer from Bukuru, of my station-master friend of 1941, who greeted me like a long-lost brother, in spite of finding me again associated with requisitions for special trains and disturbances in the station yard. There had been fighting due to tension between the 'private army' of the transport clerk, recruited from the riff-raff of Southern Nigerian towns, and the locally recruited labour who did the general work around the yard. Having the support of the station-master, I at last succeeded in getting this troublesome clerk transferred elsewhere, to the great joy of the many who had suffered from his activities.

Fortunately, we had quite a generous quota of sunny post-harvest weather when outdoor activity associated with various tasks reached its peak. 'Corn is coming in at a terrific rate, and I spend hours down by the pits where we are storing a few hundred tons of it, synchronising the rather complicated and continuous process of digging, wall-building, anti-termite lining, filling and sealing off. It's an amazing scene. First, there are hordes of the inevitable donkeys, variously loaded with corn, corn-chaff, mats, poles, ropes, braying whilst their drovers are shouting and squabbling and village headmen are trying to sort them all out. The Boguma, splendidly dressed, and the Wuroma, with the Emir of Bedde's son, look on majestically and benignly, keeping informed on the progress of village and district quotas. Mixed up in the crowd are bevies of buxom Bedde women, carrying large calabashes of grain, followed by their spouses carrying nothing. A hundred yards away, a herd of camels from Geidam and other remote places are grunting and groaning in reply to the equivalent noises of their blue-gowned, blue-turbanned, blue-masked Touareg masters persuading them to kneel, or get to their feet, as the case may be. All this in the midst of clouds of dust and such a tumult of voices, and cross-purposes of languages, that half an hour at a time is a full and adequate ration for ears, eyes, nose and throat.'

Not far away, Maina Kobbam and his mates, with warders and prisoners, had nearly finished rebuilding the walls of the old resthouse and were making sure that the top layers, on which the wall-plates and main rafters would rest, were well laced with the evil-smelling 'lumbawan'. Abba Kichi, the carpenter, was engaged on the ticklish operation of splitting the long straight trunks of doum palm which was termite-resistant and would provide wall-plates and rafters. He, Maina and I had an earnest conference to check the dimensions, allowing for the pitch of the roof and the overhang of the veranda, and confirmed, to our immense relief, that the palm trunks were long enough. I returned to the office to deal with a *bête noire*, the Native Treasury Estimates for 1944–45. This time they were for Bedde NA; in the past they had been for Katsina, and then Bornu. 'The damned NT Estimates have been returned again for *further* minor amendments. We played this extremely exasperating game with the Secretariat for Bornu NA last year, and the damned things were re-typed about five times, quite unnecessarily, due to sheer lack of consideration on the part of the bureaucrats.'

The corn-pits were now 'stuffed to the brim' with millet, and were sealed off with a thick layer of corn-chaff, mats, and a great mound of earth smoothed to a close texture with water and left to bake hard in the sun. I prayed that all would be well when they were opened, and concentrated my attention on completing the building repairs and sinking the wells for the schools and the dispensary. One of the first visitors to stay in the rebuilt rest-house was Rex Niven, recently appointed Chief Information Officer in Lagos, showing characteristic concern for the remote outposts.

I used to ride into the town most evenings, to keep an eye on things generally, and to exchange greetings with all and sundry, including the younger NA staff and their friends, who seemed to have little to do but sit around gossiping. Returning home, to get more exercise, I crossed to the south of the Gashua road into a stretch of flat, rather open country which was not farmed and through which ran a 'bush path' from Nguru to a market town in Hadejia Emirate, about ten miles away. In the late afternoon, market-goers would be returning along the path, in single file, with their purchases balanced upon their heads. There were always Fulani women in one group, carrying empty calabashes, snugged one inside the other, followed by their unladen spouses in another group at a distance conforming to accepted standards of masculine dignity. Firewood sellers would be returning to the town with their newly gathered wares. These were the regular travellers, whom I began to recognise, but there was nearly always someone out of the ordinary run to add to my understanding of the strange channels of African trade. One evening, I met an oddly assorted group of men, young and old, who turned out to be tanners, returning to Nguru with python-skins bought from hunters who caught them in the swamps. I found one old gentleman with a freshly flayed python-skin (twenty feet long) rolled up and tied to the top of a large pot of honey on which, he said smilingly, he had spent all he had, to indulge his passion for sweet things.

I took a short cut across country to the station, through thorn-scrub and low bushes with the occasional doum palm. Over short stretches, I was able to canter quite briskly, and it occurred to me that it would be possible with little effort to clear a patch of this ground and level it for use for football or polo or even as a racetrack. The next morning I spoke to the Boguma, who made enquiries and found that the area was of low fertility and had not been farmed for many years. With the help of prisoners released from building tasks, and some long ropes and a few wooden stakes, we soon cleared and roughly levelled an area the size of a football field and a half-mile stretch for horse-racing alongside it. The area was soon being used for football, rather wild polo, and even wilder horse-racing. I hoped that the enthusiasm would continue after my departure, when the rains would consolidate the ground and produce new grass.

On a journey to Kano for eye treatment, I shared a compartment with Robert Eustace, the DO, Hadejia, who joined the train at Mallamaduri. He was going home to his native Ireland on leave, and there was quite a gathering of notabilities at the station to see him off. Chief among these was the octogenarian Emir of Gumel (a small NA in the north of Hadejia Division), who was in tears. 'I shall never see you again. This is our last farewell,' he said. Robert tried in vain to comfort him, said he would surely return by the end of the rains, and finally embraced him. As the train pulled out, the old man uttered a last blessing and waved; Robert and I just looked at each other, both much moved.

Shortly after my return, we had an outbreak of cerebro-spinal meningitis in Nguru, and I sent an SOS to the Medical Officer at Hadejia, who arrived post-haste. We improvised an isolation camp for cases, suspected cases and contacts, and alerted district and village heads to be on the look-out for symptoms. Fortunately, sulphanilamide was available, and was an effective cure if properly administered. One morning, the Wuroma arrived in my office looking very seedy and complaining of headache and lassitude. I sent him to the dispensary for examination, and soon he, too, was under treatment. In the midst of this upset, we received news that the Emir of Gumel had contracted the disease and died. Wuroma became convinced that he would die too, but we managed to pull him through. This disease was a terrible annual affliction in Northern Nigeria, arising in the cold dry Harmattan season, when there was much dust, and families would huddle together for warmth in ill-ventilated huts.

From mid-March onwards, it became very hot in the middle of the day, and travelling, when necessary, was best done in the very early morning. Even Arthur Pretious reduced the length of his journeys and expressed his concern that the missionary ladies had pushed off on a 'walking tour' of south Bedde, covering about fifteen miles a day and sleeping in the villages. I shared his concern, partly because it was a rather wild and ineffectively administered area and also because one of the girls was not very fit or strong to cope with such travelling. I sent off a messenger, asking them not to travel too far from their base, to let me know their current programme and to inform me of any future touring they had in mind. A few days later, I set off on a brief tour of southern Bedde, returning via Gorgoram and Gashua. The ladies had returned, none the worse for their experience, and I felt that perhaps I had been too alarmist.

Travelling along the well-worn bush path between Gorgoram and Gashua in the early morning, I noticed that, apart from minor deviations, the path showed a remarkably steady continuity of direction, and could, with some bush-clearing and levelling, be widened to become a motorable dry-season track. There was still a small balance in the Bedde NT account which might be used for this purpose, and the Emir was, understandably, quite enthusiastic, as the track would link the old, traditional centre with the pro- posed new headquarters of the NA. The work proceeded at an amazing rate, and in April I had the rewarding experience of driving the thirty-odd miles from Gashua to Gorgoram in a little over an hour. I like to think that this is the road shown linking the two places on a recent map of Nigeria.

On 2 April came a telegram from the Resident: 'Synge will relieve Kerslake when latter proceeds leave.' As April wore on, I had another attack of fever, the meningitis epidemic continued, and there was an outbreak of smallpox which helped to launch a successful vaccination campaign. We were all praying for rain, which would bring down the temperature, lay the dust, and put an end to the meningitis.

A passage was booked for me, and I left Nguru on 24 April en route for Lagos and England. The station was tidy and in good repair, corn-pits full and snugged down, Bedde Emirate showing signs of waking from its long sleep, and most of the local thieves were back from Jos. The new DO, whom I never met, should have found little to complain about in my brief handing-over notes, but he was probably surprised to find a forty-four-gallon drum of aviation spirit sitting in one corner of the office. It had arrived one day in January by rail without indication of origin, and the office seemed to be the only place where it could be stored safely.

Research revealed that it had been sent at the request of RAF Maiduguri, and was intended to refuel a plane which would, one day, bring the Resident to Nguru where I had spent eight months, and my predecessor I know not how long, awaiting a visit. Perhaps it happened for my successor.[1]

---

[1] The Resident's relationship with his superiors was probably better than that experienced by his subordinates. His record was deemed sufficient to justify his translation to Kano (the top Resident's job) in 1946, becoming Chief Commissioner 1947–51 and Lieutenant Governor (when the old title and status were restored) 1951–52.

32

A Wife to the Rescue

❦

I LEFT Bornu with some bitterness of spirit, and in the following months I was glad to let kinder influences purge the less happy memories of it from my mind. Later, I felt regret that I had known it only under the pressures of war, which allowed so little time to understand its proud and ancient traditions, and the better qualities of its gifted people. In spite of a harsh experience of its climate and the morality of its indigenous hierarchy, I remember it with a strange nostalgia, and my African colleagues and friends there (for whom the years that followed must have brought hard vicissitudes) with affection and respect.

The voyage home was surprisingly comfortable, the pleasantest of all my war-time sea-passages. The ship was a small passenger liner belonging to the (South African) Bank Line and was well supplied with amenity space for its size so that it was possible to enjoy some degree of privacy. In convoy, somewhere in the Atlantic approaches, we had a prolonged submarine alert, and my last recollections of the trip are of standing in the cabin corridor below deck clad in a life-jacket, listening to the thuds of the scattered depth-charges impacting against the ship's sides.

Jocelyn confirms my recollection of having arrived on the doorstep at Hampstead with the milk on a fine May morning after an overnight journey from Glasgow. Her parents must have got tired of having us around, endlessly talking, and planning to go here and there but not doing it. I was soon aware of the serious nature of the food problem and the constant worry, for Jo's mother, of how to produce one edible (and enjoyable) meal after another from the meagre resources of available rations. The V1 missiles, the so-called 'flying bombs', were an added annoyance which became wearing to the nerves after a time. Jocelyn's father, Geoffrey

Bostock, seemed rather to enjoy observing the pattern of the late evening volleys from a skylight window in one of the attics. Many passed over Hampstead, made visible by the jet flame from the tail, and often one would hear the engine cut out, measure the silent interval of descent before the explosion and wonder who might have been the unfortunate recipients. Most of the bombs passed on towards Finchley or Mill Hill, but a few fell in Hampstead, one quite near the hospital on the other side of Rosslyn Hill, opposite the Bostocks' house.

Some time in the first week or two I reported, as instructed, to the Colonial Office medical consultant in a room on the top floor of the Crown Agents' building in Millbank, from which there was a long view eastwards across Lambeth Bridge towards Southwark and dockland. 'That's one end of Bomb Alley, with a lot of damage,' said the doctor. 'The rest seem to pass over our heads to land in north-west London.' He attributed my run-down condition and attacks of vertigo to 'tropical neurasthenia' and advised rest and recuperation away from the tensions of life in London. We spent some time quietly vegetating in a small farmhouse near Caernarvon. It was all very remote and somewhat unreal, especially for Jocelyn who had recently been so deeply immersed in the intelligence networks of the war at sea, and we both felt an uncomfortable restlessness. Into this setting there was suddenly injected, on 6 June, the radio news of the landings in Normandy. It is difficult to describe the effect it had upon us, although the memory of the announcement is, for me, undimmed, as is the recollection of the sense of elation, mixed with deep concern for those involved, knowing from my own small-scale experience how easily things military can go wrong, through weather and human failing or miscalculation. How near it came to going wrong is only too clear from reading the various histories of the operation.

We returned to what London could offer, including the removal of my tonsils in Hampstead General Hospital while the flying bombs buzzed away overhead. The Colonial Office had promised Jocelyn a passage, and so we concentrated on collecting what we needed for the approaching tour, including clothing, for which no extra ration coupons were available. We were told, at last, that we would sail from Greenock on 4 November, and it was arranged that we would spend the night of 3 November in Glasgow, as guests of one of Jocelyn's aunts. We reached her house in the black-out, and left it in the early morning, in mist, so that our impression of Glasgow was of massive Victorian houses of grey stone turned to black in the prevailing gloom. Our welcome, though, was warm, and helped to cheer the sadness of Jocelyn's parting from her parents for whom, under the paths of the V1s and V2s, we were much concerned.

The SS *Johan de Witt* was a vessel bearing a great name, but even in its heyday of carrying the Dutch to Java and Sumatra it could not have measured up to the standards of P & O. In 1944 it was an overcrowded, run-down troopship, its deck-space so cluttered that it was hardly possible to take any exercise. The voyage was made tolerable, even agreeable, by some of our travelling companions, to whom we said goodbye at Takoradi, and I suppose it was there that we received the routine 'appointment cable' informing me of my posting to Adamawa Province. Most of the Northern Nigerians on board shared my view of it as 'less than ideal but there are worse!' In Lagos we were most kindly met by Rex Niven who, with Dorothy, his wife, made us very welcome in their comfortable house in Ikoyi. The next morning gave Jo her first impression of the chaotic hubbub of an African railway station, and then at noon, having found most of our baggage and got it loaded, we sat briefly on the blazing hot seats of our compartment while the train got under way. Then it was better to stand near the window and try to catch something of the passing air as well as the passing scene: the small villages of red earth set in the green of the rainforest, black children running, waving, shouting, laughing, jumping up and down in the streams as we clanked across bridges and culverts. With nightfall, between Ibadan and Ilorin, there was some slight relief from the heat, and the villages showed as little pools of hurricane-lamp light, with the sound of children still awake and enjoying the cooler hours. The next day, as always, contained the worst of the unbearable heat, with the peak at Jebba during lunch. This was the point at which, traditionally, husbands became concerned about the discomfort, even distress, of their wives on their first tour. Certainly mine found the heat, to which she was very vulnerable, quite devastating and beyond her previous imagining. Unfortunately, much that was as bad, if not worse, lay ahead of us.

During a rather long evening wait at Kaduna, we met a shy but friendly Arthur Pretious on the platform. He boarded our train to take him to Kano for Nguru, while we waited for the connection to Jos. Soon after dawn the next morning, we looked out from our compartment on the pleasant, cool, green country on the edge of the Plateau near Kafanchan, and Jo was delighted with the change to a pastoral scene: encampments of Fulani with their cattle and groups of people with their donkeys on their way to market. In Jos, we met Alhadji and Francis with broad smiles and a warm welcome for the *uwar gida* (mother of the house), which was very comforting for Jocelyn amidst the rather drab amenities of the government (allegedly furnished) rest-house. She went shopping, accompanied by a newly recruited 'small boy', to carry whatever she managed to buy, while I tried to find a reliable lorry and driver for our 420-mile journey to Yola (the headquarters of Adamawa Province). Both missions were successful, and the day was rounded off pleasantly when we were kindly rescued from the rest-house by Bernard Fagg who gave us dinner and showed us some of his Nok culture terracotta figures.

The next morning – I suppose it must have been end-November – was bright and cool in Jos and for the first stage of our journey, travelling east towards Bauchi, but as we descended from the Plateau, the heat increased, and with it the dust, the haze and the jolting-jarring transmitted faithfully from the corrugated road-surface through the tyres and the frame of the lorry to the hard bench alongside the driver on which we were perched. Even I, used to this sort of thing, was fairly exhausted by the last fifty miles into Gombe which we reached in the late afternoon, and for Jocelyn the experience of the train journey seemed mild in comparison. Fortunately, the Gombe rest-house was reasonably comfortable, and the young DO, Bernard Halstead, was kind, hospitable and understanding, and so there was some rest and refreshment before we set out on the final stage of the journey. After our experience of the midday heat, we decided to make a 3 a.m. start, most wisely as it turned out, with the road deteriorating into a deeply rutted track through black cotton soil as we approached the valley of the river Benue. The last few yards of the road ran in a cutting through the river-bank, obscuring our view of the river until we emerged on the sandy bed which formed the northern terminal of the car ferry. We surveyed the scene while we waited for the ferry to arrive from the terminal on the far bank, near the trading-centre of the town of Numan, HQ of one of the three divisions of Adamawa Province.

33

Yola is Worse than Katsina

ॐ

FRICA'S major rivers are very much associated with its exploration and development, and the first sight of any one of them was for me an exciting experience. Of the four great African river systems, the Nile, the Niger-Benue, the Congo and the Zambesi, I must be content with having seen something of the first two, and am glad to have many memories of the Benue to share with my wife. That morning, as we looked across the 600 yards or so of its impressive breadth to the DO's bungalow perched on a little hillock on the south bank, we could not guess that the longer view northwards from that bungalow would later become so important to us. The ferry, consisting of a large pontoon with a flat deck and hinged loading ramps, was guided by a cable slung across the river which served also as a means of hauling it, with the help of some poling on the part of its energetic crew, who brought it to a crunching halt on the sand and jumped down to greet us in true Hausa fashion. The lorry was quickly loaded and we were soon gliding across the relatively shallow water, some fifteen feet below the level reached in the rainy season. We took an instant liking to the ferry skipper, the Hausa Sarkin Ruwa, who was most competently in charge of the operation, and his two sons, who formed the crew.

At the DO's bungalow, we were made welcome by one Delves-Broughton and his wife and given an impromptu and much-needed breakfast. We pressed on with a minimum of delay, to cover the remaining forty miles of good road to Yola, anxious to find our house and get settled at last. Journey's end, however, brought no joy; I learnt that I was to be ADO Provincial Office and that we were to live in the concrete box which went with the job.

A small group of men – a few dozen engineers or architects of the Nigerian Public Works Department – must be held responsible for the acute discomfort suffered by the much greater number of those who occupied the houses and offices designed and constructed by the PWD over the years in various stations. The houses in Yola, including the one we occupied, had been built as late as 1937 and appeared to have been designed to no obvious standards except that of minimum cost. They were two-storeyed, with practically no veranda or roof overhang, and were flimsy in construction, allowing the penetration of heat at all times, particularly sun-heat. All this would have been bad enough even if the site of the station had been the best available, but, in fact, its situation on a rocky bluff overlooking a curve in the Benue containing a mosquito-swarming marsh was widely recognised as the worst in Nigeria. In 1929, after twenty-three years' service, G. S. Browne (Chief Commissioner 1933–36) minuted:

> I have no hesitation in saying Yola is the hottest station I know. In no other part of Nigeria have I been kept awake by heat, though my bed was thirty yards from the house and I had nothing but a towel round my waist. The sheets and pillows were so hot that I had to throw water on them at intervals. In no other station have I suffered from prickly heat, and nowhere else have sandflies been such a pest. One puts up with the hot season in other stations because it is over in six weeks, but at Yola I have known it to begin in mid-January and last till June, with a return in October and November. The only pleasant month is August, which is always the time when Governors and Lieut. Governors go there and that is why the station was not moved long ago. If only someone would motor from Jos to Yola in April and stay there a few days on the hill, and not in a stern-wheeler with electric fans and iced drinks, there would be no further argument.

The argument went on, in fact, until 1933, when financial stringency was added to the reluctance of the Lamido, the Fulani Paramount Chief, to move from Yola as reasons for retaining the status quo. Browne, now Chief Commissioner, commenting on the financial and political cost of a move to the cool heights of Song, sixty miles north of the Benue, minuted: 'All this would be a heavy

price to pay for a lower night temperature.' It is not really surprising that junior officers became disillusioned and cynical in their
attitudes to some of their seniors whom they regarded as careerist
and lacking in principle and integrity.

Adamawa contains some of the most beautiful, spectacular
country in Nigeria, and also some of the best and most delightful
touring areas, including Mubi, in the north, where my old friend
Sam Bradshaw and his wife had spent a happy tour. Unfortunately,
we were not to experience any of this, and I was deeply concerned,
from the first days of our stay in Yola, that Jocelyn's initiation
into the Nigerian way of life (which was also the beginning of our
domestic life together) happened under the worst possible conditions. Our excellent staff were kind and helpful, but we did not
find a very warm welcome among the white population of the
station, though we made two or three very good friends.

The nearly bare rock on which the station was built acted as a
vast heat-storage reservoir, of which I was immediately conscious
each morning when setting out on the half-mile walk down hill to
the Provincial Office, which lay between the station and the river-
side town of Jimeta, from which a ferry ran across the Benue to
the Biu–Damaturu–Jos road. Additionally, after returning from
breakfast, I had to make at least one trip per day to the Resident's
Office in the Residency, and I found all this walking on the hot
rock surprisingly tiring, even exhausting. The Resident, who maintained the ridiculous custom of working in the Residency (perhaps,
as in Katsina, because of a designed lack of space in the Provincial
Office) was a man who had once been Secretary, Northern Provinces and as such a dedicated paperman and a thorn in the flesh of
some Residents (like mine in Katsina). The Provincial Office had
been without proper supervision for several months, and the files
were in the most appalling mess, which I was expected to put right
in a matter of days. Jocelyn, who hoped to have my company at
the end of a hot and lonely day, found that I brought home huge
bundles of files on which I would spend hours in search of continuity of papers on the Resident's favourite subjects – mostly those
related to the latest fashionable theme, provincial development. I
was, inevitably, the unfortunate secretary of the Provincial Development Committee, and was always searching, before, during, and
after its meetings for papers relevant to its past, present and future
discussions. I hated my job, I did not get on with the Resident,

and was worried about my wife who was obviously unhappy and in need of my support while I was distracted by the exacting demands of my work.

The Resident was a bachelor who probably wanted to be friendly, but after many years of living alone seemed to have lost the ability to make real contacts with people. He had a very white face – perhaps from years of office work – which carried a twisted half-smile of welcome on the few occasions when he was pleased to see me. He always wore a bow tie in the office even on the hottest days, something incongruously formal in conjunction with his short-sleeved shirt; this was somehow characteristic of the man and his attitude to the job. The Residency was situated on the edge of the bluff, looking out towards the infamous marsh, from which arose swarms of mosquitoes and sandflies whenever there was a breeze from the east. To mitigate this situation, the building had been completely fly-proofed with wire gauze, producing a dark and rather claustrophobic impression. Soil had been imported to form a garden in part of the compound, and there was a swimming pool, which we were invited to use, adjacent to the station tennis court. These were the only amenities the place offered, apart from the polo ground, which was so dusty that the players wore masks, muffling to some extent the streams of abuse and bad language which were always provoked by this game when played in Nigeria. Possibly this was a tradition established by the Waff?

We survived Christmas, and a party at the Residency, in reasonably good humour and health. The office began to function properly, and I found leisure to enjoy tennis and music with Jocelyn and with some of our friendly neighbours, including Ralph Maiden, the DO, and his wife. We delighted in the company of Major Chipper, retired from the army and a variety of overseas jobs, but now back in Nigeria as a war-time volunteer willing to tackle any task that might arise. I had met him briefly in Bornu in 1943 when he was touring through the bush in the north of the province, organising the anti-locust campaign. Now, in Adamawa, he was in charge of the company of Nigerian Police who were stationed in Yola, available to help to deal with any tribal unpleasantness which might arise. (Adamawa contained a number of tribes which had successfully resisted the Fulani, before the advent of the British, and could still show an independent attitude towards law and order, and particularly the payment of tax.) As a young man, Chipper had served with the Waff but had none of their style and he still had a very useful command of Hausa. Subsequently, he commanded the tiny army of the Yemen, in the tradition and style of Glubb Pasha whom he resembled quite remarkably. He had the most charming natural good manners, which were equally evident whether he was addressing his police orderly, Jocelyn, or Mrs Nottingham, the wife of his visiting senior officer from Kaduna. I had met, and liked, the Nottinghams on the voyage out in 1938 and in Kaduna. They were both very tall, very fit, grey-haired but full of fun and quite without self-importance. As we relaxed with them after tennis, I could not help thinking that Yola might have been tolerable, even enjoyable, if they had been the occupants of the Residency.

We never knew how much we would have become reconciled to the Yola way of life. One morning in January, the Resident informed me that the Delves-Broughtons were going on leave, and that we were to go to Numan in their place. Within a day or two we were packed and ready to go, saying a glad goodbye to the rocks, the concrete box with its electric fans endlessly and uselessly churning the hot air, the Provincial Office, and the Residency which together had comprised our total world during the past weeks. I did not say goodbye to Yola town and the Adamawa NA because no one had found the time (or made time for me) to take me there, and we had no transport of our own for even the most local exploration. In retrospect, I was fortunate in having no involvement with the Adamawa NA which was probably even more corrupt than its northern neighbour, Bornu, and was also purged by Sharwood-Smith in the 1950s.

A lorry was found to take us to Numan, a mere forty miles away, and we accepted the Maidens' kind invitation to breakfast on the morning of our departure. As we were finishing breakfast, the lorry, fully loaded and piled high with domestic staff, their wives and effects, rolled slowly round the Maidens' drive and stopped just outside the dining-room. Of all our personal equipment thus displayed to public view, the most prominent item was the folding camp latrine which had been tied to the framework of the lorry on the outside. Perhaps this was a most appropriate farewell gesture to this detested station, but at the time it was a matter of embarrassment, combined with hilarity, to my wife!

233

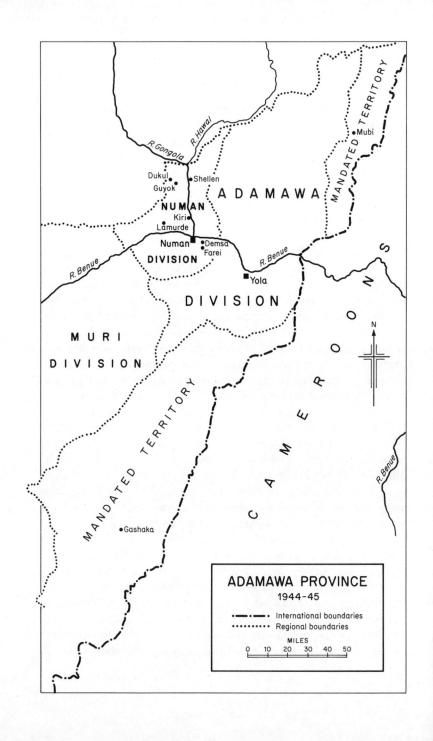

ADAMAWA PROVINCE
1944-45

— ·— ·— International boundaries
· · · · · · · · Regional boundaries

MILES
0   10   20   30   40   50

34

Escape to Independence: Numan

✑

I SUPPOSE that I ought to have asked the Resident to give me some sort of briefing before taking over the Numan Division, but I had by now come to accept, as a matter of routine, the operation of moving into a job with a minimal hand-over. Certainly, I did not receive any briefing, before leaving Yola, on the division's problems, sensitivities or urgencies. Delves-Broughton faced a long journey to Lagos to catch a boat, and I do not blame him for reducing the hand-over to what could be fitted into twenty-four hours. Leaving Jocelyn and the staff to unpack for a short sojourn in the rest-house, I spent the rest of the morning with D-B in Numan town meeting various notabilities and in the station meeting Mr Obba, the Ibo divisional clerk, the postmaster, and some of the Danish staff of the Sudan United Mission. In the afternoon, as I recollect, we drove forty-odd miles up the Gombe road to Shellen to meet the Shellen District Head and the Shellen Native Treasurer, and to check the work remaining to be done in building the new NA school there. The following day Jocelyn and I moved into the DO's bungalow, and we realised that we were, at last, on our own.

In 1930, at the height of the debate on the siting of the provincial headquarters, a committee had considered Numan a possibility, but had found it politically unacceptable to site the headquarters outside Adamawa Emirate, the major emirate and division of the Province. Against this, it might have been argued that rather less than 30 per cent of the population of the province was Muhammadan and 67 per cent pagan, and that Numan and the surrounding terrain was somewhat representative of this situation. In fact, the whole of the Province, with its tribal diversity, offered a wealth of opportunity for anthropological research and administrative development.

When the Protectorate of Northern Nigeria was formally established in 1900, the British found that the Fulani conquest of the territory was by no means complete, and that even the predominantly Islamic emirates such as Sokoto, Katsina and Zaria contained pockets of paganism. Further south, in the hills of the Plateau, and along the banks of the Niger and the Benue, substantial tribal groups such as the Tiv, the Igala and the Igbirra had managed to maintain their independence. In the region which was to become Adamawa Province, a large number of smaller tribes opposed the Fulani with fierce determination and considerable success, and nowhere more completely than in the area which was ultimately to become the Numan Division. This, with its seven or eight tribes free from Muslim domination, was regarded in 1945 as a shining example of a progressive and well-organised pagan division, in spite of the many reorganisations and administrative upsets which it had suffered between 1907 and 1936. I was to find that there was still need for improvement.

On the map, the division is seen as roughly pear-shaped, about 2200 square miles in area, with the Benue running east–west through its lower half, and the Gongola flowing north–south to the confluence at Numan. The eastern and western boundaries north of the Benue contain lines of hills where lived, in 1945, the shy and primitive Lala and Piri tribes, and the rather backward and superstitious hill-Longuda. In the south, the three dominant tribes settled astride the river Benue – the Bachama, the Batta and the Mbula, who had much in common culturally and linguistically – had been loosely joined since 1936 in the Numan Federation, a Native Administration with a court and a Treasury serving a population of about 70,000. In the north, there was a separate NA based on the Kanakuru town of Shellen with a Kanakuru district head responsible for the administration of the Longuda and Lala as well as his own tribe, making a population of about 50,000. With a total population of about 120,000, the division's population density of roughly 50 per square mile was about half that of Katsina Emirate and about twice that of Bornu.

Numan had been an important fuelling and trading centre for the steamer traffic on the river since the early years of the century and had developed a certain cosmopolitan air which combined quaintly and rather charmingly with the unsophistication of most of its inhabitants. The town had a population of about 6000 and lay about three-quarters of a mile to the west of the government station, which comprised the Divisional Office, the post office, the rest-house and the DO's bungalow. A short straight road ran between the station and the town, and there was a parallel road along the river-bank, which served the warehouses of several trading firms, the most important being those of the UAC and John Holt, which operated steamers on the river during the rainy season between Garua, in the Cameroons, and the Niger delta ports of Burutu and Warri, a voyage of about 1000 miles. Between the station and the town, on the other road, lay the headquarters and hospital of the Danish branch of the Sudan United Mission.

I began by underrating the power and influence of the mission and failing to recognise the ambivalence of the attitudes of the tribal chiefs towards it. The chiefs and permanent officials of the NA, even the schoolmaster and the government messengers, saw DOs come and go with disturbing and disorganising frequency, while the mission, which came to Numan in 1913, continued to develop its installations and activities within the division and in the larger neighbouring Muri division. Churches, schools, hospital and dispensaries evidenced a more widespread satisfaction of needs, and some would say a greater usefulness than the government could show. The war cut the mission's communications with its supply and finance base in Denmark, and kept some of its staff trapped at home under the German occupation, but those who remained continued to run the very considerable establishment with great dedication. Characteristic of them, in devotion and continuity of service, was Laura Madsen who came to Numan in 1919, and was, as nursing sister, in charge of the hospital and all the medical services in the absence of the medical officer who was stranded in Denmark.

Numan had been the seat of the Bachama district head since 1921, when the chief moved from Lamurde, the traditional tribal centre about ten miles away to the north of the river. This gave him a strong influence on the town administration and development, and on the affairs of the Federation, as well as close contact with the DO. In fact, I saw Ngbale (his name) every day at 10 a.m. and discussed with him a wide range of matters. He was a sensible, shrewd and reliable counsellor, with a delightful sense of humour, who remained very much a Bachama tribesman beneath his rather formal, Hausa style of dress. He had a network of useful contacts among the polyglot community of the town, and was, surprisingly, a good friend of the Alkali, whose court had been established to deal with litigation arising among the considerable Muhammadan population, most of whom were Hausa by origin. The 'foreign' community, in fact, was fairly representative of the trading tribes and settlements to be found all along the course of the river and especially in the big market towns such as Lokoja and Makurdi. The river had been the trading highway for these people for genera-tions, and they often had family connections in towns on the river hundreds of miles away.

The Numan Native Authority establishment was very small, and its physical assets – courts, Treasury, general office and the in-evitable prison – formed the boundaries of a small town square. The one rather unexpected amenity was a reading-room which unfortunately had little on offer except material supplied by the Lagos Information Office. The NA Chief Scribe, as he was called, was a young, cheerful and very energetic Hausa, Mallam Ma'azu, who was liked and trusted by the three district heads and was invaluable to me. The NA Treasurer was a Fulani, rather effeminate and diffident in manner, contrasting oddly with his extrovert col-leagues, among whom I include the Alkali, also a Fulani, but plump and jolly and broad-minded. The chiefs of Batta and Mbula were also very different personalities. Batta was small and shy and nervous, and I imagined him to be strongly influenced by the priest-witch-doctor hierarchy associated with the fetish at Farei which was very near Demsa, his HQ town. Mbula was tall and burly, blunt and direct in manner, typical of his tribe who occupied the best land in the area, grew large crops and fed well. The Farei fetish was held in awe by the majority in all three tribes, and was the focus of a well-attended annual festival, associated with some sexual licence, held in May at the end of the dry season. Farei was a thorn in the side of the missionaries, who regarded the festival as a dreadful temptation to backsliding among their converts.

The leading spirits of the Numan NA were certainly a very mixed bunch, so varied in their motivations and attachments that they produced an effective system of checks and balances in the overall administration of the area. There seemed to be relatively little corruption or maladministration, judging by the small number of complaints, and this was certainly a relief, after my previous experience in Bornu. However, I did find that the mechanics of the job, for the DO, were quite different from those normally found in an emirate, where the NA organisation could be described as pyramidal. In Numan the organisation was much more flat-topped, and the DO had to supply more coordination and intercommunication. Shellen NA, in the northern half of the division, was quite another matter, as we shall see later.

The spate of paper-work which had been such a burden in Nguru was also fully manifest in Numan, with the addition of the correspondence relating to the 1500 or so soldiers who had been recruited into the Nigeria Regiment from the division – the highest recruitment-rate in the country. (One of them, Corporal Yaro Lamurde, a Bachama, had been in my Intelligence Section in 1NR.) Many of them were now in Burma, from whence there issued a surprising number of letters, mostly concerned with the payment of allotments to their wives. The payment system had been devised by the government to ensure that soldiers' wives (and by imputation their children) received adequate maintenance during their husbands' absence from Nigeria on active service. In fact, the soldiers used the system, quite irregularly, to make various payments, via a real or putative wife, to suit their own personal requirements. Probably about half the payments were made to a genuine wife, for her support, as intended. The remainder were devoted to the payment of a bride-price, purchase of a farm, settlement of debts, or the amassing of savings against the day of the soldier's return. Whether the payments were made and used as the government intended or not, a substantial proportion of them gave rise to queries or complaints from the soldiers, all of which passed across the desk of the DO.

The DO's desk was too small for the work, but too large for the ridiculous little concrete box of an office which had replaced the original mud-and-thatch building in the previous year. The adjacent office of the District Clerk, who was also local Treasurer, was even smaller, but had somehow to accommodate the clerks who worked on the soldiers' allotments. When these were being paid, during several days of each month, the noise and general chaos around the office was intolerable, and I had to let Mr Obba bring his typewriter into my office so that he could work in relative peace. The immediate problem was solved by building a *rumfa* (grass shelter) office for the allotment clerks at a respectable distance from my own, but since this would obviously be inadequate when the rains began, I decided to repair and re-roof the old office. No money was available, so I had, as before, to use prison labour, but this time there was no headman of the calibre of Maina Kobbam, and it fell to me to boss the work along. Obba's house needed repair, and we also dealt with that, without much show of gratitude from Obba who, like many Ibos at this time, seemed to have a large chip on his shoulder, acquired perhaps from too much reading of the *West African Pilot*, then at its most virulent under the editorship of future President Azikiwe. The two allotment clerks were also Ibos, but had no liking for Obba, to whom they were nominally subordinate, and there was a steady crop of tiresome disputes on which I had to arbitrate.

The payments to soldiers' wives required a considerable flow of cash which was financed from the NA treasuries as the government share of tax collected by the NAs. Much of it was spent by these same wives on the purchase of cloth, mainly from the UAC store, and they were certainly a colourful sight when assembled for payment of allowances, reminding me of the scene at Bukuru in 1942. The UAC made large and increasing purchases of hides and skins at record prices, leading to a net input of money into the division, and inflation became quite a serious worry which was diminished, to our great relief, by the excellent harvests in 1944 and 1945.

The DO's bungalow was sited between the office and the Benue on a small bluff, from which the ground fell along a fairly steep path to the river some hundred feet below. The house was essentially a rectangular box divided into four compartments. At the west end was a small dining-room, connecting through an opening with the somewhat larger sitting-room. Between the sitting-room and the bedroom at the east end was a compartment which contained a store, a sort of dressing-room, and a bathroom. Outside the bathroom, under the veranda, was a large water-tank, which was kept filled by the garden-boy with the assistance of a donkey which made many trips to the river, returning with a full load of two petrol cans full of water (eight gallons) drawn from a hole in the sandy shore of the river where there was some degree of natural filtration. All water for drinking was, as ever, boiled and filtered, under Alhadji's personal supervision. The corrugated-iron roof of the house had been covered with thatch, which helped to keep it cooler than the Yola inferno, but encouraged the growth of a numerous colony of bats, which arrived and departed in dense swarms at dawn and dusk. The associated smell became very oppressive during the hottest weather, when the house was kept closed and curtained to keep out the heat and the sun. The site had more soil cover than the Yola station, but there was rock, and, in any case, the whole of the Benue valley was notoriously hot and humid in the months before the rains. I felt sorry for Jocelyn, who had to bear the heat of the middle of the day without the distractions of work which helped me to face the worst of it. However, despite her aversion at that time to arithmetic and accounts, she bravely undertook the monthly checking of the Native Treasury accounts, thus saving me many hours of work, and she also typed confidential memoranda which, for various reasons, I could not entrust to Obba. Alhadji and Francis sought and accepted her advice on household management, meals and food supply, and she did much to restore the self-confidence of Francis which had been damaged by my shortness of temper and intolerant stomach in the last months in Nguru.

Whatever one might say against the house, it certainly had one great asset, its view to the north across the river, and from the veranda along the river in each direction. In our first months of residence, the water was at its lowest, and the stream followed the winding course of the lowest bed, among the many sand-banks which patterned the breadth of the river to the far shore. Only a tiny trickle of water emerged from the mouth of its tributary, the Gongola, which appeared as a wide sandy gap in the tall waving grass of the bank opposite the house. Downstream, to the west, was the line of hills beyond Lamurde, some twenty miles away, often outlined against the spectacular sunsets which spread their glow along the paths of the water. To the east, the river curved nearer to the house, and was somewhat deeper; it was the scene of fishing, by humans, and by the occasional flock of pelicans. The human fishers were highly skilled, using a variety of techniques suited to the depth of water and to breeding and feeding areas known to the fishermen and handed down as secrets of the craft for generations. The most intriguing operation was the netting and spearing of fish by a line of men supporting themselves on large gourds, maintaining their position in the stream by gentle flips of their legs. (The same technique was used in hunting the dugong or manatee to provide oil for the ritual anointing of the priestess at the Farei festival.) The Fulani would bring their cattle to the river to drink, and sometimes, at low water, would drive them across it to find fresh grazing; in the early morning or late afternoon, the scene was of a struggling mass of splashing, bellowing animals, plunging through the water, urged on by their masters.

35

Anthropologists'
Paradise

⳩

I n the great heat of March, April and early May, the last
months of the dry season, we slept out on camp-beds (with
mosquito-nets) set up just before sunset by Alhadji on the veranda or the grassy terrace below the house. In this situation we
enjoyed whatever breeze passed along the valley and often slept
well, so that our first awakening was at dawn, in time to see the
quiet figure of the police guard making his way to the flag-staff at
the edge of the terrace to raise the flag. Then Alhadji, having said
the first prayer of the day, would bring tea, and we would briefly
enjoy the coolness, the view of the river, its sights and sounds. By
seven o'clock, I was at work in the office, leaving Jocelyn to whatever ploys suited her in these pleasant first hours of the day. The
approach to the office, some 300 yards from the house, was through
an avenue of silk-cotton trees, which were very impressive with
their smooth pale grey bark and strongly buttressed trunks, and I
made the journey on foot, unless intending to visit the town, when
I would take a bike, or even a horse. In the latter case, my arrival
would create a flutter among the messengers waiting on the office
veranda. I was glad to have someone to hold and tether the horse,
but could have dispensed with having someone seize the handle-
bars of the bike while I alighted. It was all so well meant that I
never suggested any change in the proceedings for fear of hurting
feelings.

The three messengers, Cheji, Barracki and Sale, were rather
under-employed, but they were needed as interpreters, into Hausa,
of the various languages which were spoken by my 'clients'. Cheji
was a rather tiny Longuda in his early thirties who also spoke

Kanakuru and some Lala. Barracki (his name implied that he had been born near the station or the barracks in the early, military, days) was a Bachama of about the same age, mission-educated and usefully literate. He was a large shambling bear of a man with a great sense of humour, who spoke Mbula as well as his native tongue. Sale was a Fulani who could read and write Ajami (Hausa in Arabic script). He was much older than the others and had a certain elegance of deportment and charming manners. He had travelled extensively throughout the division with several DOs and knew it, and its leading personalities, very thoroughly.

Two or three mornings a week, after a brief call at the office, I rode on into town, enjoying the exercise in the fresh morning air, finding plenty to do in visiting the various NA establishments, and occasionally penetrating as far as the mission schools on the far side of the town. Mallam Ma'azu's office was always well organised, and he and the Treasurer produced up-to-date situation reports on tax-collection, which gave less trouble in Numan than in any place I had known previously. (Perhaps this relatively fertile and well watered area was under-assessed, but I did not have the time to make the sort of in-depth survey of the local economy which was probably needed.) I had to make a regular quarterly check of the Native Treasury cash, and also make surprise checks, which I regarded as much more important. In a trading town like Numan, there was always a shortage of ready cash for speculative transactions and money could be lent at high rates of interest for relatively short periods. It must have been very tempting for a modestly paid treasurer to take a chance on lending cash for a week or so, and I am glad that all those I knew, and liked, managed to keep on the straight and narrow.

It was always profitable to visit and examine the records of the courts – the Chiefs', which administered tribal law and custom, and the Alkali's, which administered Muhammadan law – before going on to the prison. Most of the cases before them were civil matters, marital disputes or property claims of some kind, but there was a small proportion of petty offences, usually theft or assault, which accounted for the modest population, sometimes reaching a score or so, of the prison across the way. It seemed to me that there was something Gilbertian about the near-domesticity of the Numan prison, so different from the stark, sombre establishments I had known in Katsina and Maiduguri. It was Ma'azu's direct responsibility, and he tackled the job with typical conscientiousness. Never were prisoners better fed, housed and clothed for the standard per capita charge, and my morning visit found them all smiles, bursting with rude health, standing beside their 'kit' for inspection. The three warders were rather elderly, and appeared to maintain a very mild regime, with some of my informants claiming that the cells were often empty at night while the inmates were patronising the nearby brothel. I tried to redress the balance by working the prisoners very hard, but their life was certainly much pleasanter than one would expect to find in any African prison today.

Breakfast on the veranda with Jocelyn, looking out across the river, was probably the pleasantest meal of the day, enhanced and prolonged to the full hour between nine and ten by *The Times* crossword of some two months' earlier date, tackled solemnly in correct sequence. When I returned to the office, Jocelyn would have her daily session with Francis, agreeing his market list (which contained some remarkable spelling) and the prices attached to each item. On some mornings, catering would be simplified by the arrival of the Sarkin Ruwa (Chief of the River), accompanied by a rather reluctant fisherman, who had been persuaded to bring his catch, whole or in part, for disposal to the DO's household. Sometimes, the offering would be part of a large Nile perch, and there would always be some grumbling that the calculated value, based on weight (on our scales) and the controlled price per pound, was too low. Fishing was a monopoly activity by a strictly limited craft group, and its practitioners did not enjoy much public sympathy.

I spent the period from ten till two in and around the office, where there was usually a mass of papers for attention, including the various returns demanded by Kaduna or Lagos, which had not diminished since I left Nguru. The prisoners worked hard on the rebuilding of the old office, but the heat was so intense that I was persuaded to release them at about 1 p.m. Obba and I were thankful to escape an hour later, with the prospect of a cool drink and lunch to restore our flagging energies.

Jocelyn kept most of the house shut up, and windows curtained, in the heat of the day, but the dining-room was opened up partially for lunch, and the garden-boy or small boy set to work the *punkah* (made of cotton material on an oblong frame), which was pulled to and fro stirring the air between the ceiling and the table.

Sometimes we were too tired or heat-exhausted to eat much, but we tried to do justice to Francis's dishes, in which he made good use of the limited raw materials available. After lunch came the inevitable siesta, when sleep was welcome if not made impossible by the heat.

Life began again about 4 p.m., with a cup of tea and change into casual clothes for some outdoor activity. If Jocelyn had not been riding in the morning we might decide to ride along the sandy stretches in the river-bed, which were quite extensive in the dry season. We had acquired, from the Delves-Broughtons, a lively little chestnut for Jocelyn. This horse had very dainty feet and seemed to find the soft going in the sand very exciting, setting off at a brisk gallop for the first half mile or so and occasionally unseating his rider. Many Nigerian ponies had hard mouths (like this one), perhaps from the use of the cruel native bits, and could be hard to control when using the standard humane curb or snaffle. However, we both enjoyed these wild scurries as a refreshing start to the second enjoyable spell of the day – the brief interval between the slackening of the heat of the afternoon, around 4.30 p.m., and sunset, around 6.30. There was always enough water in the river to enable us to make use of the one perquisite attaching to the Numan job, a dug-out canoe which could accommodate two 'passengers' and one man to pole it, punt-fashion, from the stern. We used the canoe as a most convenient, and restful, means of approaching the farmland and neighbouring bush which lay beyond Numan town, the area most productive for an hour's hunting of guinea-fowl and bush-fowl. Jocelyn accompanied me on these expeditions, and enjoyed the canoe-trips but found the long, hot walks in search of game very tiring.

The care and custody of the canoe was the responsibility of the Sarkin Ruwa, who always detailed one of his two sons, Musa or Sajo, to pole it, to search for game and generally to look after us. We enjoyed the company of these two young men, their simple conversation and homespun philosophy, so full of humour, expressed in clear slow Hausa for Jocelyn's benefit. The late afternoon light on the river provided a splendid background for spectacular displays of formation-flying by flocks of birds which were probably small waders such as stints. On one memorable occasion, we crossed the river to get a closer view of a group of crested cranes dancing their courtship ritual in which they were so absorbed as to be oblivious of our near approach. The broad sweep of the river was otherwise empty, quiet, utterly peaceful, and one had the feeling of sharing a timeless experience with these birds.

On our more sociable days, we would take exercise with Mathiesen, of the mission, or John Elliott, the UAC manager. Mathiesen was a quiet, gentle man in his thirties, deputy to Engskov, the head of the mission, who was a very dominant character. We played tennis at the mission on a court which had a surprisingly good surface of baked mud, tough enough to survive about three months' play in the dry season. On entering the mission compound, we would be greeted by a smiling row of African children, some of them Laura Madsen's 'orphans' (who had started life as babies in one of the rooms of her bungalow), standing at the salute; these were our team of ball-boys. Mathiesen seemed to enjoy having company outside the mission circle, and we persuaded him occasionally to join us, with John Elliott, for table-tennis or tenniquoit, played on the grassy terrace below our bungalow. John, who was a specialist in the hides and skins trade, was a marvellous person to find as the only other Britisher in this small station; we might so easily have had someone quite incompatible. He was always cheerful, helpful and supportive, never demanding, and we found the same qualities in him years later when he spent a family holiday with us in Norfolk. In Numan, he had a radio and motor transport which he shared with us who had neither, making our life more agreeable and my job more feasible.

After bath and dinner, we spent our evenings quietly, either reading or listening to records on our EMG gramophone. In the dry season, we sat on the veranda where a small cohort of toads welcomed the lamplight which enabled them to catch mosquitoes and other insects, leaping high with amazing speed and accuracy. At ceiling level, a similar service was rendered by a resident company of lizards, helping to keep the insect menace at a bearable level. In the rains, the insect population increased enormously, and we were driven to take refuge within a mosquito-net 'room', an eight-foot cube which I had purchased, in an inspired moment, from a tropical outfitters in London. Certainly, insects were always a nuisance after dark and it was something of a relief to be in bed at last, with mosquito-net tucked in, and, before sleep came, to listen to the night noises as an auditor and not as a combatant.

There was much to do in and around Numan, and much to

learn, but I was aware of the urgent need to spend as much time as possible in Shellen District, where Amna Shellen, the youngish district head, had a bad reputation for autocratic behaviour giving rise to many complaints, particularly among those people – the Longuda and the Lala – who were not of his tribe. Shellen was only forty-five miles from Numan, but to reach it I had to hire motor transport from the Adamawa NA, ferry it across the Benue, take it up the dry-season road to the village of Lakumna and thence proceed on horseback across the Gongola to Shellen. This was the fast, dry-season, transit. In the rains, when the rivers were in flood and the dry-season road became a morass of sticky black cotton-soil, the only approach was by barge.

Shellen was little more than a village, and we enjoyed the rural quiet of the place, the simple but spacious round thatched rest-house and the climate, which seemed fresher and somewhat cooler than at Numan. These things were some compensation for the large number of complaints and other evidences of maladministration which were the main subjects discussed at my meetings with Amna Shellen who seemed to be suspicious of me and my intentions, and was surly and even arrogant on most occasions. He was on very bad terms with the mission who had closed their school in Shellen after much disagreement and decided to concentrate their efforts at Guyok, in Longuda country, a few miles from Shellen, west of the Gongola. This left a gap in the divisional education scheme, and my predecessor had started the building of a Native Authority school at Shellen which was progressing well under the foremanship of a mission-trained carpenter who, like his counterpart in Nguru, suffered from a stammer which considerably lengthened our technical consultations.

With the school nearing completion, I had to make sure that the initial intake of pupils (inevitably all boys) was reasonably balanced as between the Kanakuru (the local tribe) and the Longuda, who would need to find local accommodation for their children, possibly with relations or fellow tribesmen who had settled in Shellen. It had also been agreed in Yola that every effort should be made to persuade two of the Lala village heads to send their sons to the school. I was assured by Amna Shellen that this would be impossible, and so one day I set off to spend a night in the Lala hills, leaving Jocelyn in Shellen. I met the two village heads, quiet, shy, and perhaps rather frightened people, and had quite a long chat with them, using Cheji as interpreter, with some help from a Lala who spoke Kanakuru. They were obviously afraid to expose their children to the influences and adverse pressures of the school, as they saw it, and were also worried about accommodation for them. I tried to convince them that the tribe could not remain isolated for ever, and that they should try to avoid a situation, some years in the future, in which they, unlike their neighbours, would have no one with education to represent them. When I left next morning, I was given a reluctant promise that they would produce two Lala boys from somewhere to attend the school before the end of the year.

My overnight stay in Lala had provided an opportunity for Cheji to make some enquiries about a former village head who had just returned to his home after serving a sentence in Kaduna jail. I had received a telegram from the prison governor warning me of the man's release, and had read the divisional file on the case which revealed a strange story of Lala primitive beliefs and attitudes. It seemed that a woman from a village plagued by a man-eating leopard had been killed by the leopard while walking along a bush path past a small farm which was enclosed, in the common local fashion, by a thorn fence. When she failed to return home, a search party, armed with spears, went out to look for her and found her body. They also found the owner of the farm working on his land inside the fence. Paw-marks and the woman's injuries left no doubt that she had been killed by a leopard which appeared to have jumped over the fence into the farm. The searchers, who included the woman's husband and the village head, looked for tracks made by the leopard when it left the farm and failed to find any. They were convinced that the farmer was a were-leopard, and the village head thereupon killed him with his spear. The farmer's relatives informed Amna Shellen, who informed the DO, and the village head fled to escape arrest. He remained in hiding for some months but was finally traced by skilful shadowing of the movements of his wife. The DO took a detachment of armed police (a normal precaution for many years during a dispute with an 'unsettled' tribe), surrounded the hiding-place, a very remote village, by night and secured the surrender of the village head.

At the trial, the judge (I think it was my wise old friend Judge Ames) took an understanding and lenient view of the affair and imposed a moderate sentence of imprisonment. It then remained for the DO to inform the Lala that the village head they considered to be a hero and a protector was really an ignorant and misguided man and adjudged a criminal. He, they, and everyone must accept the greater wisdom of the wider world that were-leopards did not exist and that it was wrong to accuse someone of being a part-time leopard. They were told to choose another village head but refused again and again before they finally accepted the prisoner's brother.

Cheji knew the history of the case very well, though he had not been involved in the affair at the time. He was regarded with some suspicion by the Lala, and it was only by helping them to consume large quantities of their home-brewed beer that he obtained the information I needed as to whether the authority of the new village head had been destroyed by the return of his brother. It seemed that the official position was sustained but the new village head acted now only after consultation with his hero-brother. The man-eating leopard had not reappeared, and the Lala were convinced that they (unlike the DO and similar misguided fools) knew the reason why.

On our way back to Numan, we made a diversion to spend a night at Guyok, where we found an American missionary couple, and the impressive village head, full of complaint against Amna Shellen. This was the country of the Longuda of the fertile plains, well nourished, vigorous people, increasingly exposed to the influence of the mission but respecting and fearing the ancient tribal cults based on Dukul, the chief village of the Longuda hill-country some miles to the west of Guyok. I met the chief of Dukul, the priest of the cult and rain-maker, a pathetic bleary-eyed figure, but obviously a person of much influence and authority for a people who did not dare to disbelieve in his power to produce or withhold the rain needed to grow their crops. Superstition and fear of anything new caused some Longuda to continue living in the old hill-villages (sanctuaries in the times of the tribal wars), even though most of them farmed in the plain. With poor water supplies and insanitary housing, they had a sorry health record, including a high incidence of leprosy. Altogether, this was a thoroughly frustrating state of affairs for any DO, and one longed to charge in and sort out the situation on a basis of reason and common sense, but caution, and awareness of the almost certain disapproval of my seniors for any precipitate course of action, prevailed.

I worked off my frustration in the neighbouring village of Bobini, on the main road. This was a recognised overnight stop for travellers, which had lived down its former reputation for cannibalism (described pithily in Hausa: 'Bobini, where the stranger doesn't complain of feeling cold') and had a thriving market which I found to be filthy beyond any previous experience. I suggested to the village head that we should pull down all the stalls, burn them, and make stallholders build anew on an adjacent site with shade trees, which fortunately was available. The idea proved popular, and I have never seen people work so fast. As we left for Numan in the late afternoon, the new stalls were being thatched while a vast column of smoke ascended from the site of the old market.

It was now the turn of Numan and the surrounding villages to experience the scourge of cerebro-spinal meningitis which had caused so much distress in Nguru the previous year, and I was thankful, this time, to have the help of the mission and, in particular, Sister Laura Madsen and her staff, to cope with it. A team of African nurses went out into the villages to treat cases on the spot and to bring in to our improvised isolation hospital those which required nursing. The new wonder-drug M&B 693 proved its worth in curing most cases, and my information was that very little of it found its way to the black market for the treatment of VD, which said much for the integrity of the mission staff.

April and early May found everyone praying for rain to bring an end to the meningitis, to the heat, humidity and dust, and to start things growing again. We, Jo and I, decided to do a classical horse-trek, with carriers, into Batta district, to reach some of the 'inland' villages while the paths were still open. We left at dawn one morning, intending to breakfast at Demsa, a trek of ten miles or so. We had been going for about an hour when a violent storm blew up, with amazing suddenness, from the south. The wind, at tornado strength, was soon accompanied by sheets of rain which turned the bush path into a stream of mud in which the horses slithered uncontrollably. We dismounted, and slithered, utterly drenched, with staff and struggling carriers, back to Numan, to baths and breakfast, produced with remarkable speed and cheerfulness by our efficient staff. This marked the beginning of the rains, and in the following weeks the Benue and the Gongola came into flood and began to dominate our lives and influence all our movements.

36

Final Scenes and Farewell

❦

THIS rapid filling of the rivers was our great local event, but we were aware, increasingly, from the early months of 1945, of greater developments in the larger world. The DO Numan, unlike the DO Nguru, was unprovided with a radio set, but our good friend John Elliott invited us very often to join him, over the evening drink, to listen to the BBC World Service news with comment supplied, I think, by Vernon Bartlett or someone of similar calibre. So we were able to share, in our remote outpost, in the excitement which grew, day by day, in April and early May as German resistance began finally to crumble.

At about this time my relations with Engskov, the head of the mission, had become distinctly cool. I had sensed, since our arrival, that the mission was becoming increasingly intolerant of tribal cults, and that there were indications that it was developing an open attack on them. One morning, I found the Sarkin Bachama and the Sarkin Batta awaiting me, with long faces, at the office after breakfast. They complained that the mission had built a church (a round, thatched hut) within earshot of the cult-house at Farei, where the famous (or infamous) fertility festival was due to take place within a fortnight or so.

This was bad enough, but there was also a bell, which was rung for services, and this they could not tolerate. I promised to look into the problem, and sent a note to Engskov, asking him to call in to discuss the matter. We had a distinctly unpleasant meeting, at which he insisted that they had as much right to open a church in Farei, where they claimed a few converts, as anywhere else. He refused to accept the fact that Farei was a very special place, or that the ringing of the bell was a provocative action, particularly at this time of year, and I listened to a long defence of the mission's attitude, which amounted to clear and open opposition to all pagan beliefs and practices. I could understand, and even sympathise with, his views, but could not allow the mission to incur the risk of serious disorder, possibly even a large-scale riot, during the festival period. I advised him to stop the bell-ringing, and hoped that he would agree at once, to avoid any need for formal legal procedures. Reluctantly, he complied, but there was no meeting of minds. I considered him to be too actively propagandist, ambitious and self-important. He regarded me as an unsympathetic reactionary, a view to which I may have contributed by my recent lenient treatment of a group of adherents of the Mam cult. Mam was a brotherhood, fairly widespread along the upper Benue, characterised by some unpleasant practices, including arm-cutting and ritual mutual blood-drinking. As a kind of freemasonry, with a binding commitment to mutual support, it had an appreciable following among a number of otherwise unrelated tribes. It was proscribed by government (which was understandably opposed to anything which might undermine, or be alternative to, the established power-structure) and hated by the missions because it was a pagan cult which transcended tribal boundaries and beliefs, and could be regarded as a direct challenge to their own activity. There had been unconfirmed reports of Mam rituals among the Bachama on the western boundary of the division, but the Sarkin Bachama made light of these until information was laid against a group of young men by a mission evangelist who was working among the villages to the north of the river. The Sarkin Bachama brought them to Numan together with the ironmongery and other paraphernalia of the cult, which were destroyed, after a trial of the case in the Federation court. I decided not to report the affair to Yola, which would have produced masses of paper-work for me and Kaduna prison sentences for the young men. Instead, the head warder gave each of them 'six of the best' in public, and they were returned to their village with a warning.

A day or two after the bell-ringing argument (it must have been 5–6 May), one of the messengers reported that Mr Engskov was walking up the road towards the office, and my heart sank in anticipation of more acrimonious discussion. To my surprise and relief, he entered the office with a radiant expression and hand outstretched to express, on behalf of all 'his people', their gratitude and joy at the liberation of Denmark by British forces. He was particularly delighted that those forces had been commanded by a true, professing Christian, Field-Marshal Montgomery!

On 8 May, the chiefs mustered as many people as possible into the little town square, and I rode down, in some state, to announce the end of the war in Europe. I had to moderate my own feelings and expression, realising that this happening was of limited significance for many in the audience whose husbands, sons and brothers were still fighting the Japanese in Burma, where 'Commonwealth' troops had retaken Rangoon on 3 May. I, too, was thinking of my old comrades who were still involved in the bloody battles of a half-forgotten army, and regretting my own forgetfulness of them.

We were a thousand miles from Lagos, and had no radio set, but we were made increasingly aware of the pressures which were building up within Nigeria, partly as a result of the war, but also through the spread of ideas and ideology, increasing 'middle-class' affluence, and the growing influence in the villages of Christian missions and Islam. I had the impression, as ever, that the DO on the spot was expected to get on with the job, making as little fuss as possible and not asking questions to which there were probably no answers. The Resident sat tight in Yola, or toured elsewhere, and we in Numan, a little over one hour's drive from the Provincial HQ by an all-season road, saw him not at all. The first-ever general strike in Nigeria, which appeared to be Ibo-inspired from Lagos, caused the Resident to sit tighter still, and we discussed my local situation by telephone on the Yola–Numan telegraph line, a facility normally denied to us by the P & T. I dealt very firmly with my clerk, Mr Obba, and his colleagues, who reluctantly agreed to carry on working. I had another row with Obba at about this time, provoked by his attempt to propagate a scandalous accusation, which had been published in the West African Pilot. It began one morning when he entered my office brandishing a copy of the Pilot carrying banner headlines alleging a plot by the Governor to assassinate Dr Azikiwe, the editor, who had 'fled into hiding'. Obba was wildly excited, almost incoherent, and I asked him whether he believed this rubbish. He said that he did, and that he intended to spread 'the news'. I suspended him from duty forthwith, and promised him further discipline if he attempted to spread the rumour. The next day he came to apologise, saying it was 'all a mistake'. The strike and Azikiwe's journalistic antics had little or no effect in the North, but were regarded more seriously in the South. Strangely, the published memoirs of Niven and Sharwood-Smith and others who attained high office and knighthoods contain no reference to these occurrences, perhaps in recognition of the fact that Azikiwe had, after all, as the first President, finally joined the establishment, with all sins forgiven.

In remote Numan, we were aware of these events only as sudden ripples on the ebb and flow of our daily lives, but they were evidence of the increasing pace of change, and I was concerned to know what should be done to help the people of the division, so varied in their cultures and their 'development', to cope with the imminent problems of the future. I could have discussed these matters with Niven, Tupper-Carey, or even Money, but this Resident seemed too cold and bureaucratic for the kind of down-to-earth talk which I needed. More than anything, the division needed the services of a trained anthropologist to help the DO to develop and strengthen the native institutions and traditional authority structures, to enable them to deal more effectively with the organised pressures from the outside world. Such help was not forthcoming, and I had to rely on the useful but rather sketchy notes on the tribes produced by C. K. Meek, the one and only 'Government Anthropologist' in the 1920s and 1930s. Jo was very understanding of my preoccupation with these problems, and was really the only person with whom I could discuss them. She helped me to draft, and finally typed, the confidential proposals for the reorganisation of the division, which were put into effect, with some improvements, a few years later.

I took as my starting point the undoubted success of the Numan Federation of the Bachama, Batta and Mbula tribes, and considered ways of enlarging the Federation to include the remainder of the division. People (such as Amna Shellen and the Chief of Guyok) were available to represent the Kanakuru and the Longuda, but the more backward elements such as the Lala would continue to need the special protection of the DO while they 'grew up'. I realised that this arrangement might involve some dilution of the effectiveness and cohesion of the existing Federation, but felt convinced that the enlargement would provide some kind of education and mind-broadening for all concerned. I saw it as an exemplar of what would need to be done throughout Nigeria to develop regional cooperation in administration as one of the essential steps towards ultimate self-government, and it became a matter of urgency amounting to obsession to produce firm proposals for the reorganisation and feed them into the bureaucratic channel before I left the division, probably, on past experience, never to return.

My state of health may have added to the sense of urgency. The rains brought a great increase in the mosquito and sandfly population, and one got bitten by day as well as by night. Dengue fever came on me quite suddenly, with aching bones and muscles and painful swollen glands. I ran the office from bed or armchair for three weeks with Jocelyn's help and nursing, and then, a little later, developed an ear infection which required treatment in Jos, 520 miles away by the all-season road through Yola, Biu and Damaturu. Fortunately, we were able to travel fairly comfortably with our kind friend John Elliott, and I was soon back on full duty, as the river trading season began to reach its peak.

The river steamers, operated by the United Africa Company and John Holt, were paddle-boats of shallow draught which possessed none of the glamour of their Mississippi counterparts. They were highly functional transporters of tropical produce, with a few deck passengers sprawling at ease on the upstream journey or perched among the sacks and bales on the heavily loaded return trip. Some of the passengers were rogues and tricksters from the big towns, hoping to make easy money in trading with the simple peasantry, and there were criminals, too. The police resources of Numan (normally a handful of Native Authority policemen) were augmented during the river-season by a detachment of armed Nigerian Police from Yola. They met all the steamers, and kept an eye on the movements of travelling strangers. Nevertheless, we had a pathetic case of the rape and murder of a very young girl, which remained an unsolved mystery.

I suppose we must count ourselves fortunate that we did not 'lose' any of our few possessions, with the sole and extraordinary exception of a pot of Jocelyn's very precious (almost unobtainable) face-cream. We were convinced that it was stolen from her dressing-table near an open window by one of a gang of prisoners who were cutting grass around the house. We had been so plagued by mosquitoes that I decided to clear the grass and rank vegetation which grew in the creek between our house and the John Holt bungalow, which was occupied by one of their people during the steamer season. The work took a week or so, and produced some moments of drama and comedy to enliven Jocelyn's quiet mornings. One day, as we were finishing breakfast, there was a great commotion in the compound, and as I went out to investigate I met the garden-boy holding by the tail the still-twitching corpse of a puff-adder which had just been killed by a prisoner. Seconds later, a large black and white mongoose broke cover from the grass in the creek, and was pursued by the entire gang of prisoners brandishing machetes and shouting wild hunting cries. The warders, waving their batons, brought up the rear of the hunt which soon spread out over most of the road into the town, with the mongoose well in the lead. There was no mongoose soup in the prison that night, and, being soft-hearted, I did not impose any other restriction in rations on account of this breach of discipline.

There was another, more serious, incident a few days later. I was working quietly in the office when Sale, the Fulani messenger, trying hard to combine his natural dignity with a sense of urgency, entered swiftly to announce that a prisoner had escaped into the river. I ran to the house and found Jocelyn, servants, prisoners and warders watching the bobbing head of the fugitive as he swam strongly towards the far shore. Responding to the shouts and appeals of the warders (one of whom was nursing a nasty wound from the prisoner's machete), a canoe carrying three or four people tried to head off the swimmer who responded by capsizing the canoe and continuing on his way. He emerged on the far bank and disappeared into the long grass, never to be seen again. I was informed that this was really no violent criminal; he had been convicted of wife-stealing and was described by the Alkali as an incurable and highly successful philanderer. 'You have seen that he is a very strong man; the women cannot resist him; even those in purdah are not safe.' We assumed that he had gone to torment the husbands in his native Gombe district. I warned the DO there, but we heard no more.

The maintenance of purdah was a kind of status symbol in all Muslim communities of Northern Nigeria. It was not practised by the poorer folk or the nomadic Fulani, whose wives worked and went to market. In a town such as Numan, with a very mixed population, it must have been particularly frustrating for women in purdah to be aware of the freedom and educational opportunities available to other women. Islamic schools for girls had been established, after much conservative opposition, in several major emirates, but they experienced great difficulties through the operation of purdah. They were staffed initially, at great expense, by British women, and it was planned to appoint African women staff (Northern Muslims, for the Emirs would not tolerate Southerners although they were available) as and when suitable candidates became qualified. Unfortunately, nearly all the girls who emerged from the top forms of the schools and then became teachers were soon married, entered purdah, and were lost to the cause of women's education. For the mission schools the situation was quite different, Christian girls being very willing to become teachers, whether married or not, and the girls' school of the Numan mission became one of the best, perhaps *the* best, in the whole of the North. I always felt unhappy about purdah, the loss of liberty and sociability that it involved in the context of a Nigerian town or village. It was one of the many inevitables of the environment in which we worked.

Another seeming inevitable was the lack of equipment and resources to do the job. People with experience of Malaya and other well-endowed territories were horrified by the poor quality of our housing and the absence of the high-quality support facilities and competent subordinate staff to which they had been accustomed. Roads and transport available to us during the dry season were bad enough, but at least it was then possible to cover the ground, however slowly and uncomfortably. In the rainy season, it simply was not possible to travel by horse or on foot because so much of the land was flooded and the paths a morass of mud. However, the main rivers were navigable for several weeks during the height of the rains, and the government recognised this fact by providing the loan of a Marine Department barge for this period. This vessel was always referred to as 'the Resident's barge' and it was made very plain to me that I was no. 4 on the list of those entitled to use it, below the Resident, the DO i/c Adamawa and the DO i/c Muri (my neighbour on the Benue, downstream, whom I never met). The Resident made use of the barge for what proved to be his sole visit to us in Numan. Travelling only along the Benue, he made up for the lack of any mechanical motive-power in the barge by the simple expedient of attaching it to one of the steamers. Clad in shorts and bush-shirt, he seemed to have assumed a different persona, something like a boy on holiday. We had a pleasant dinner-party, and he disappeared downstream next day, never to be seen by us again.

The competition for the use of the barge was not as great as I had feared before experiencing its slowness and lack of amenities and we had no difficulty in securing it for the essential monthly visits to Shellen and occasional short trips along the Benue. The vessel was, I suppose, about thirty feet long and six feet wide, and was divided into three compartments covered by a light timber roof. The central section served as living-room, bedroom and tiny separate bathroom; the galley and servants' quarters were in the stern, and the crew (when present) occupied the bow section. The 'captain' of the barge, an ancient gowned and turbanned gentleman from Lokoja (on the Niger) where it spent the dry season, sat on the roof, pulled the rudder strings and shouted instructions to the crew which were generally disregarded. Eight local men, selected for their muscle-power and endurance, constituted the crew who propelled the barge, against the current, by all the force they could bring to bear on their long bamboo poles. All of us, including the normally critical Alhadji, regarded the equipment, the operation, the journey, as a great institutional joke, something foisted upon us by the Marine Department a thousand miles away in their Lagos harbour heaven of chugging engines, teak decks, polished brass and white drill uniforms. I remembered the launch in which I travelled the fifty-odd miles from Lagos to Badagry in about four hours, and felt deeply aggrieved that our equipage was so inferior and was, apparently, accepted by my seniors without protest.

A trip to Shellen began after an early breakfast. We crossed the Benue easily enough, and then entered the Gongola which, in full flood, had a very strong current, particularly in its narrower reaches. At the end of a hard day's poling, including several hours of intense heat, we had covered some twenty to twenty-five miles, about half the journey. The course of the river was a strange mix-ture of narrows with sharp bends alternating with broad, multi-channelled stretches in which the stream ran between sandbanks, where the problem was to locate the main stream and avoid going aground. The crew's appetite for food was prodigious, and the actual poling strength at any moment was seldom more than six, with two absentees away buying food in a nearby village, relieving nature, or perhaps (as I suspected) renewing acquaintance with some local light o'love. There were periods of swift current when we seemed to make hardly any progress at all and I threatened dire reprisals for absenteeism. This, however, was Africa, and we learned to laugh when we collided with the bank bringing a cascade of soil into our living quarters. The most comic, but slightly alarming, moment occurred when I shot at a group of whistling teal which took off as we rounded a bend. Most of the crew dived spontaneously into the water to retrieve the birds (which they hoped to share), leaving us drifting downstream, all of us madly seizing the abandoned poles and trying to check our gathering speed.

Mosquitoes were a fearful plague on the river after dusk, and so we had an early meal and retired to bed. Poling began soon after dawn, and we were thankful to reach the relative comfort of Shellen rest-house in the late afternoon. The return journey was comparative bliss. Leaving mid-morning, and with a break for lunch, we could reach Numan by sunset after about six hours of actual travelling. Manoeuvring round the bends at speed, the advantage of a poling crew was shown in skilful avoidance of collisions with the bank and grounding in the shallows. Only once did we run fast aground, on our last trip, as we emerged from the Gongola and tried to cross the rapidly falling Benue towards the lights of our bungalow on the far shore.

A small fleet of poling barges, carrying ten tons each, was used by the UAC at high water to evacuate produce from the trading-stations on the Gongola to their depot at Numan. It was an effective operation with a basic simplicity which was well suited to the local circumstances, including the absence of all but the most primitive technology. At about the same time, the fearful fruit of the highest technological endeavour of Western science descended upon two Japanese cities and a few days later I informed the assembled populace of Numan town that the Japanese war was officially at an end. It all seemed very unreal, perhaps the more so because I was one of the very few people in Nigeria who understood the nature of the atom bomb, the paradox of the high achievement and its threat of impending catastrophe for us all. As the rains came to an end, we began to look forward to the prospect of touring among the hill tribes in the remoter areas of the division. There was even the possibility that we might have six months in the delightfully cool Northern touring area, based on Mubi in the Cameroons, about ninety miles north-east of Yola. Then, two things happened, one much hoped for, and one quite unexpected. Either, alone, would have been sufficient to cause me to reconsider the Colonial Service as a life-career; together they compelled me to a decision which had probably been forming subconsciously for some time. That lay in the future; early in November 1945 we rejoiced that Jocelyn was expecting a baby, and hoped that my transfer to the Lagos Secretariat, so suddenly announced one morning by telegram, would be helpful to her pregnancy in providing a better diet and more comfortable accommodation. We hurried to complete my report on the reorganisation of the division, and I handed over to my successor, whose seniority and urbanity seemed more suited to service in Lagos than were my own qualities. Our farewells to our African friends were sad, almost tearful, the saddest perhaps being the farewell to the Sarkin Ruwa as we drove away from the north bank of the Benue where he had first greeted us in the previous year. His son, Sajo, a young man of great charm and simplicity, was coming with us as assistant to that hard taskmaster, Alhadji, to whom he was completely devoted.

I had by this time experienced so many removals from one African scene to another and said so many farewells to people who had been dear to me in some measure, that I found the only way of coping with the sense of loss and disruption was to con-centrate hard on the practical tasks that lay ahead. I had no idea of what would be my job in Lagos, but the preoccupations of travelling and relocating were sufficient to help me forget the work left undone in Numan and the mistakes made which might have been corrected, given a longer stay in the division.

My hopes of having an interesting and worthwhile job to do were soon dispelled. I was the Import Control Officer, in charge of the office which issued permits for the importation of goods from countries outside the sterling area. There was a monthly allocation of foreign currencies to meet the permitted importation of foreign goods, and the allocation of hard currencies such as Swiss francs and dollars was meagre indeed. My chief occupation – an unpleasant one – was to receive a never-ending stream of people, mostly Yorubas and Ibos, who wanted to import spare parts for watches, vehicles, mechanical and electrical equipment of all kinds. I investigated the bona fides of applicants and tried to be fair to everyone, but it was all very difficult and very wearing.

It was pleasant to cycle the mile or so along the Marina to the

Secretariat at 8 a.m. when it was fairly cool and before there was much traffic about. Later in the day, toiling in the heat, one was painfully aware of being squeezed to the edge of the road by African drivers, particularly a new, brash breed of taxi-driver with a special insolence towards whites, which seemed to herald the shape of things to come. These pests were everywhere touting for custom, even penetrating into the narrow, sandy track which led through the mangroves to the wide expanse of Victoria beach.

Jocelyn, in the early stages of pregnancy, found the climate particularly trying, but she, too, cycled to work at the Police HQ beyond the racecourse where she had a part-time job examining the papers relating to German personnel employed by firms in the territory (including the Woermann shipping line) in the years immediately before the war. This occupation, like my own, proved to be rather futile, but helped to relieve boredom. She was not really well, and a blood test showed that she had a malarial infection. She was advised to take the opportunity of a passage to the UK in January, and we both agreed, regretfully, that this was the sensible thing to do. I was rather concerned that she would be travelling on a twelve-cabin cargo-liner without a doctor on board, but in those days there was very little choice. In the event, it was fortunate indeed that she had, as fellow passenger, a trained nurse, who almost certainly helped her to avoid a miscarriage.

After her departure, I reverted to the single person ménage of earlier years, and found it intolerable. I remember spending a whole evening making a thorough review of the life colonial as I had known it, and as it promised to be in the future. I could not avoid the conclusion that the best years, almost certainly, lay behind me. Lagos, and other large towns had become the homes of demagogues and tribal agitators, breeding-grounds of corruption and future exploitation. The new and rising power-holders were conveniently on view for inspection at a garden-party at Government House just before Jocelyn sailed. There seemed to be a preponderance of brash, hard faces and loud voices with clothes to match. The Governor, Richards, later Lord Milverton, was, in contrast, quiet-mannered but without the warmth which was so attractive in his predecessor, Bourdillon.

It was common knowledge that the path of advancement to senior posts lay through service in one of the Secretariats, and that appointment to the Lagos Secretariat, as a junior, was a mark of official favour and approval. The prospect of spending years on this kind of treadmill to win promotion was even less inviting than the alternative of provincial service, often in hard stations inimical to health and, though interesting and worthwhile in many ways, involving separation from wife and family.

I mentioned none of these matters in my brief letter of resignation, but the Secretary i/c Personnel was anxious to know the reasons for my decision. He assured me that salaries would soon be increased, and seemed surprised that pay had not been, for me, a determining factor. It seemed pointless to go through the whole argument, much of which was a personal matter, and I confined the discussion to the question of health, which was easily understood, and was recognised as strong enough to override all other considerations – the unwisdom of discarding a promising career in particular.

I secured an early passage in a very uncomfortable ship, and had just enough time to dispose of most of my unwanted kit. There was enough money to provide some recognition to Alhadji and Francis for their faithful service. Alhadji planned to buy 'housing' (as he put it) in Yola or Jos, while Francis found another, well-paid, job as a cook. Sajo sensibly returned to Numan, to his farm and his barge-pole, symbol of his separation from the fleshpots. We said our sad farewells, speaking and thinking of the life we had shared together and the travels to so many remote places, knowing that this was a final parting, unlike the earlier ones that Alhadji and I had lived through.

As I stood in the stern of the boat sailing out of Lagos harbour in February 1946, it was exactly nine years since my first sight of it. The rippled water, the white buildings, the flaming trees and the green sward, all gleaming under the sun, seemed little changed, but behind the façade, as I knew, things were very different, and changing faster all the time. For me, too, this was the end of a chapter, in a way, the end of my youth, in that my earliest idealism had finally come to terms with reality. I had plenty of opportunity, on the voyage, to ponder the experience of my nine years, its satisfactions and its disappointments. As the view became more distant, more detached, possibly more objective, I concluded, sadly, that I had achieved very little, least of all in the fight against corruption and exploitation which had absorbed so much of my time and energy. Most of my colleagues, being honest men, would have assessed their service in similar terms. To some of us it seemed that our efforts had been directed towards training and educating an élite who, on our departure, would be all the better fitted to exploit those beneath them. Would this be the verdict of history: that our endeavours had been largely a waste of time, or even that, in the longer term, we had made matters worse?

37

Return and a Postscript

❧

I N March 1973 I returned to Nigeria on a short visit, as a director of an international company, to brief myself on the serious local problems of staff recruitment and training. I travelled by plane to Kano, thence by car to Zaria and Kaduna, by air to Lagos and Benin. In all these places the transformation, from the state in which I had known them, into Westernised environments containing the whole range of social and economic hardware, from the plastic shoddy to the near luxurious, was unbelievable – a sort of nightmare experience from which one did not wake up. Vast sums of money, derived from, or supported by, oil, had been spent on a variety of installations in all the major towns. Some hotels, a few public utilities and most of the factories, where European or Asiatic supervision was still effective, were acceptably operational, even efficient. Elsewhere, the departure of the contractors, builders and engineers, and the handover to Nigerian managers all too often marked the beginning of operational decline. Nigerians had one symptom of the English disease very badly; among the well-educated there were few who were willing to take a management job in industry, most preferring law, medicine or government service in which money came more easily. Food prices were controlled to keep the townsfolk happy, farmers and their sons left the villages to join the supposed bonanza in the towns. Unfortunately, my commitments left neither time nor opportunity to visit Adamawa, Bornu or Katsina or to see anything of life in the villages, which was said to have changed little, except for the worse, in the quarter-century of my absence. The following extracts from my diary of the tour may give some idea of the changes I was able to observe, not always with approval.

'I was lodged in the Central Hotel, Kano, in one of the over-lavish VIP suites dotted around a central dining-room/reception/bar area. Slept fitfully with the air-conditioning full on in a vain attempt to discourage vagrant mosquitoes, there being no sign of a mosquito-net. The railway worked noisily, and in close proximity throughout the night. After a very indifferent breakfast, very indifferently served, I made a tour of the new industrial area. Quite an impressive collection of light industrial developments: groundnut oil extraction and refining; production of corned beef; a tannery; plastic moulding; a small brewery, and many other activities designed to satisfy a growing consumer demand. Mixed in with all this were a great number of entertainment establishments, minor hotels, pubs, discothèques, cinemas and nightclubs.

'The Sales Manager drove me to Kaduna, via Zaria, in a comfortable, air-conditioned car. We called first at the Bagauda Lake Holiday Resort development. This is located around the smaller of two lakes formed by damming the Kano river and comprises an hotel, a restaurant, cinema, nightclub, swimming-pool, bars and other "amenities". There is water-skiing on the lake. All this has a bizarre artificiality in a large area of empty bush almost bare of vegetation, the heat and sun-glare being almost unbearable.

'The Ahmadu Bello University at Samaru, just outside Zaria, is growing into a sizeable complex covering a wide range of disciplines from veterinary science to the liberal arts. Soldiery very much in evidence following a student "demo" the day before against a government proposal to establish a Youth Service Corps. I discussed with Dr Laing, the director of the Agricultural Research Institute, the possibility of growing barley in Nigeria, and agreed that the scope for this crop would be very limited. Maize much more promising. I was impressed by this establishment, and the competence and enthusiasm of its staff.

'We were very hungry when we reached the Zaria Club at about 1.45 p.m., but had to be content with sandwiches. I well remember this place, from my army days in 1939, as being one of the most "pukka" of the Nigerian station clubs of the old imperial establishment. Now it is beginning to look tatty, with the lawns unkempt, the flower-beds untended, the buildings unpainted. Inside, the cups for the club competitions and race meetings still stand on the mantelshelf, soon perhaps to be sold off, like the remnants of the library (mostly novels of the 1930s) for what they will fetch. I wonder whose property, in law, they are? We had some awful sandwiches with a bottle of beer, and came away sadly, leaving the bar to a group of giggling non-Hausa Nigerians, a down-at-heel Italian building contractor, and a few rather miserable-looking Britishers.

'We came on to Kaduna, driving at 60 mph along the road (now tarmacadammed) which I had route-marched so painfully in 1940 with the rest of the 1st Battalion. After a brief stop at his office, the manager dropped me at the Haamdala Hotel, a tower-block with gardens and swimming-pool, more or less on the site of the house which I occupied with "Swig" Swainson et al. in the autumn of 1939. The clientele was impressively cosmopolitan and well-heeled, and the swimming-pool was full of youngish people of all colours and both sexes. I walked past the old Club to the polo field, where people were "knocking up" before a chukka, with the usual amount of dry-season dust hanging over the whole area. Some very choice horseflesh around – imported from the Sudan, I imagine – and the usual bevy of grooms, genuine Hausas, speaking the language with a swift, soft fluency. They, and the dust, remained from the past, in the midst of so much change, and I enjoyed some lighthearted banter with them. Later, at dinner, I met a number of the new élite, including some impressive Northerners who had emerged from Kaduna College in its heyday, when it was still staffed by Oxbridge graduates. Nearly all of them have made their mark in some way since Independence, and all speak excellent English with a public school accent.'

Thursday 1 March. 'We made a tour of the extensive new industrial development, including several textile factories. Interested to learn that the one owned and operated by Hong Kong Chinese is larger and more efficient than the adjacent Japanese factory. It has taken sixty-odd years since Lugard moved his headquarters into this place, then a pleasant wilderness of empty bush, to turn most of it into a jungle of concrete. I tried, briefly, to find the old 1NR Mess but it seemed to have been submerged within a greatly enlarged military establishment. Soldiers were swarming everywhere, with no appearance of former standards of discipline.

'Met at Ikeja (Lagos) airport by the Managing Director and taken to his very pleasant house in which I was given a large, air-conditioned bedroom and bathroom. An agreeable dinner, recalling old acquaintance and experience with "old-timer" guests from the UAC.'

The following day I visited Benin: 'I had not realised that Benin was a walled town, rather like Kano, and that the Oba had a mud palace, again like Kano. We drove around part of the town and saw much recent development, including the new university. Then to the airport for another long wait before flying to Ikeja via Ibadan, which is now enormous. I got a very good view of the enlarged town area, and of the very extensive Ibadan University complex.'

Saturday 3 March. 'Dined at the Mandarin Chinese Restaurant in Ikeja, where we had some of the best Chinese food I have tasted anywhere, including Singapore. This restaurant is one of the peripheral enterprises started up by the Hong Kong Chinese, who are much involved in the textile industry here, as in Kaduna. It does a thriving trade, not only with white faces but with Indians, Japanese and, of course, the Nigerian moneyed classes. These were very much in evidence and included not only the traditional "important" man, wearing gown and gold-braided cap, together with his ample, be-turbanned spouse, but also some glamorously dressed younger wives with their successful businessmen or bureaucrat husbands. It seems as though most of the additional wealth which is being generated in this country is being creamed off by the wealthier classes, and the poor (as evidenced by the shanty dwellings along most of the roads in the towns) are mostly as poor as ever. ... One wonders whether the student population is militant because it feels that the government is making very little headway against the problem of mass poverty. Certainly there is plenty of student unrest, and also an awareness among them of the needs of the underprivileged. In Benin yesterday, students were around in large numbers, in the hotels, the streets and the airport, collecting for the "poor and disabled" and the police and the military, who were patrolling everywhere, did nothing to hinder them.'

Sunday 4 March. 'Set off on a tour of Yaba, Apapa, Ebuta Metta, Ikoyi and Victoria island (reclaimed from mangrove swamp), all of which now constitute one vast, messy conurbation. The areas under government development or residentially "ex-patriate" are kept reasonably clean, but the rest of the development is like old Lagos, and the living conditions are generally appalling.

'The whole of Apapa, including the aerodrome which we guarded in 1942, is now built up and merges with Ebuta Metta, through which we drove to cross the new bridge into Lagos and so along the Marina to Five Cowrie Creek. The yacht club is still there, but the house in which Jocelyn and I lived in 1945–46 has, with its neighbours, been pulled down and is now the site of the Prime Minister's house. From this house, in the first army coup, the Federal Prime Minister, Abubakar Balewa, was taken and shot.

'We crossed the creek to Victoria island and followed the road (formerly a sand-track) that led to the beach. A large crowd was assembled on the sand-dune at the end of the road, listening to a service conducted by the Cherubims and Seraphims, a new pseudo-Judaic sect which has a considerable following among the credulous but is accused, in the local papers, of many scandalous practices. Returning, a new road across the reclaimed land took us past the diplomatic residences and embassies (including that of China behind a high wall and solid steel gates) until we reached a complex of large new buildings – the Nigerian Institute of Law, a fitting memorial to the national passion for litigation.

'There is a new road to Ikoyi which avoids the cemetery, for so long a reminder of the high mortality rate among the British who laboured here. No. 6 Glover Road, the ugly concrete box which I once occupied, surprisingly still stands, and the various roads named after early proconsuls are not much changed except where houses have been demolished to make way for more luxurious dwellings. We went to a "pool lunch" at a house in Bank Road. This is a new form of hospitality, spanning the hours between twelve and three, providing drinks, buffet lunch, swimming and card games. Barclays' General Manager, the host, had assembled some of the modern top brass, including the Dutch Ambassador and the vice-chairman of the Federal Central Bank (a Yoruba graduate of the LSE, and chairman of the Capital Issues Committee). The latter is a man of much power and influence at this time, when the government is enforcing greater Nigerian participation in foreign enterprises, at share prices arbitrarily fixed at a fraction of their true value.

'We came back to Ikeja along the old road, which I knew so well, and which is little changed, except that the slums are more crowded than ever, and there are sky-scrapers by the approaches to Carter bridge. The road between Carter bridge and Ikeja is said to be the most dangerous in the world, and I can believe it, from the standard of driving and the evidence of very recent accidents. On a normal weekday, the fifteen-mile journey can take two hours.'

Monday 5 March. 'Had talks with a number of people in Engineering, Production and Distribution departments. The British were communicative, but some of the Africans seem very introverted, and most of them articulate English poorly, and very softly, in almost a whisper. The Training Engineer believes that most of the men working on the shop floor are suffering from psychological as well as physical stress, and all their reactions are slowed down in defence. At home, they live in crowded, relatively primitive conditions, and at work have to adapt to the unremitting demands of high-speed, sophisticated machinery. At night, they fail to sleep properly in hot, cramped dwellings, and tend to fall asleep on the job during the day. These views were confirmed by the African Personnel Manager.'

Wednesday 7 March. 'At the airport we hung around (after the usual tedious formalities) for nearly two hours before departure was finally announced, then another half hour before actual take-off. I flew by Nigerian Airways rather than Swissair or Luft-Hansa, but once aboard, I realised that I had made a bad choice, the only other first-class passengers being four Nigerian businessmen who arrived half-drunk and kept on drinking. They appeared to be travelling to Italy on some kind of purchasing mission, and were soon on intimate terms with the Yoruba air-hostess, who had the style and manners of a Lagos market-mammy. We spent over an hour in Rome, apparently through administrative incompetence in revictualling the aircraft. The American pilot was furious.'

These brief impressions of my return to Nigeria are included as a tailpiece to the account of the last months of my colonial service, in Lagos. They convey something, but certainly not all, of my feeling of disillusion, and sadness, that the efforts and dedication of so many of my former colleagues have been largely obliterated, since Independence, by rabid selfishness and materialism. Corruption has been thriving within a legal, bureaucratic, economic and social framework. Nigeria has had one terrible civil war, and serious racial tensions remain. In nearly all parts of Africa, there are similar, or worse, stories to be told. In several territories, the evils to be found in Nigeria are compounded by unchecked tribalism, which the British suppressed in their colonies, but are unable to control in Britain, whether in Northern Ireland or in the immigrant ghettos of its mainland cities. Africans of many tribes, Indians and white South Africans fought under British leadership to 'liberate' Ethiopia, Eritrea and Somalia. All these have been disaster areas, devastated by tribal warfare, imported ideologies, incompetence, massive debt and – the final straw – drought. The fearful burden of debt which is a major element in the African tragedy, as it is in so many parts of the Third World, is something for which the 'developed' world, and the international bankers, must bear the blame.

Those who served in Malaysia can feel happier. The country was saved, by enormous and devoted effort, from a communist takeover in the post-war period, and the two dominant races, the Malays and the Chinese, appear to have achieved a *modus vivendi* after narrowly averting a drift into civil war. My visit to Malaysia in 1971, discovering the beauty of the country, the charm and friendliness of its people, their industry and efficiency (the Chinese setting the example) left an impression of positive achievement and hope, in marked contrast to what I found a year later in Nigeria.

Was any of it, then, worthwhile? The answer must be yes, for I should not, otherwise, have spent so much time, since my retirement, in writing this record of nine years. The job was there to be done, and someone had to do it. My abstention would not have changed British colonial policy by one iota, and my place would have been filled by someone perhaps even less able, even more opinionated. I tried to do the job conscientiously, and have few regrets, after this detailed remembering, almost reliving, of the experience. Chiefly, I blame myself for having failed to support my senior colleague in Bornu in 1943–44, Guy Money, in his opposition to the recruitment of labourers from the towns and villages of Bornu to work in the tin-mines around Jos. Foolishly, I had assumed that they would be adequately protected by our colleagues in Plateau Province, to ensure that their working conditions and pay were satisfactory. Unfortunately, as I learned subsequently, the supervision and inspection, by government, of the enlarged mines operation appears to have fallen short of what was required, and the sickness and death rate among these labourers was significantly higher than the provincial average. These people suffered hardship and some of them died so that our forces in the battlefields, including their own brothers in Burma, could continue to receive their tinned rations to enable them to fight on and win. I regret that I did not urge Guy Money to articulate his opposition to the scheme (which might have produced some guarantee of satisfactory working conditions), instead of assuming, as I did, that his silent non-cooperation was simply his characteristic recalcitrance.

On the positive side, I am glad to have battled against widespread oppression and corruption, dirt, dark ignorance and disease, to have planned villages, done much building in traditional style, road-making and repairing and tree-planting. I taught what I knew about various useful skills and procedures, and perhaps some of it endured after my departure.

However, all these things which took up so much time and energy probably weigh far less, in total, than the contribution made to the well-being of the people by just being there, to help maintain Pax Britannica. I shall always remember Alhadji's reply when I asked him once what it was like to live in his village, about fifty miles north of Yola, before the British occupation. 'It was just slavery. When the tribes weren't fighting the Fulani, they fought each other. Those who were captured became slaves. Many were taken far away and were never seen again.' Nigeria has not reverted to that state of affairs, and, one hopes, never will. Elsewhere, there are probably many territories where the common folk would gladly welcome the return of a benign protecting power.

I can affirm that it was enormously worthwhile for me, as a personal experience. It was a great privilege to live with Africans, to work with them and get to know them intimately. It was a constant delight to discover their great sense of humour and their underlying philosophy of life, with its acceptance of hardship and freedom from self-pity. The climate was sometimes harsh and enervating, but there were often the compensations which are to be found in many of the wild and relatively empty parts of the world. In most of my travelling in the bush, I was meeting people who were still almost untouched (I was about to say uncontaminated) by the outside world. Journeys to the more remote areas had a special excitement, a feeling akin to exploration when one was aware that they had seldom, if ever, been toured before. One had this very precious experience of knowing people who were still immersed, and I believe happy, in their age-long culture, of speaking their language and helping, where one could, to make their lives a little easier, kinder, healthier. I saw the last of that brief span of British tutelage in Northern Nigeria, when we tried to let it develop at its own natural pace. World War II changed all that, and no part of Africa will ever again be as we knew it. That is why I have added this record to those already written by my predecessors and erstwhile colleagues who shared a unique and now vanished way of life.

Index

Adams, Sir Theodore, 21, 22
Alhadji, Yaro Mohammed Ben, 8, 10,
    12, 13, 16, 31, 40, 44, 53, 54, 60,
    76, 85, 136, 157, 167, 190, 191,
    192, 218, 228, 240, 241, 243, 259,
    261, 263, 272

Bain, Louis, 16, 20, 85, 196
Baron, The (Lieut. R. W. Dodds),
    100, 113, 117, 121, 142
Bourdillon, Sir Bernard, 5, 37, 41, 42,
    43, 143
Bradshaw, Sam, 16, 231

Cameron, Sir Donald, 17, 18, 21, 25,
    26

Drake, H. W., 15
Drummond-Hay, Toby, 25, 31, 39, 41,
    43

Fagg, Bernard, 105, 158, 228
Francis, 29, 31, 53, 54, 55, 157, 174,
    228, 241, 245, 263
Funtua, Ibrahim, 23, 103, 116

Gass, Sir Michael, 141
Gilbert, Guy, 174, 197, 214

Hadow, Bernard, 18, 20, 22, 23, 44,
    45, 46, 47, 60, 63, 74, 75

Jorn, Dougie, 173, 174, 185, 195, 214

Lodge, Sergeant Frank, 21, 105, 119,
    121, 130, 154
Lugard, Lord, 10, 17, 22, 25, 26, 32,
    40, 41, 69, 105

MacBride, Desmond, 5, 6, 8, 15, 22
Macfarlane, Brian, 25, 29, 39, 63, 66
Madsen, Laura, 237, 251

Nagogo, Usuman, 31
Nigra, Capitano Luigi, 157
Niven, Sir Rex, 5, 6, 158, 160, 161,
    166, 170, 221, 227, 255

O'Flynn, Capt. Garry, 141
Owen, Lt.-Col., later Brigadier, 82,
    83, 89, 161, 169, 211

Perham, Dame Margery, 17, 18, 25,
    27, 176, 189
Pretious, Arthur, 206, 207, 209, 222,
    227

Rogers, Capt. John, 105, 116, 117,
    119, 120, 121, 122, 142

Swainson, O. S. (Swig), 82, 93, 147,
    267

Tupper-Carey, H. D., 169, 170, 172,
    173, 174, 175, 176, 178, 179, 180,
    181, 182, 183, 184, 185, 186, 187,
    188, 191, 194, 195, 198, 214, 255
Turing, Alan, 88

Wali, 170, 171, 172, 181, 182, 183
Ward, L. S., 16, 17
Wright, Derek, 178, 186, 214
Wright, The Rev. Ruthven, 11, 154,
    169

Yakub, Umar, 172